教育文论选读

主　编　孙二军　王嘉铭
编　者　原　昉　陈　熙　张迪晨
主　审　李　辉

北京大学出版社
PEKING UNIVERSITY PRESS

图书在版编目(CIP)数据

教育文论选读:英文/孙二军,王嘉铭主编. —北京:北京大学出版社,2014.9
ISBN 978-7-301-24716-7

Ⅰ.①教… Ⅱ.①孙… ②王… Ⅲ.①英语—教学研究—文集 Ⅳ.①H319.3-53

中国版本图书馆CIP数据核字(2014)第198900号

书　　　名：教育文论选读

JIAOYU WENLUN XUANDU

著作责任者：孙二军　王嘉铭　主编
责任编辑：李　娜
标准书号：ISBN 978-7-301-24716-7/G·3867
出版发行：北京大学出版社
地　　址：北京市海淀区成府路205号　100871
网　　址：http://www.pup.cn　新浪官方微博:@北京大学出版社
电子信箱：nklina@gmail.com
电　　话：邮购部 62752015　发行部 62750672　编辑部 62759634　出版部 62754962
印　刷　者：北京鑫海金澳胶印有限公司
经　销　者：新华书店
　　　　　　720毫米×980毫米　16开本　21印张　394千字
　　　　　　2014年9月第1版　2016年3月第2次印刷
定　　价：46.00元

未经许可，不得以任何方式复制或抄袭本书之部分或全部内容。
版权所有，侵权必究
举报电话：010-62752024　电子信箱：fd@pup.pku.edu.cn

序

　　随着我国外语教育事业的蓬勃发展,社会对英语专业人才培养的规格和质量提出了新的要求与挑战。英语教师教育改革与发展的出发点即是要着力提升英语教师队伍建设的层次与质量,并最终通过"英语+教育"的复合型人才培养模式改革适应未来社会的国际化发展趋势及其教育需求。

　　英语教师教育具有典型的"双专业特征",即兼顾了英语学科与教育学科的专业特征。前者主要解决"教什么"的问题,后者则主要解决"如何教、如何成长"的问题。因此,英语教师教育ESP(特殊用途英语)课程开发及其教材建设需要立足于"双专业"的协同发展,达成融合共生的课程理念,既重视职业倾向性的专业用途英语学习,也重视学术性研究对于学生的专业发展需求。《教育文论选读》是西安外国语大学英语教育学院近些年来教育教学改革的尝试与探索。具体而言,该教材首先立足于英语学科的专业优势,将相关的教育学科内容融入英语的课程与教学之中(诸如阅读、翻译、写作和听说等),使得学生在增强英语专业技能的同时更多地关注教育学科的相关内容;其次对教育学科内容进行"精加工",使学生掌握基本的教育理论,领悟经典的教育思想,关注教育研究的前沿动态。这不仅有利于实现复合型英语教师的人才培养理念,扩展其后续的专业学习或职业生活的发展空间,而且有利于实现教育学科与英语学科的融合共生,提升英语教师教育的层次与质量。

　　《教育文论选读》的设计理念与编写特点主要体现在以下几个方面,即"方向明、特色强、选材精、设计活、内容全"。"方向明"强调英语教师教育人才培养的适用性,在教材的编写中突出"复合型"、"应用性"和"实践性"的课程开发方向;"特色强"强调在教材编写中突出"英语+教育"的融合与兼顾,突出英语语言素养与教育素养的双重提升;"选材精"强调题材内容、体裁类型的多样性和教育内涵的丰富性,重视教材对学生未来专业发展的知识引领;"设计活"强调学生的学习兴趣和学习习惯,在教材编写中加大互动性、趣味性的教学环节;"内容全"强调教材编写要围绕教育名家、教育热点问题、学生发展、教师发展、英语学习、英语教学等方面,向学生呈现出较为系统化的教育主题学习。此外,《教育文论选读》在满足传统泛读教材对阅读技能和能力提高的基础上,通过课堂任务、课后小组活动和视听材料等培养学生逻辑思维能力、分析反思能力、问题解决能力和语言运用能力,力求改变传统泛读教材模式单一的语言技能训练。在选材上,主要以英语语料中涉及教育的文献、资料、报刊、图书等内容为蓝本,结合复合型专业特色、学生学习兴趣和社会热点教育话题组织编排,力求在帮助学生巩固语言能力的同时,引导和开拓学生对教育和教师职业的认识和视野,为今后就业和深入学习奠定教育专业基础。

此外,西安外国语大学英语教育学院2011年获批成为陕西省"国际化外语教师教育人才培养模式创新实验区","教育文论选读"课程开发及教材建设是人才培养创新实验的重点项目之一,其团队成员都是英语教育学院的优秀青年教师,他们或是具有教育学博士学位的青年学者,或是具有TESOL专业留学背景的教学能手。近几年来,该团队先后获得陕西省教育厅资助项目两项,陕西省教育科学规划资助项目两项,获批陕西省教学改革研究项目一项,发表教学科研论文十余篇,其中以《对英语教育专业建设的思考及其改革策略》为代表的论文先后被刊载于《外语教学》和《中国教育学刊》等核心期刊。

总之,经过该团队成员坚持不懈的努力,在"教育文论选读"的课程开发及教材建设中,我们取得了一些成绩,总结归纳了一些关于ESP课程的规律性认识,积累了一些课程开发经验,但应该看到当前的研究主要集中于英语专业阅读类课程的特色改造,对于ESP课程的一般性研究还有待进一步拓展和深化。我们需要加快英语教师教育ESP课程系统开发的节奏,为英语教师教育的人才培养模式改革与创新,探索出切实可行的发展道路,谋求有效的ESP课程开发及教学策略。

李　辉
2014年8月于西安

前　言

随着我国外语教育事业的蓬勃发展，社会对英语专业人才培养的规格与质量提出了新的要求，英语教学改革面临新的挑战。复合型、应用型的培养目标成为英语专业人才培养模式改革与发展的关键所在，英语专业的课程与教材体系需要顺应这一趋势，改革固有的课程理念与模式，在课程与教材建设方面寻求突破与创新。"教育文论选读"是在原有英语专业泛读课程基础上予以改造的特色课程，是构建复合型外语教师教育专业课程体系中的核心课程。本课程以英语专业教学大纲中对英语专业阅读课程的要求为基本出发点，同时以国内外教育理论与实践的研习为方向，在培养学生语言综合运用能力的基础上，提高学生的教育专业素养，实现复合型的人才培养目标。

教材特色：

《教育文论选读》旨在通过对教育学科知识内容的填充，改造传统语言课程只注重语言而忽视学科内容的弊端，从教育学科与英语学科融合提升的角度提升教材内涵。本教材的特色在于：

第一，语言技能（Academic English）。语言技能训练侧重以学术英语阅读为主的阅读技能，并兼顾听、说和写作技能，力求使学生了解和认识学术语言，并通过大量分析性阅读的语言输入，培养学生学术的语体意识和批判的思维习惯。在文本体裁上体现学术性，在练习形式上凸显新题型和反思性。

第二，学科素养（Subject Quality）。在课程与教材的设计中，我们努力将教育理论素养的提升融入阅读教学之中，通过课文内容组织、小组活动安排和课堂教学任务训练使英语学习和专业学习交叉融合，真正实现英语与教育专业结合的教育理念。

第三，学习技能（Learning Skills）。学习技能旨在帮助学生建立良好的学习习惯，培养其建立自主、合作与探究的学习方法，实现被动学习向学会学习转变。本教材按不同单元依次建构了一套以学生学会学习为目标的学习技能体系，通过课堂教学与小组学习相结合的方式将课堂教学与课后练习有机结合，充分发挥学生的主动性与创造性。

组织编排：

《教育文论选读》编排分为上、下两篇，上篇的主题是"学习与学生"，下篇的主题是"教学与教师"。在单元主题设置上涉及与教育相关的重点和热点话题，兼有学习心理、教育比较、教育经济、学习方式、学科学习、课程教学、高等教育、教师发展、教育公平、教育技术等。本教材选材文章来源广泛，包括国外综合杂志的教育专栏、重要报纸的教育专刊、教育类电子杂志、教育类专著和期刊、著名教育家（哲学家）的论著和演讲、教育统计报告、名人自传、诗歌、戏剧等多种形式。

上篇	下篇
1. 名家谈学习	6. 名家谈教学
学习技能 I: 图书馆资料查阅技能	学习技能 VI: 记笔记技能
2. 中外教育之我见（学习篇）	7. 中外教育之我见（教学篇）
学习技能 II: 课堂演讲技能	学习技能 VII: 批判性写作技能 I
3. 基于多元智能的学生发展	8. 基于教育叙事的教师发展
学习技能 III: 学术报告写作 I	学习技能 VIII: 批判性写作技能 II
4. 外语学习的新视野	9. 外语教学的新进展
学习技能 IV: 学术报告写作 II	学习技能 IX: 学术写作技能
5. 合作学习与美国内战	10. 探究教学与亨利八世
学习技能 V: 合作学习技能	学习技能 X: 探究学习技能

本教材在编排中遵循由浅入深、由易至难、循序渐进的原则。每单元设置四篇课文，课文层级组织充分结合英语学习与教育专业学习，围绕学术英语、教育知识、学习技能三个目标展开。

第一篇文章为每一单元的主题导入，在内容上反映本单元的主题内容，重在知识性内容的介绍和主题内容的探讨。后续三篇文章 Text A, B, C 为本单元的核心课文，在内容上与单元主题保持一致，在语言文本上综合了学术语言与通俗语言，充分考虑了文本选择的趣味性、内容的广泛性和体裁的多样性。

教学安排：

本教材供英语（教育）专业高年级学生或教育专业研究生使用，也可供非英语专业研究生或高校教师学习，并配有教材同步慕课学习资源，详情请参考链接 http://ptr.chaoxing.com/course/962373.html。

前　言

教材每单元四篇文章。结合自主、合作、探究的教育理念,每单元后都为学生设计了小组活动和自我评价表作为教师检查和形成性评价的参考。

教材创新:

本教材在编写之初就确立了创新、求变的思路,经过课题组成员的共同调研和思考最终形成了以 ESP(特殊用途英语)为基本理论,结合 CBI(内容依托教学)和现代教育理念的课程教材建设思路,并在教材编写中不断实践和创新如下理念:

第一,传统英语教材或英语泛读教材选材较为宽泛,内容排列缺乏逻辑性,知识体系不系统。本教材以教育学学科背景为基础,以教育学科知识和要素为基本框架,是结合语言与专业,融合学科知识和跨越学科界线的新教材。

第二,传统英语教材按语言技能划分教材类型,忽视综合语言能力的培养,人为割裂语言能力的内在联系。本教材在编写中充分考虑各项语言技能的综合与运用,以语言输入技能为主体,兼顾其他技能,强调语言的综合性和交际性。

第三,传统英语教材不区分一般英语学习与特殊用途英语学习,也很难建立二者之间的联系。本教材旨在帮助学生认识和了解学术英语语体和学术规范,更重要的是为学生搭建了由一般英语学习向学术英语学习过渡的桥梁和纽带。

第四,能力培养一直是传统教学的短板,也是传统教材本应该重视而没有重视的重要内容。本教材将学习能力培养通过学习技能训练的方式展示出来,使学生学会学习方法而不是学习知识,并通过教学活动设计体现平等合作、自主学习、知识建构的现代教育理念。

鉴于时间仓促和课题组成员水平所限,本书在内容和形式上难免有所疏漏,还请使用本书的教师、学生和教育同行不吝赐教,我们热切地盼望大家对我们的工作提出批评指正,以期实现更高层次的课程开发。

本教材的编写历时4年,先后经过两次大的调整,最终成稿。课题组成员中,孙二军老师负责教材的理论框架构建和教学内容的甄选,王嘉铭老师负责教材的章节设计和第1、4单元的编写,原昉老师负责第3、9单元的编写,陈熙老师负责第2、8单元的编写,张迪晨老师负责第5、6单元的编写,其中第7、10单元为共同编写完成,每人承担工作量9.85万字,全书共计39.4万字。

《教育文论选读》课题组
2014/8/21

Contents

上　篇

Unit 1　Educators Philosophies and Learning Theories
Introduction: Nature of Learning ·· 3
Text A: Of Studies ·· 6
Text B: What Knowledge Is of Most Worth? ·· 10
Text C: The Differences Between Learning by Instruction and Learning by Discovery　15
Learning Skills: Library Skills ·· 20

Unit 2　My Perspectives on Education Between China and America
Introduction: Defining Comparative Education: Conceptions ·························· 24
Text A: Re-education ·· 26
Text B: The Social Logic of Ivy League Admissions ·· 32
Text C: Is College Really Worth the Money? ·· 39
Learning Skills: Oral Presentation Skills ·· 46

Unit 3　Education and Students' Development
Introduction: Student Diversity ·· 52
Text A: MI(Multiple Intelligence), IT (Instructional Technology) and Standards: The Story of Jamie ·· 57
Text B: The Man Who Couldn't Forget: The Story of Solomon's Memory ············ 65
Text C: The Boy Who Needed to Play: The Story of Dibs ···························· 71
Learning Skills: Academic Report Skills I ·· 78

Unit 4　English Language and Learning
Introduction: Learning English ·· 86
Text A: Mother Tongue ·· 89
Text B: Identity, Motivation and Autonomy in Second Language Acquisition from the Perspective of Complex Adaptive System ·· 95

Text C: Development: Some General Principles ········· 101
Learning Skills: Academic Report Skills II ········· 108

Unit 5　Learning Model-cooperative Learning

Introduction: What Is Happening to Cooperative Learning? ········· 114
Text A: Cooperative Learning: What Makes Groupwork Work? ········· 118
Text B: "The Union Is Unbroken" March 4, 1861 ········· 124
Text C: To Save the Union: 1861—1863 Moving Toward Emancipation ········· 128
Learning Skills: Cooperative Learning Skills ········· 133

下　篇

Unit 6　Educators Philosophies and Teaching Theories

Introduction: Early Teaching Models ········· 145
Text A: My Pedagogic Creed ········· 147
Text B: Jerome Bruner: The Lesson of the Story ········· 153
Text C: Curriculum Development from a Constructivist Perspective ········· 159
Learning Skills: Note-taking Skills ········· 164

Unit 7　My Perspectives on Education from Pedagogies to Globalization

Introduction: Education and Globalization: Some Hypotheses ········· 173
Text A: Tiger Moms: Is Tough Parenting Really the Answer? ········· 176
Text B: The Tutorial System: The Jewel in the Crown ········· 182
Text C: Education, the Nation-State, and Global Movement ········· 188
Learning Skills: Critical Reading Skills I ········· 194

Unit 8　Education and Teachers' Development

Introduction: Defining Teaching and Teacher Education ········· 201
Text A: The Novice Teacher: Armed and Dangerous
　　　　——A Cautionary Tale ········· 203
Text B: Teaching Teachers: Professional Development to Improve Student Achievement
········· 210
Text C: An Education President for the 21st Century ········· 218
Learning Skills: Critical Reading Skills II ········· 225

Unit 9 English Language and Teaching

Introduction: Approaches to Language Learning and Teaching ·················· 232
Text A: Illiteracy at Oxford and Harvard: Reflections on the Inability to Write ········ 236
Text B: TESOL in China: Current Challenges ······························· 241
Text C: From Reading to Writing, from Elementary to Graduate Students ············ 247
Learning Skills: Academic Writing Skills ··································· 253

Unit 10 Learning Model-inquiry Learning

Introduction: Bibliography of Henry VIII ··································· 264
Text A: Handling Henry VIII ··· 266
Text B: The Six Wives of Henry VIII ······································ 274
Text C: Who Were the Early Reformers in England? ························· 288
Learning Skills: Inquiry Learning Skills ···································· 296

References ·· 318

上 篇

Unit 1

Educators Philosophies and Learning Theories

Introduction

Nature of Learning[1]
Christina Hinton & Kurt W. Fischer

Learning Is Constructive

The constructivist view of learning has nowadays become more or less common ground among educational psychologists. But, what does this mean exactly? There is strong evidence now that learning is in some sense always constructive, even in environments with a predominantly guided learning approach. This is convincingly demonstrated by the research showing the occurrence of misconceptions (such as "multiplication makes bigger") and defective procedural skills among students in traditional mathematics classrooms. As expressed pithily by Hatano: "It is very unlikely that students have acquired them by being taught."

What is essential in the constructivist perspective is the mindful and effortful involvement of students in the processes of knowledge and skills acquisition in interaction with the environment. This is illustrated nicely by the solution strategy of first graders for one step word problems mentioned in earlier short description of constructivism.

There are, however, many versions of constructivism in the literature spanning a wide variety of theoretical and epistemological perspectives, as described by Phillips in his article "The good, the bad, and the ugly: The many faces of constructivism". This characterization still holds true today, so that at present we cannot yet claim to have a fully-fledged, research-based constructivist learning theory. The present state of the art thus calls for continued theoretical and empirical research to give a deeper understanding and a more fine-grained analysis of constructive learning processes that promote the acquisition of worthwhile knowledge, cognitive and self-regulation skills, and the affective components of adaptive competence. We need more research into the role and nature of teaching to foster such learning.

---

[1] Excerpt from "Historical Developments in the Understanding of Learning", *The Nature of Learning—Using Research to Inspire Practice,* OECD Publications, 2010.

Learning Is Self-regulated

Constructive learning, being about the process rather than the product, is also "self-regulated". This captures the fact that "individuals are metacognitively, motivationally and behaviorally active participants in their own learning process". Although research on self-regulation in education began only about 25 years ago, a substantial amount of empirical and theoretical work has already been carried out with interesting results.

First, we now know the major characteristics of self-regulated learners: they manage study time well, set higher immediate learning targets than others which they monitor more frequently and accurately, they set a higher standard before they are satisfied, with more self-efficacy and persistence despite obstacles. Second, self-regulation correlates strongly with academic achievement, and this has been found in different subject areas. Third, recent meta-analyses of teaching experiments show convincingly that self-regulation can be enhanced through appropriate guidance among primary and secondary school students. Important recent research by Anderson shows that the learning and achievement of disadvantaged students can be improved significantly by teaching self-regulatory skills.

There is still need for continued research in order to gain a better understanding of the key processes involved in effective self-regulation in school learning, tracing the development of students' regulatory skills, and unraveling how and under what classroom conditions students become self-regulated learners. That is, there is much still to be understood about how students learn to manage and monitor their own capacities of knowledge-building and skill acquisition and about how to enhance the transition from external regulation(by a teacher) to self-regulation.

Learning Is Situated or Contextual

It is also widely held in the educational research community that constructive and self-regulated learning occurs and should preferably be studied in context, i.e. in relation to the social, contextual and cultural environment in which these processes are embedded. In the late 1980s, the importance of context came into focus with the situated cognition and learning paradigm. This, as described above, emerged in reaction to the view of learning and thinking as highly individual and involving purely cognitive processes occurring in the head, and resulting in the construction of encapsulated mental representations. The situated view rightly stresses that learning is enacted essentially in interaction with, and especially through participation in, the social and cultural context. In mathematics, the situational perspective has stimulated the movement toward more authentic and realistic mathematics education.

The "situated cognition" perspective has nevertheless also come in for criticism. It has been criticized for being only "a 'loosely coupled' school of thought", for making inaccurate and exaggerated claims from which inappropriate educational lessons might be drawn and for downgrading or at least not appropriately addressing the role of knowledge in learning. There is therefore a need for further theoretical inquiry and empirical research to better integrate the positive aspects of both cognitive psychology and situativity theory.

Learning Is Collaborative

The collaborative nature of learning is closely related to the situated perspective that stresses the social character of learning. Effective learning is not a purely solo activity but essentially a distributed one, involving the individual student, others in the learning environment and the resources, technologies and tools that are available. The understanding of learning as a social process is also central to socio-constructivism, and despite the almost idiosyncratic processes of knowledge building, it means that individuals nevertheless acquire shared concepts and skills. Some consider social interaction essential, for instance, for mathematics learning as individual knowledge construction occurs through interaction; negotiation and cooperation.

The available literature provides substantial evidence supporting the positive effects of collaborative learning on academic achievement. It suggests that a shift toward more social interaction in classrooms would represent a worthwhile move away from the traditional emphasis on individual learning. It is important to avoid going too far to the opposite extreme, however: the value for learning of collaboration and interaction does not at all exclude that students develop new knowledge individually. Distributed and individual cognitions interact during productive learning, and there remain numerous unanswered questions relating to collaborative learning in small groups. For instance, we need a better understanding of the ways in which small-group activities influence students' learning and thinking, of the role of individual differences on group work and of the mechanisms at work during group processes.

In addition to the four main characteristics of the CSSC[①] conception of learning, two other aspects can be mentioned briefly: learning is cumulative and individually different. That it is cumulative is implied in it being constructive—students develop and build new knowledge and skills on the basis of what they already know and can do. Ausubel argued already in 1968 that the most important single factor influencing learning is the learner's prior knowledge. That claim has been vindicated by the studies showing that prior knowledge explains between 30% and 60% of the variance in learning results. The importance of prior knowledge clearly also underscores the value of linking formal to informal learning.

Learning is also individually different, which means that its processes and outcomes vary among students on a variety of pertinent variables. Prior knowledge is one of these variables, but so are ability, students' conceptions of learning, learning styles and strategies, their interest, motivation, self efficacy beliefs and emotions. Encouraging and sustaining effective learning therefore means that school should provide as much as

---

① CSSC 表示前文提到的 constructive self-regulated situated colcaborative.

possible adaptive education to take account of these differences.

Questions after reading:

Why is learning constructive, self-regulated or collaborative? Can you take examples from your own experience to illustrate?

Group work:

Topic: Before we further the theme, we need to reflect on what learning beliefs people have as either an individual or a group, such as objectives of learning, methods in learning experience.

Directions: Work as a group and share your ideas with others.

Text A

Brainstorming

Francis Bacon

Humanism: The term "humanism" has come to represent diverse philosophical and religious movements over the centuries. In general, humanist thought rejects belief in the supernatural, focusing instead on a human-centered view that emphasizes reason and scientific inquiry. During Europe's Renaissance, between roughly 1400 and 1650, humanism came to dominate social philosophy, literature and intellectual debate. The period marked a fascination with the Greek classics and secularism, the idea that religion and government should be separated. Individual expression and personal independence were greatly valued. Notable humanist thinkers included Italian Niccolo Machiavelli, author of *The Prince*, and Englishman Francis Bacon.

Empiricism: It is a theory of knowledge that asserts that knowledge comes only or primarily via sensory experience. Empiricism emphasizes the role of experience and evidence, especially sensory perception, in the formation of ideas, over the notion of innate ideas or traditions. In the philosophy of science, it emphasizes evidence, especially as discovered in experiments. It is a fundamental part of the scientific method that all hypotheses and theories must be tested against observations of the natural world rather than resting solely on a priori reasoning, intuition, or revelation.

Unit 1　Educators Philosophies and Learning Theories

Questions before reading:
Do you know anything that Confucius said on learning?
What do you know about Francis Bacon?

Of Studies[①]
Francis Bacon[②]

Studies serve for delight, for ornament, and for ability. Their chief use for delight is in privateness and retiring; for ornament, is in discourse; and for ability, is in the judgment and disposition of business.

For expert man can execute, and perhaps judge of particulars, one by one; but the general counsels, and the plots and marshalling of affairs, come best from those that are learned. To spend too much time in studies is sloth; to use them too much for ornament, is affectation; to make judgment wholly by their rules, is the humour of a scholar.

They perfect nature, and are perfected by experience: for natural abilities are like natural plants, that need pruning by study; and studies themselves do give forth directions too much at large, except they be bounded in by experience.

Crafty men contemn studies, simple men admire them, and wise men use them; for they teach not their own use; but that is a wisdom without them, and above them, won by observation.

Read not to contradict and confute; nor to believe and take for granted; nor to find talk and discourse; but to weigh and consider.

Some books are to be tasted, others to be swallowed, and some few to be chewed and digested; that is, some books are to be read only in parts; others to be read, but not curiously; and some few to be read wholly, and with diligence and attention. Some books also may be read by deputy, and extracts made of them by others; but that would be only in the less important arguments, and the meaner sort of books; else distilled books are, like common distilled waters, flashy things.

Reading maketh a full man; conference a ready man; and writing an exact man. And therefore, if a man write little, he had need have a great memory; if he confer little, he had need have a present wit; and if he read little, he had need have much cunning, to seem to know that he doth not.

Histories make men wise; poets witty; the mathematics subtle; natural philosophy deep; moral grave; logic and rhetoric able to contend. *Abeunt studia in morse*[③].

Nay there is no stond or impediment in the wit, but may be wrought out by fit

---

① Excerpt from *The Essays—Francis Bacon*. Ebooks@Adelaide, 2014.
② Francis Bacon (1561—1626) was an English lawyer, statesman, essayist, historian, intellectual reformer, philosopher, and champion of modern science. Francis Bacon is the father of the scientific method, which is fundamental to natural philosophy.
③ 拉丁文:凡有所学皆成性格。

studies; like as diseases of the body may have appropriate exercises. Bowling is good for the stone and reins; shooting for the lungs and breast; gentle walking for the stomach; riding for the head; and the like. So if a man's wit be wandering, let him study the mathematics; for in demonstrations, if his wit be called away never so little, he must begin again. If his wit be not apt to distinguish or find differences, let him study the schoolmen; for they are *cymini sectores*①. If he be not apt to beat over matters, and to call up one thing to prove and illustrate another, let him study the lawyers' cases. So every defect of the mind may have a special receipt.

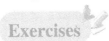

1. Reading Comprehension:

There are four suggested answers marked A, B, C and D. Choose the best answer for each question.

1. Which one of the following statements is not Bacon's attitude towards learning?
   A. While reading, people need to think, analyze and reason.
   B. While reading, people should treat books differently according to their real value.
   C. People who do not have the habit of reading must be cunning.
   D. Different subjects have different values and help build different character.

2. What is the correct understanding of this sentence "To spend too much time in studies is sloth"?
   A. People who spend too much time in studies will be regarded lazy.
   B. People should not waste too much time on studies as it is not worthwhile.
   C. People should not devote whole-heartedly in learning as there are much more valuable things to do in life.
   D. Spending too much time influences the efficiency of learning.

3. What writing techniques does Bacon employ to develop the article?
   A. Cadence and reasoning.
   B. Symmetry, allusion and metaphor.
   C. Parallelism, ellipsis and analogy.
   D. All of the above.

4. Which one of the following characteristics can be best summarized as Bacon's writing style in this essay?
   A. Simplicity, clarity.
   B. Brevity, compactness and reasoning.
   C. Witty, brief and humorous.
   D. Critical, ironical.

---

① 拉丁文:吹毛求疵。

Unit 1 Educators Philosophies and Learning Theories

II. Summary:

Summarize Text A and match information into different categories.

Learning subjects	1. 2. 3.
Learning methods	1. 2. 3.
Reading books	1. 2. 3.

III. Judgments and Implications:

Do the following statements agree with the information given in the passage?
True   if the statement is true according to the passage
False   if the statement contradicts the passage

1. In this essay, "study" itself actually includes a variety of meanings, such as reading, learning and studying.
2. According to the essay, men with great experience govern affairs better than men who are learned.
3. The solutions of diseases of the body and the disadvantages in mind share similarities as they both can be resolved through physical and mental exercise.
4. If one is not able to find out the differences, learning math could make people subtle, exact and concentrate on his studies.
5. The use of Latin in the text is to show the nobility of Bacon as well as his knowledge.

IV. Critical Questions:

1. Read the following quotes from <u>Analects</u> and translate them into Chinese.

Confucius said, "To study and not think is a waste. To think and not study is dangerous."

Confucius said, "Yu, shall I teach you about knowledge? What you know, you know, what you don't know, you don't know. This is knowledge."

Confucius said, "Isn't it a pleasure to study and practice what you have learned? Isn't it also great when friends visit from distant places? If people do not recognize me and it doesn't bother me, am I not a Superior Man?"

Confucius said, "Reviewing what you have learned and learning anew, you are fit to be a teacher."

The Master said, "They who know the truth are not equal to those who love it, and they who love it are not equal to those who delight in it."

2. Discussion.

Under the topic of learning, can you find certain similarities between Confucius and Bacon? How can these learning methods benefit your learning of English?

Text B

Brainstorming

Queen Victoria

Victorian era: The Victorian era of British history was the period of Queen Victoria's reign from 20 June 1837 until her death on 22 January, 1901. It was a long period of peace, prosperity, refined sensibilities and national self-confidence for Britain.

Curriculum and Instruction (C&I) is a field within education which seeks to research, develop, and implement curriculum changes that increase student achievement within and outside of schools. The field focuses on how students learn and the best ways to educate. It tries to find answers to questions such as "why to teach", "what to teach", "how to teach" and "how to evaluate" in instructional process.

Questions before reading:

Which subjects have impressed you most at university? Why?

What Knowledge Is of Most Worth?[1]
Herbert Spencer[2]

It has been truly remarked that, in order of time, decoration precedes dress. Among people who submit to great physical suffering that they may have themselves handsomely tattooed, extremes of temperature are borne with but little attempt at mitigation. Humboldt tells us that an Orinoco Indian, though quite regardless of bodily comfort, will yet labour for a fortnight to purchase pigment wherewith to make himself admired; and

---

[1] Excerpt from *What Knowledge Is of Most Worth?* General Books LLC, 2009.
[2] Herbert Spencer (27 April 1820 — 8 December 1903) was an English philosopher, biologist, sociologist, and prominent classical liberal political theorist of the Victorian era.

that the same woman who would not hesitate to leave her hut without a fragment of clothing on, would not dare to commit such a breach of decorum as to go out unpainted. Voyagers uniformly find that coloured beads and trinkets are much more prized by wild tribes than are calicoes or broadcloths. And the anecdotes we have of the ways in which, when shirts and coats are given, savages turn them to some ludicrous display, show how completely the idea of ornament predominates over that of use. Nay, there are still more extreme illustrations: witness the fact narrated by Capt. Speke of his African attendants, who strutted about in their goat-skin mantles when the weather was fine, but when it was wet, took them off, folded them up, and went about naked, shivering in the rain! Indeed, the facts of aboriginal life seem to indicate that dress is developed out of decorations. And when we remember that even among ourselves most think more about the fineness of the fabric than its warmth, and more about the cut than the convenience—when we see that the function is still in great measure subordinated to the appearance—we have further reason for inferring such an origin.

It is not a little curious that the like relations hold with the mind. Among mental as among bodily acquisitions, the ornamental comes before the useful. Not only in times past, but almost as much in our own era, that knowledge which conduces to personal well-being has been postponed to that which brings applause. In the Greek schools, music, poetry, rhetoric, and a philosophy which, until Socrates taught, had but little bearing upon action, were the dominant subjects; while knowledge aiding the arts of life had a very subordinate place. And in our own universities and schools at the present moment the like antithesis holds. We are guilty of something like a platitude when we say that throughout his after-career a boy, in nine cases out of ten, applies his Latin and Greek to no practical purposes. The remark is trite that in his shop, or his office, in managing his estate or his family, in playing his part as director of a bank or a railway, he is very little aided by this knowledge he took so many years to acquire— so little, that generally the greater part of it drops out of his memory; and if he occasionally vents a Latin quotation, or alludes to some Greek myth, it is less to throw light on the topic in hand than for the sake of effect. If we inquire what is the real motive for giving boys a classical education, we find it to be simply conformity to public opinion. Men dress their children's minds as they do their bodies, in the prevailing fashion. As the Orinoco Indian puts on his paint before leaving his hut, not with a view to any direct benefit, but because he would be ashamed to be seen without it; so, a boy's drilling in Latin and Greek is insisted on, not because of their intrinsic value, but that he may not be disgraced by being found ignorant of them—that he may have "the education of a gentleman"—the badge marking a certain social position, and bringing a consequent respect.

Thoroughly to realize the truth that with the mind as with the body the ornamental precedes the useful, it is needful to glance at its rationale. This lies in the fact that, from the far past down even to the present, social needs have subordinated individual needs, and that the chief social need has been the control of individuals. It is not, as we commonly suppose, that there are no governments but those of monarchs, and parliaments, and constituted authorities. These acknowledged governments are supplemented by other unacknowledged ones, that grow up in all circles, in which every man or woman strives to be king or queen or lesser dignitary. To get above some and be reverenced by them, and to propitiate those who are above us, is the universal struggle in which the chief energies of life are expended. By the accumulation of wealth, by style of living, by beauty of dress, by display of knowledge or intellect, each tries to subjugate others; and so aids in weaving that ramified network of restraints by which society is kept in order. It is not the savage chief only, who, in formidable war-paint, with scalps at his belt, aims to strike awe into his inferiors; it is not only the belle who, by elaborate toilet, polished manners, and numerous accomplishments, strives to "make conquests;" but the scholar, the historian, the philosopher, use their acquirements to the same end. We are none of us content with quietly unfolding our own individualities to the full in all directions; but have a restless craving to impress our individualities upon others, and in some way subordinate them. And this it is which determines the character of our education. Not what knowledge is of most real worth, is the consideration; but what will bring most applause, honour, respect—what will most conduce to social position and influence—what will be most imposing. As, throughout life, not what we are, but what we shall be thought, is the question; So in education, the question is, not the intrinsic value of knowledge, so much as its extrinsic effects on others. And this being our dominant idea, direct utility is scarcely more regarded than by the barbarian when filing his teeth and staining his nails.

If there needs any further evidence of the rude, undeveloped character of our education, we have it in the fact that the comparative worths of different kinds of knowledge have been as yet scarcely even discussed—much less discussed in a methodic way with definite results. Not only is it that no standard of relative values has yet been agreed upon; but the existence of any such standard has not been conceived in any clear manner. And not only is it that the existence of any such standard has not been clearly conceived; but the need for it seems to have been scarcely even felt. Men read books on this topic, and attend lectures on that; decide that their children shall be instructed in these branches of knowledge, and shall not be instructed in those; and all under the guidance of mere custom, or liking, of prejudice; without ever considering the enormous importance of determining in some rational way what things are really most worth learning. It is true that in all circles we have occasional remarks on the importance of this or the other order of information. But whether the degree of its importance justifies the expenditure of the time needed to acquire it; and whether there are not things of more importance to which the time might be better devoted; are queries which, if raised at all, are disposed of quite summarily, according to personal predilections. It is true also, that from time to time, we hear revived the standing controversy respecting the comparative merits of classics and mathematics. Not only, however, is this controversy carried on in an empirical manner, with no reference to an ascertainment; but the question at issue is totally insignificant when compared with the general question of which it is part. To suppose that deciding whether a mathematical or a classical education is the best, is deciding what is the proper curriculum, is much the same thing as to suppose that the whole of dietetics lies in determining whether or not bread is more nutritive than potatoes!

The question which we contend is of such transcendent moment, is, not whether such or such knowledge is of worth, but what is its relative worth? When they have named certain advantages which a given course of study has secured them, persons are apt to assume that they have justified themselves: quite forgetting that the adequateness of the advantages is the point to be judged. There is, perhaps, not a subject to which men devote attention that has not some value. A year diligently spent in getting up heraldry, would very possibly give a little further insight into ancient manners and morals, and into the origin of names. Any one who should learn the distances between all the towns in England, might, in the course of his life, find one or two of the thousand facts he had acquired of some slight service when arranging a journey. Gathering together all the small gossip of a county, profitless occupation as it would be, might yet occasionally help to establish some useful fact—say, a good example of hereditary transmission. But in these cases, every one would admit that there was no proportion between the required labour and the probable benefit. How one would tolerate the proposal to devote some years of a boy's time to getting such information, at the cost of much more valuable information which he might else have got. And if here the test of relative value is appealed to and held conclusive, then should it be appealed to and held conclusive throughout. Had we time to master all subjects we need not be particular. To quote the old song:

Could a man be secure
That his days would endure
As of old, for a thousand long years,
What things might he know!
What deeds might he do!
And all without hurry or care.

"But we that have but span-long lives" must ever bear in mind our limited time for acquisition. And remembering how narrowly this time is limited, not only by the shortness of life, but also still more by the business of life, we ought to be especially solicitous to employ what time we have to the greatest advantage. Before devoting years to some subject which fashion or fancy suggests, it is surely wise to weigh with great care the worth of the results, as compared with the worth of various alternative results which the same years might bring if otherwise applied.

In education, then, this is the question of questions, which it is high time we discussed in some methodic way. The first in importance, though the last to be considered, is the problem—how to decide among the conflicting claims of various subjects on our attention. Before there can be a rational curriculum, we must settle which things it most concerns us to know; or, to use a word of Bacon's, now unfortunately obsolete—we must determine the relative values of knowledges.

Exercises

I. Reading Comprehension:

There are four suggested answers marked A, B, C and D. Choose the best answer for each question.

1. From the first paragraph, it can be inferred_____.
   A. primitive men are able to appreciate natural beauty
   B. natural ornaments were prevalent paints
   C. human beings concerned more about quality than quantity from the primitive stage
   D. exteriority overpasses pragmatism originally

2. In the sentence "it is less to throw light on the topic in hand than for the sake of effect", "it" indicates that _____.
   A. subjects learned at school are of little usefulness
   B. many subjects learned at school are meaningless to the public
   C. many subjects learned at school can be hardly taken effect to solve problems
   D. many subjects learned at school can only be selected to explain issues than consequences

3. Why does the author say "social needs have subordinated individual needs" in paragraph 3?
   A. Because monarchs and parliaments are involved.
   B. Because energies of life are wasted to propitiate the superior.
   C. Because all of us restlessly impress our individuality to others.
   D. Because social needs bring most applause, honour, and respect.

4. From the quoted poem, the author implies that _____.
   A. a man can be educated in a lifelong time
   B. a man does need to learn whatever things gradually
   C. a man can hardly learn all subjects
   D. a man does not need to learn subjects urgently

5. Which one of the following writing styles describes the organization of the whole text?
   A. An argument which presents statements and opinions.
   B. An argument which induces views by cases.
   C. An argument which examines and illustrates principles.
   D. An argument which deduces ideas for examples.

II. Summary:

Complete the summary below. Choose ONLY ONE WORD from the text for each answer.

It has been truly remarked that, in order of time, decoration precedes dress. Indeed, among mental as among bodily acquisitions, the ornamental comes _____ the useful. The knowledge has been _____ to that which brings applause. From the far past down even to the present, social needs have _____ individual needs. The character of our education is not the intrinsic _____ of knowledge, but what will bring most applause, _____ and respect. In fact, the comparative worth of _____ kinds of knowledge have been as yet scarcely even discussed. The question which we contend is not whether such or such knowledge is of worth, but what is it _____ worth? The first in importance is the problem—how to decide among the conflicting claims of _____ subjects on our attention.

III. Judgments and Implications:

Do the following statements agree with the information given in the passage?
True   if the statement is true according to the passage
False   if the statement contradicts the passage

1. In the Greek schools, music, poetry, math, and philosophy were the dominant subjects.
2. Men in most cases would rather equip their children's minds with knowledge in use than that in popular fashion.
3. Men learn things according to the custom, preference and the relative worth of knowledge.
4. There is little link between required labour and the probable benefit.
5. We must weigh and consider which things are the most relevant to us to know, before we set up a sensible curriculum.

IV. Critical Questions:

Whether professional knowledge or practical skills should be taught in university has become an arguable issue, and how would you comment on it?

Text C

Brainstorming

> *Discovery learning:* Discovery learning takes place in problem solving situations where the learner draws on his own experience and prior knowledge and is a method of instruction through which students interact with their environment by exploring and manipulating objects, wrestling with questions and controversies, or performing experiments.

Questions before reading:

What kind of learning activities do you always have in the classroom? Are there any differences in learning activities between college and high school?

The Differences Between Learning by Instruction and Learning by Discovery

David H. Jonassen

Getting more information is learning, and so is coming to understand what you did not understand before. But there is an important difference between these two kinds of learning.

To be informed is to know simply that something is the case. To be enlightened is to know, in addition, what it is all about: why it is the case, what its connections are with other facts, in what respects it is the same, in what respects it is different, and so forth.

This distinction is familiar in terms of the difference between being able to remember something and being able to explain it. If you remember what an author says, you have learned something from reading him. If what he says is true, you have even learned, you have gained nothing but information if you have exercised only your memory. You have not been enlightened. Enlightenment is achieved only when, in addition to knowing what an author says, you know what he means and why he says it.

It is true, of course, that you should be able to remember what the author said as well as know what he meant.

Montaigne speaks of an abecedarian ignorance that precedes knowledge, and a doctoral ignorance that comes after it. The first is the ignorance of those who, not knowing their ABC's, cannot read at all. The second is the ignorance of those who have misread many books. They are, as Alexander Pope rightly calls them, bookful blockheads, ignorantly read. There have always been literate ignoramuses who have read too widely and not well. The Creeks had a name for such a mixture of learning and folly which might be applied to the bookish but poorly read of all ages. They are all sophomores.

To avoid this error—the error of assuming that to be widely read and to be well-read are the same thing—we must consider a certain distinction in types of learning. This distinction has a significant bearing on the whole business of reading and its relation to education generally.

In the history of education, men have often distinguished between learning by instruction and learning by discovery. Instruction occurs when one person teaches another through speech or writing. We can, however, gain knowledge without being taught. If this were not case, and every teacher had to be taught what he in turn teaches others, there would be no beginning in the acquisition of knowledge. Hence, there must be discovery—the process of learning something by research, by investigation, or by reflection, without being taught.

Discovery stands to instruction as learning without a teacher stands to learning through the help of one. In both cases, the activity of learning goes on in the one who learns. It would be a mistake to suppose that discovery is active learning and instruction passive. There is no inactive learning, just as there is no inactive reading.

This is so true, in fact, that a better way to make the distinction clear is to call instruction "aided discovery". without going into learning theory as psychologists conceive it, it is obvious that teaching is a very special art, sharing with only two other arts—agriculture and medicine—an exceptionally important characteristic. A doctor may do many things for his patient, but in the final analysis it is the patient himself who must get well-grow in health. The farmer does many things for his plants or animals, but in the final analysis it is they that must grow in size and excellence. Similarly, although the teacher may help his student in many ways, it is the student himself who must do the learning.

The difference between learning by instruction and learning by discovery—or, as we would prefer to say, between aided and unaided discovery—is primarily a difference in the materials on which the learners works. When the help of a teacher—the learner acts on something communicated to him. He learns by acts of reading or listening. If we ignore the minor differences between these two ways of receiving communication, we can say that reading and listening are the same art—the art of being taught. When, however, the learner proceeds without the help of any sort of teacher, the operations of learning are performed on nature or the world rather than discourse. The rules of such learning constitute the art of unaided discovery. If we use the word "reading" loosely, we can say that discovery—strictly, unaided discovery—is the art of reading nature or the world, as instruction (being taught, or aided discovery) is the art of reading books or, to include listening, of learning from discourse.

What about thinking? If by "thinking" we mean the use of our minds to gain knowledge or understanding, and if learning by discovery and learning by instruction exhaust the ways of gaining knowledge, then thinking must take place during both of these two activities. We must think in the course of reading and listening, just as we must think in the course of research. Naturally, the kinds of thinking are different—as different as the two ways of learning are.

The reason why many people regard thinking as more closely associated with research and unaided discovery than with being taught is that they suppose reading and listening be relatively effortless. It is probably true that one dose less thinking when one reads for information or entertainment than when one is undertaking to discover something. Those are the less active sorts of reading, but it is not true of the more active reading—the effort to understand. No one who has done this sort of reading would say it can be done thoughtlessly.

Thinking is only one part of the activity of learning. One must also use one's senses and imagination. One must observe, and remember, and construct imaginatively what cannot be observed. There is, again, a tendency to stress the role of these activities in the process of unaided discovery and to forget or minimize their place in the process of being taught through reading or listening. For example, many people assume that though a poet must use his imagination in writing a poem, art of reading, in short, includes all of the same skills that are involved in the art of unaided discovery; keenness of observation, readily available memory, range of imagination, and, of course, an intellect trained in analysis and reflection. The reason for this is that reading in this sense is discovery, too—although with help instead of without it.

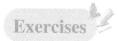

I. Reading Comprehension:

There are four suggested answers marked A, B, C and D. Choose the best answer for each question.

1. What is the main argument of the text?
   A. Learning is to be informed and tutored through instruction.
   B. Thinking is the utmost important activity of learning.
   C. The nature of learning is the distinction between instruction and discovery.
   D. The nature of learning is the distinction between instruction and thinking.
2. Which one of the following sentences indicates the difference between learning by instruction and learning by discovery?
   A. To be informed is to know simply that something is the case.
   B. There is no inactive learning, just as there is no inactive reading.
   C. The activities of reading and listening are both learning by instruction.
   D. The differences between learning by instruction and learning by discovery is the differences between thinking and reading.
3. Which one of the following statements is not true?
   A. People regard thinking as more closely associated with research and unaided discovery, because those are the less active sorts of reading.
   B. Thinking, senses and imaginations have to be integrated in the learning process.
   C. The art of reading has been regarded as unaided discovery.
   D. Since thinking exists in both aided and unaided learning, learning means thinking.
4. The example from Montaigne is used to illustrate _____.
   A. reading and learning is essentially integrated
   B. extensive reading does not mean intensive reading
   C. misreading is one cause of inefficient learning
   D. the fundamental distinction of reading reflects its relation to learning
5. The tone that the author used to write this article is _____.
   A. ironic
   B. critical
   C. analytical
   D. objective

Unit 1　Educators Philosophies and Learning Theories

II. Judgments and Implications:

Do the following statements agree with the information given in the passage?
True　if the statement is true according to the passage
False　if the statement contradicts the passage

1. Enlightenment is achieved only when you know what the author means and why he says it.
2. In the process of learning, discovery is more important than instruction because we can gain knowledge without being taught.
3. Both instruction and discovery are active learning.
4. Instruction can be called "aided discovery" because it is similar to agriculture and medicine.
5. The difference between instruction and discovery is primarily a difference in the materials on which the learner works.
6. Discovery is the art of reading nature or the world, and instruction is the art of reading books.

III. Matching:

　　Read the following items (from A to E). They are all related to learning by instruction or learning by discovery. Categorize them into corresponding groups.

　　A. The process of learning something by research, by investigation, or by reflection, without being taught.
　　B. Aided discovery.
　　C. One person teaches anther through speech or writing.
　　D. Learning by acts of reading or listening.
　　E. Thinking.

Learning by Instruction:

Learning by Discovery:

IV. Critical Questions:

　　Do you have any experience of discovery learning? What is it? If not, can you work out a learning activity of discovery learning?

Learning Skills

Library Skills

I. Read the following terms and check your understanding with their definitions.

> Journal
> Specialized sources (research papers)
> Encyclopedia
> Specialist dictionaries
> Magazines & newspapers
> Online resources (general websites)

Journal: It is sometimes used as a synonym for "magazine", in academic use, a journal refers to a serious, scholarly publication that is peer-reviewed. A non-scholarly magazine written for an educated audience about an industry or an area of professional activity is usually called a professional magazine.

Specialized sources: Academic papers, thesis or dissertations have always been referred as a specialized source.

Encyclopedia: It is a type of reference work—a compendium holding a summary of information from either all branches of knowledge or a particular branch of knowledge.

Specialist dictionaries: Dictionaries provide lexis or discourse in a particular register or genre, which specialists or professionals have to consult for terminologies.

Magazines & newspapers: Daily information resources that people may always refer to as a mean to indicate fact or truth.

Online resources: The fast development of Internet prompts varied combinations of information resources ranging from general websites to communication tools.

II. Using the Library Catalog

To identify specific books or journal titles in the library use the Library Catalog located on the Library Website homepage. You can search by words or phrase (keyword), author, title, subject, or periodical title. To search, click on the Library Catalog and type in your topic. If you don't see any relevant books available, try typing in broader or related terms to describe your topic.

Library Catalog

Write down the following information for one book, and then go to the book shelves to find it.

Unit 1　Educators Philosophies and Learning Theories

Title: _____
Author: _____
Date of Publication: _____

III. Collecting Reference Books

Reference books provide great overviews of a topic and are extremely credible sources. These are examples of some of the reference books in the discipline of education available at the Library.

Reference Books:

A. Higher Education

Higher Education in the 21th Century
The Marketisation of Higher Education and the Student as Consumer
The Benefits of Higher Education for Individuals and Society
Higher Education and International Student Mobility in the Global Knowledge Economy

B. English Language Teaching

Teaching Grammar in Second Language Classrooms—Integrating Form—Focused Instruction in Communicative Context 2010
Effects of the Second Language on the First Communicative Language Teaching
Second Language Listening
Register, Genre, and Style

Use library catalog to select one book from Reference Collection Books above, and then fill in the missing information.

Title of reference books you used:	Page numbers where you find your topic:
Sample: Second Language Listening	Sample: The nature of spoken language: pp.47—59

IV. Finding Articles

You use articles from journals to update the information you found in books and to find discussions of current theories and developments in your topic area.

Libraries subscribe to many journals, magazines, and newspapers. These publications are called periodicals because they are published over and over again... periodically. Libraries are adding many of these periodicals to their collections electronically via databases and getting rid of paper or print copies.

Browse through a few e-journals. Find an article of interest to you, and write:
Title of article: _____
Author: _____
Title of journal: _____
Date of issue: _____
Volume number: _____ Issue Number: _____ Page article begins: _____

V. Using Internet

Sometimes, it is useful to collect general information from a searching engine or encyclopedia, when Internet is easily accessible or it requires only basic facts.

Log onto the website below to find an interesting topic and complete the form.
http://en.wikipedia.org/wiki/Main_Page
Topic: _____
Categories it refers to: _____
Other related terms or websites: _____

Use searching engines to look for a topic in your area and evaluate valid (useful and good quality) information.
http://www.google.com.hk/webhp?rls=ig&hl=zh-CN
http://cn.yahoo.com/
Topic: _____
Valid sources: _____ (in numbers)
Author: _____
Title of page or document: _____
Date of your Web page: _____
URL of your document or page: _____
Is it clear who wrote the material?
Are the author's qualifications stated?
Is there a phone number or address of the sponsoring organization?

👉 *Group Work Activities*

Work in groups to complete the following two tasks:
1. Based on what we have discussed in learning, you are supposed to use at least two above-mentioned ways in the Library Skills to search for resources referring to knowledge learning, learning method, learning style or learning outcome.
2. When you have found the materials, you are required to write a summary as a book report to present what you have learned useful from it.

Unit 1 Educators Philosophies and Learning Theories

Self-evaluation Form

What are the main objectives in this unit?
___
___
___

What useful vocabularies and expressions have you learned from this unit?
___
___
___

What key terms and educational knowledge have you learned?
___
___
___

Have you used the learning skills before? Why do you think they are useful or not useful?
___
___
___

If possible, what would you like to add to make learning more interesting and relevant?
___
___
___

Unit 2

My Perspectives on Education Between China and America

Introduction

Defining Comparative Education: Conceptions[1]
Harold J. Noah

The last decade has witnessed not only a vast burgeoning of the literature in and about comparative education, but also a radical change in the rationales, methods, and goals of the field. Whether this change in landscape has been for the better or the worse I shall leave for colleagues to judge.

Consider what is happening to the term "comparative" in the title that denotes our field. I believe that we are about to move rather rapidly away from the everyday meaning of the word to a much more technical meaning. This rather radical redefinition of the term "comparative education" will involve at once a limitation and an extension of its scope. The impulse toward limitation will arise because we have come to realise that many studies that happen to use international and foreign data are not to be considered "comparative" simply by virtue of that fact; and the impulse toward extension will occur because many studies conducted on the basis of data drawn from within a single country nevertheless have a valid claim to be considered comparative, once we define the term in a way that reflects the function of comparison in systematic explanation.

Clearly, while this process is continuing we can expect a rather lively controversy on just what the term should and does mean. The summary of our deliberations may legitimately expect to record what is happening to the nature of our field, and if we are optimistic, we can even hope to influence it.

Comparative education has mistakenly come to be identified either with the study of education in another country, or with studies using data drawn from more than one country. This view of what constitutes comparative education enjoys the sanction of both common usage and common sense. One finds out what is going on abroad and compares it with what is happening at home, often with a practical programme of amelioration in

---

[1] Excerpt from "Defining Comparative Education: Conceptions," in Reginald Edwards et al, eds. *Relevant Methods in Comparative Education.* Hamburg: UNESCO Institute for Education, 1973.

view. Certainly, many essays in comparative education are of this type. Alternatively, one uses a collection of multi-national data to identify, describe, and compare relationships (usually correlations) within education, or between education and other social phenomena. Again, I must emphasize that to call such studies "comparative" agrees with common sense and usage. But the weakness of that position is that it establishes as the criterion for classification as a comparative study, the mere presence or absence of foreign or multi-national characteristics of data, and by implication ignores, or even denies, the existence of a characteristically comparative method. We are hindered from asking a set of key questions: Are all inter-, cross-, or multi-national studies ipso facto comparative? Are all comparative studies necessarily either inter-, cross-, or multi-national? What, indeed, are the necessary and sufficient conditions for a study to be comparative? Does there exist a characteristic comparative approach to a problem? If so, what is it?

Nations constitute one important set of systems that attract our attention, and we have employed so-called comparative studies largely to identify and describe the attributes of such national systems. We have ended up with "nominal" statements of the type: "In country A, the secondary school curriculum is such-and-such; while in country B. it is so-and-so; and in countries C, D, and E, it is something else". Or, we might say in quantitative terms: "In country A, the fraction of the GNP spent on education is high (7—8 percent); in country B, it is moderate (5 percent); in country C, it is low (2.5—3 percent)".

However, as the social sciences have extended the range of questions they ask and as comparative studies (among them, comparative education) have matured, so we have begun to comprehend a fundamentally different role for comparison, whether conducted on the basis of national systems, or of other units. The key to this transformation in our thought lies in the attempt inherent in the social sciences to explain and predict, rather than merely to identify and describe. A simplified example may, perhaps, help illustrate the new emphasis in comparative work:

Let us assume that we wish to explain (and, perhaps predict) the relationship between the size of a family's income and the probability of the children in the family enrolling in full-time post-secondary education. If we find mirabile dictu that this relationship is the same from country to country, then we have no need to proceed further. We can immediately make a general (that is, a non-system-specific) statement defining a relationship between family income and the probability of post-secondary enrolment that is valid without including the names of any countries. But matters are more complicated if we are faced with the more likely case in which relationships differ from country to country. For example, we might find that while all countries exhibit a positive relationship between these two variables, the correlation is very strong in some countries, only moderate in others, and rather weak in a third group. Or, putting it in the language of least-squares linear regression analysis, we find that our best fitting equation explains different proportions of the observed variance in different countries. Let us assume, too, that no amount of within-system adjustment of either the independent or dependent variables alters the fundamental fact that in different countries similar levels of family income are associated with (or, "produce") different probabilities of a family's children attending post-secondary institutions.

This is the paradigm situation calling for employment of the comparative method. We now have to ask, what are the system-level factors that are at work, influencing the interaction of within-system variables? As we shift the level of analysis from consideration of within-system to system-level factors, we are engaged in trying out the effect upon these different within-system relationships of introducing additional, theoretically justifiable independent variables, in the form of system characteristics. We continue to do this until we can no longer (a) increase further the proportion of observed variance explained within each country; and, (b) reduce further the differences among countries in the proportions of observed variance explained.

Questions after reading:
What are the two different conceptions of comparative education mentioned above?

Group work:
Topic: Do you agree that children from rich families are more likely to receive higher education in all countries? What are the factors influencing the possibilities of college enrollment? Do all the factors work the same from country to country? If these factors can be adjusted, is it possible to change the enrollment of students between rich and poor families?

Directions: Work as a group and share your ideas with others.

Text A

Brainstorming

Decentralization: It is defined as the transfer of decision-making authority closer to the consumer or beneficiary. This can take the form of transferring powers to lower levels of an organization, which is called deconcentration or administrative decentralization. A popular form of deconcentration in education is to give additional responsibilities to schools. This is often called school autonomy or school-based management and may take the form of creating elected or appointed school councils and giving them budgets and the authority to make important educational decisions. Deconcentration may also take the form of empowering school directors or directors and teaching faculty to make decisions within the school.

Unit 2 My Perspectives on Education Between China and America

> *University systems:* Higher education functions as a system to complete missions of teaching, research and social service, university as an organization includes both the undergraduate level (sometimes referred to as tertiary education) and the graduate (or postgraduate) level (sometimes referred to as graduate school). Universities are generally composed of several colleges. In the United States, universities can be private and independent, like Yale University, they can be public and State governed, like the Pennsylvania State System of Higher Education, or they can be independent but State funded, like the University of Virginia.

Questions before reading:
Can you illustrate any differences on education between China and America?

Re-education[1]
Ann Hulbert

"Definitely wake me up around 9!!! I have an important presentation... wake me up at that time please... Thanks!! Meijie."

The e-mail message, sent to me at 3:55 a.m. under the subject line "yeah!" was my enthusiastic welcome to Harvard from a freshman named Tang Meijie. That was last May, nine months after she arrived on campus from mainland China. Except for the ungodly hour at which the message was dashed off, you wouldn't have guessed that its author had come to Cambridge trailing accomplishments and expectations that were impressive even by Harvard standards. Nor was there obvious evidence of a student superstar in the tousled figure in a sweatshirt and khakis who appeared at the Greenhouse Café in the Science Center at around 10 a.m. Greeting me with a reflexive bow, as she had at our first meeting a couple of months earlier, Meijie apologized for taking a few minutes to finish up the talk she had been assigned to give that morning in one of her courses.

Her topic gave her away. What Meijie was editing between bites of a bacon cheeseburger and sips of coffee was a short presentation for an expository-writing class called Success Stories. The questions addressed in the course, which focused on "what philosopher William James once called 'our national disease,' the pursuit of success", have become newly urgent ones in Meijie's own country. "What is 'success'?" the course introduction asked. "Is it a measure of one's financial worth? Moral perfection? Popularity? How do families, schools and popular culture invite us to think about success? And how are we encouraged to think about failure?" At Harvard, she and her classmates were discussing those issues as they read, among other things, *The Great Gatsby* and David Brooks on America's résumé-rich "organization kids" and watched

---
[1] Excerpt from "Re-education", *The New York Times Magazine*, April 11, 2007.

movies. In China, a nation on a mission to become a 21st-century incubator of "world class" talent, Meijie is the movie. As she progressed through her classes in the cutting-edge city of Shanghai, spent a year abroad at a private high school in Washington, D.C., and came to Harvard, she became a celebrated embodiment of China's efforts to create a new sort of student—a student trying to expand her country's sometimes constricting vision of success.

Downstairs in the computer room of the Science Center, Meijie showed me the thousands of Chinese citations that come up when you Google her name. "That's very crazy," she said with a laugh, a girl all too familiar with the Chinese ardor for anything associated with the name Harvard. Getting in "early action" in December 2004 set off a media frenzy at home, where it's still relatively rare for students to enroll as undergraduates at elite American schools, and study abroad promises to provide a crucial edge in a jammed job market. A packet of press coverage her parents gave me—Meijie rolled her eyes at the trove—portrayed her as every Chinese parent's dream child. Child magazine accompanied photos of Meijie and her parents with counsel on how to "raise a great child". The winner of no fewer than 76 prizes at the "city level" or above, as one article marveled, she was a model that top Chinese students themselves were dying to emulate. "What Does Her Success Tell Us?" read a headline on an article in *The Shanghai Students' Post*. "Meijie Knocked at the Door of Harvard. Do You Want to Copy?" asked *The Morning News Express* in bold Chinese characters. For months, she was besieged by journalists begging to profile her; publishers, she recalls, clamored to sign her up to write her life story and companies asked her to advertise their products. A director of Goldman Sachs's China division wanted her on the board of the private school he recently helped found, which was then under construction in an erstwhile rice field outside Shanghai.

But what was truly exceptional about Meijie was how she responded to the adulation. The fervent worship back home made Meijie uncomfortable and anxious to clarify what she wasn't. "Don't call me 'Harvard Girl,'" she told one of many magazine interviewers. She was referring to a student six years ahead of her, Liu Yiting, whose arrival at Harvard in 1999 made her a huge celebrity in China when her parents published a book, *Harvard Girl*, describing the meticulous regimen that produced their star. It quickly sold almost a million and a half copies and inspired numerous how-to-groom-your-child-to-get-into-college-abroad knockoffs. For all her triumphs, Meijie wasn't obsessed with being at the head of the class and didn't want the well-programmed-paragon treatment. She excelled in assorted subjects, but her school reported that her overall ranking wasn't in the top 10 percent. Her parents had stood by, a little stunned, as their intrepid daughter won distinction in an unusual way, by accomplishing all kinds of things outside of the classroom.

Amid the hoopla, Meijie insisted that the last thing Chinese students (or parents) needed was to be encouraged in their blind reverence for an academic brand name, much less be told there was some new formula to follow and competitive frenzy to join. That was just the kind of pressure they had too much of already. It was everywhere in a culture with a long tradition of rigidly hierarchical talent selection, dating back to the imperial civil-service-exam system more than a thousand years ago—and still there in a school system driven by a daunting national college-entrance exam. The Chinese call it the Gaokao, a three-day ordeal for which the preparation is arduous—and on which a single point difference can spell radically different life options. The cramming ethos, which sets in before high school, was what Meijie had tried hard not to let erode her curiosity. In her experience, America had come to stand for a less pressured and more appealing approach to schooling. "There is something in the American educational system that helps America hold its position in the world," she told me. "Many people will think it's a cliché, but there is something huge about it, although there are a lot of flaws—like bad public schools and other stuff. But there's something really good, and it's very different from my educational system."

Once at Harvard, in the fall of 2005, Meijie figured out what she wanted to do. She would try to make liberal education's ideal of well-rounded self-fulfillment "more real in China". She plunged into conceiving a summer exchange program run by and for students. Meijie named it the Harvard Summit for Young Leaders in China, or Hsylc—pronounced "H-silk", evoking the historic trading route. In August 2006, on the campus of that now-completed private school outside Shanghai whose board she had joined, a cosmopolitan array of Harvard undergraduates would offer a dose of the more freewheeling American campus and classroom experience. Meijie and an inner circle of organizers (similarly on-the-go Harvard women, all of Chinese descent, some reared in the U.S.) envisaged nine days of small-group discussions on wide-ranging issues outside of math and science. Hsylc would also offer extracurricular excitement and social discovery—chances for students to try new things and connect with one another, rather than compete for prizes. The participants that Meijie had in mind were several hundred promising Chinese high-schoolers, to be chosen in an un-Chinese way. She and a selection committee would pick them on the basis not of their G.P.A.'s but of their extracurricular activities and their essays in response to the kinds of open-ended prompts they never encountered at school. On her list was a question that might be a banality in the U.S. but was a heresy at home: "If you could do one thing to change the world, what would it be?"

Meijie's answer to that question—help shake up Chinese education—puts her in step with the latest wave of a 30-year-old government effort to overhaul China's schools and universities to keep pace with "socialist modernization". After the chaos of the Cultural Revolution, when schools were closed and cadres of students assaulted "enemies of the state", Deng Xiaoping resumed the National College Entrance Exam in 1977, marking the start of a radical expansion of the education system. The continued growth since then has been a success in many respects; educational attainments and college attendance have surged. Yet in the process, some prominent government officials have grown concerned that too many students have become the sort of stressed-out, test-acing drone who fails to acquire the skills—creativity, flexibility, initiative, leadership—said to be necessary in the global marketplace. "Students are buried in an endless flood of homework and sit for one mock entrance exam after another, leaving them with heads swimming and eyes blurred," lamented former Vice Premier Li Lanqing in a book describing his efforts to address the problem. They arrive at college exhausted and emerge from it unenlightened—just when the country urgently needs a talented elite of innovators, the word of the hour. A recent report from the McKinsey consulting firm, "China's Looming Talent Shortage", pinpointed the alarming consequences of the country's so-called "stuffed duck" tradition of dry and outdated knowledge transfer: graduates lacking "the cultural fit", language skills and practical experience with teamwork and projects that multinational employers in a global era are looking for.

Even as American educators seek to emulate Asian pedagogy—a test-centered ethos and a rigorous focus on math, science and engineering—Chinese educators are trying to blend a Western emphasis on critical thinking, versatility and leadership into their own traditions. To put it another way, in the peremptorily utopian style typical of official Chinese directives (as well as of educationese over the world), the nation's schools must strive "to build citizens' character in an all-round way, gear their efforts to each and every student, give full scope to students' ideological, moral, cultural and scientific potentials and raise their labor skills and physical and psychological aptitudes, achieve vibrant student development and run themselves with distinction". Meijie's rise to star student reflects a much-publicized government call to promote "suzhi jiaoyu"—generally translated as "quality education", and also sometimes as "character education" or "all-round character education". Her story also raises important questions about the state's effort, which has been more generously backed by rhetoric than by money. The goal of change is to liberate students to pursue more fulfilling paths in a country where jobs are no longer assigned; it is also to produce the sort of flexibly skilled work force that best fits an international knowledge economy. But can personal desires and national demands be reconciled? Will the most promising students of the new era be as overburdened and regimented as before? As new opportunities have begun to emerge, so have tensions. If Meijie's own trajectory and her Hsylc brainchild are any guide, the force most likely to spur on deep-seated educational ferment in China may well turn out to be students themselves—still struggling with stress, yet doing so in an era of greater personal independence and international openness. Overachievers of the world unite!

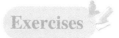

I. Reading Comprehension:

There are four suggested answers marked A, B, C and D. Choose the best answer for each question.

1. Why was Meijie considered as a celebrated embodiment of China's efforts to create

Unit 2　My Perspectives on Education Between China and America

a new sort of student?
  A. Because she went to Harvard University to pursue her higher degree.
  B. Because she is a student trying to expand her country's sometimes constricting vision of success.
  C. Because she hit the defects of China's education.
  D. Because she could study in America at such a young and tender age.
2. Why could people google Meijie's name on the Internet?
  A. Because she is the student who achieved great success.
  B. Because she won a prize in America
  C. Because Chinese are enthusiastic for anything concerning with the name Harvard.
  D. Because she is the fortuned child of the media.
3. What factor has made American school more ideal for students?
  A. America has come to stand for a less pressured and more attracting approach to schooling.
  B. American school provides a larger range of scholarship.
  C. American school provides a crucial edge in a jammed job market.
  D. American school proclaims the freedom of choice.
4. What has been the potential focus for Hsylc to provide extracurricular excitement and social discovery?
  A. To enrich their curricula.
  B. To let students involve in the social affairs.
  C. To encourage the students to try new things and connect with one another.
  D. To breed more social scientists.
5. What force might spur on deep-seated educational ferment in China?
  A. The government policy.
  B. The overseas influence.
  C. The school together with the parents.
  D. Students themselves.

II. Judgments and Implications:

Do the following statements agree with the information given in the passage?
True　if the statement is true according to the passage
False　if the statement contradicts the passage
1. At Meijie and the author's first meeting, Meijie was late as she had to finish the presentation in her writing course.
2. Before Meijie entering Harvard, she had no study experiences abroad.
3. Meijie felt glad and enthusiastic about public frenzy and adulation.
4. Meijie performs excellently in all her subjects and became a top student in Harvard.
5. According to Meijie, the American educational system put less pressure on students and adopted more flexible teaching methods.

6. Many Chinese government officials were aware of the current problems and backwardness in the educational field and tried to blend Western educational philosophies and styles into Chinese traditions.
7. The Chinese government calls to promote "character education", but it was not truly developed and did not meet the original goals.

III. Summary:

Complete the summary below. Choose ONLY ONE WORD from the text for each answer.

Tang Meijie, a Shanghai girl, was admitted by Harvard University which stirred up a media frenzy at home. She was widely advertised and even invited to join the _____ of a private school in Shanghai. In Meijie's eyes, Chinese students had too much pressure from so-called "stuffed duck" tradition and "Gaokao". As a student who achieved excellence beyond classroom, she joined a summer exchange program— _____ which offered particular excitement and social discovery. The participants were chosen not on the basis of their GPAs but on _____ activities and their responses on _____ questions. When American educators strive to emulate test-centered education from China, what Chinese students need is critical thinking, _____ and leadership from Western education. At the moment, Meijie's story could serve as a guidance to motivate educational _____ in China.

IV. Critical Questions:

What criteria do China and America have in recruiting college students? What factors may lead to these differences?

Text B

Brainstorming

The Ivy League: It is an athletic conference comprising eight private institutions of higher education in the Northeastern United States. The term is most commonly used to refer to those eight schools considered as a group. The term also has connotations of academic excellence, selectivity in admissions, and social elitism.

The term became official, especially in sports terminology, after the formation of the NCAA Division I ath-

letic conference in 1954, when much of the nation polarized around favorite college teams. The use of the phrase is no longer limited to athletics, and now represents an educational philosophy inherent to the nation's oldest schools. In addition, Ivy League schools are often viewed by the public as some of the most prestigious universities worldwide and are often ranked amongst the best universities in the United States and worldwide.

The eight institutions are Brown University, Columbia University, Cornell University, Dartmouth College, Harvard University, Princeton University, the University of Pennsylvania, and Yale University.

Questions before reading:
Can you describe the changes of college admission policies in China since 1999?

The Social Logic of Ivy League Admissions[1]
Malcolm Gladwell

In 1905, Harvard College adopted the College Entrance Examination Board tests as the principal basis for admission, which meant that virtually any academically gifted high-school senior who could afford a private college had a straightforward shot at attending. By 1908, the freshman class was seven per cent Jewish, nine per cent Catholic, and forty-five per cent from public schools, an astonishing transformation for a school that historically had been the preserve of the New England boarding-school complex known in the admissions world as St. Grottlesex[2].

As the sociologist Jerome Karabel writes in "The Chosen", his remarkable history of the admissions process at Harvard, Yale, and Princeton, that meritocratic spirit soon led to a crisis. The enrollment of Jews began to rise dramatically. By 1922, they made up more than a fifth of Harvard's freshman class. The administration and alumni were up in arms. Jews were thought to be sickly and grasping, grade-grubbing and insular. They displaced the sons of wealthy Wasp alumni, which did not bode well for fund-raising. A. Lawrence Lowell, Harvard's president in the nineteen-twenties, stated flatly that too many Jews would destroy the school: "The summer hotel that is ruined by admitting Jews meets its fate... because they drive away the Gentiles, and then after the Gentiles have left, they leave also."

The difficult part, however, was coming up with a way of keeping Jews out, because

---

[1] Excerpt from "Getting In: The Social Logic of Ivy League Admissions", *The New Yorker*, October 10, 2005.
[2] The term "Saint Grottlesex" is used to collectively refer to five famous and very prestigious boarding schools in New England. These schools graduate some of the nation's most wealthy and politically powerful individuals, with most students at the Saint Grottlesex schools going on to be educated at prestigious universities in the United States and abroad. As one might imagine, a Saint Grottlesex education comes with a hefty price tag.

as a group they were academically superior to everyone else. Lowell's first idea—a quota limiting Jews to fifteen per cent of the student body—was roundly criticized. Lowell tried restricting the number of scholarships given to Jewish students, and made an effort to bring in students from public schools in the West, where there were fewer Jews. Neither strategy worked. Finally, Lowell—and his counterparts at Yale and Princeton—realized that if a definition of merit based on academic prowess was leading to the wrong kind of student, the solution was to change the definition of merit. Karabel argues that it was at this moment that the history and nature of the Ivy League took a significant turn.

The admissions office at Harvard became much more interested in the details of an applicant's personal life. Lowell told his admissions officers to elicit information about the "character" of candidates from "persons who know the applicants well", and so the letter of reference became mandatory. Harvard started asking applicants to provide a photograph. Candidates had to write personal essays, demonstrating their aptitude for leadership, and list their extracurricular activities. "Starting in the fall of 1922," Karabel writes, "applicants were required to answer questions on 'Race and Color,' 'Religious Preference,' 'Maiden Name of Mother,' 'Birthplace of Father,' and 'What change, if any, has been made since birth in your own name or that of your father? (Explain fully).'"

If this new admissions system seems familiar, that's because it is essentially the same system that the Ivy League uses to this day. According to Karabel, Harvard, Yale, and Princeton didn't abandon the elevation of character once the Jewish crisis passed. They institutionalized it. Starting in 1953, Arthur Howe, Jr., spent a decade as the chair of admissions at Yale, and Karabel describes what happened under his guidance:

The admissions committee viewed evidence of "manliness" with particular enthusiasm. One boy gained admission despite an academic prediction of 70 because "there was apparently something manly and distinctive about him that had won over both his alumni and staff interviewers". Another candidate, admitted despite his schoolwork being "mediocre in comparison with many others", was accepted over an applicant with a much better record and higher exam scores because, as Howe put it, "we just thought he was more of a guy." So preoccupied was Yale with the appearance of its students that the form used by alumni interviewers actually had a physical characteristics checklist through 1965. Each year, Yale carefully measured the height of entering freshmen, noting with pride the proportion of the class at six feet or more.

At Harvard, the key figure in that same period was Wilbur Bender, who, as the dean of admissions, had a preference for "the boy with some athletic interests and abilities, the boy with physical vigor and coordination and grace". Bender, Karabel tells us, believed that if Harvard continued to suffer on the football field it would contribute to the school's reputation as a place with "no college spirit, few good fellows, and no vigorous, healthy social life", not to mention a "surfeit of 'pansies,' 'decadent esthetes' and 'precious sophisticates'". Bender concentrated on improving Harvard's techniques for evaluating "intangibles" and, in particular, its "ability to detect homosexual tendencies and serious psychiatric problems".

By the nineteen-sixties, Harvard's admissions system had evolved into a series of complex algorithms. The school began by lumping all applicants into one of twenty-two dockets, according to their geographical origin. (There was one docket for Exeter and Andover, another for the eight Rocky Mountain states.) Information from interviews, references, and student essays was then used to grade each applicant on a scale of 1 to 6, along four dimensions: personal, academic, extracurricular, and athletic. Competition, critically, was within each docket, not between dockets, so there was no way for, say, the graduates of Bronx Science and Stuyvesant to shut out the graduates of Andover and Exeter. More important, academic achievement was just one of four dimensions, further diluting the value of pure intellectual accomplishment. Athletic ability, rather than falling under "extracurriculars", got a category all to itself, which explains why, even now, recruited athletes have an acceptance rate to the Ivies at well over twice the rate of other students, despite S.A.T. scores that are on average more than a hundred points lower. And the most important category? That mysterious index of "personal" qualities. According to Harvard's own analysis, the personal rating was a better predictor of admission than the academic rating. Those with a rank of 4 or worse on the personal scale had, in the nineteen-sixties, a rejection rate of ninety-eight per cent. Those with a personal rating of 1 had a rejection rate of 2.5 per cent. When the Office of Civil Rights at the federal education department investigated Harvard in the nineteen-eighties, they found handwritten notes scribbled in the margins of various candidates' files. "This young woman could be one of the brightest applicants in the pool but there are several references to shyness," read one. Another comment reads, "Seems a tad frothy." One application—and at this point you can almost hear it going to the bottom of the pile—was notated, "Short with big ears."

Social scientists distinguish between what are known as treatment effects and selection effects. The Marine Corps, for instance, is largely a treatment-effect institution. It doesn't have an enormous admissions office grading applicants along four separate dimensions of toughness and intelligence. It's confident that the experience of undergoing Marine Corps basic training will turn you into a formidable soldier. A modelling agency, by contrast, is a selection-effect institution. You don't become beautiful by signing up with an agency. You get signed up by an agency because you're beautiful.

At the heart of the American obsession with the Ivy League is the belief that schools like Harvard provide the social and intellectual equivalent of Marine Corps basic training—that being taught by all those brilliant professors and meeting all those other motivated students and getting a degree with that powerful name on it will confer advantages that no local state university can provide. Fuelling the treatment-effect idea are studies showing that if you take two students with the same S.A.T. scores and grades, one of whom goes to a school like Harvard and one of whom goes to a less selective college, the Ivy Leaguer will make far more money ten or twenty years down the road.

The extraordinary emphasis the Ivy League places on admissions policies, though, makes it seem more like a modelling agency than like the Marine Corps, and, sure enough, the studies based on those two apparently equivalent students turn out to be flawed. How do we know that two students who have the same S.A.T. scores and grades really are equivalent? It's quite possible that the student who goes to Harvard is more ambitious and energetic and personable than the student who wasn't let in, and that those same intangibles are what account for his better career success. To assess the effect of the Ivies, it makes more sense to compare the student who got into a top school with the student who got into that same school but chose to go to a less selective one. Three years ago, the economists Alan Krueger and Stacy Dale published just such a study. And they found that when you compare apples and apples the income bonus from selective schools disappears.

In the wake of the Jewish crisis, Harvard, Yale, and Princeton chose to adopt what might be called the "best graduates" approach to admissions. France's École Normale Supérieure, Japan's University of Tokyo, and most of the world's other élite schools define their task as looking for the best students—that is, the applicants who will have the greatest academic success during their time in college. The Ivy League schools justified their emphasis on character and personality, however, by arguing that they were searching for the students who would have the greatest success after college. They were looking for leaders, and leadership, the officials of the Ivy League believed, was not a simple matter of academic brilliance. "Should our goal be to select a student body with the highest possible proportions of high-ranking students, or should it be to select, within a reasonably high range of academic ability, a student body with a certain variety of talents, qualities, attitudes, and backgrounds?" Wilbur Bender asked. To him, the answer was obvious. If you let in only the brilliant, then you produced bookworms and bench scientists: you ended up as socially irrelevant as the University of Chicago (an institution Harvard officials looked upon and shuddered). "Above a reasonably good level of mental ability, above that indicated by a 550—600 level of S.A.T. score," Bender went on, "the only thing that matters in terms of future impact on, or contribution to, society is the degree of personal inner force an individual has."

In the nineteen-eighties, when Harvard was accused of enforcing a secret quota on Asian admissions, its defense was that once you adjusted for the preferences given to the children of alumni and for the preferences given to athletes, Asians really weren't being discriminated against. But you could sense Harvard's exasperation that the issue was being raised at all. If Harvard had too many Asians, it wouldn't be Harvard, just as Harvard wouldn't be Harvard with too many Jews or pansies or parlor pinks or shy types or short people with big ears.

Unit 2 My Perspectives on Education Between China and America

Exercises

I. Reading Comprehension:

There are four suggested answers marked A, B, C and D. Choose the best answer for each question.

1. What measure had not been taken by the administration to limit the number of Jews in Harvard by the fall of 1922?
   A. Setting up a limiting quota.
   B. Reducing scholarship given to Jewish students.
   C. Increasing enrollment numbers in public schools.
   D. Putting more emphasis on students' characters.
2. Which of the following qualities were not valued by the new admission system?
   A. Appearance.   B. Background.   C. Manliness.   D. Wealth.
3. What kind of talents did the Ivy League schools aim to cultivate?
   A. Leaders.   B. Superstars.   C. Millionaire.   D. All of the above.
4. What is the distinction between treatment effects and selection effects?
   A. The logics between induction and deduction.
   B. The logics between generality and particularity.
   C. The logics between excellence and average.
   D. The logics between selection and nomination.

II. Judgments and Implications:

Do the following statements agree with the information given in the passage?
True   if the statement is true according to the passage
False   if the statement contradicts the passage

1. By 1922, Jewish students increased greatly in Harvard which upset the administration.
2. Harvard's administration succeeded to limit the number of Jewish students by setting a quota limiting Jews to 15%.
3. Harvard, Yale and Princeton would choose the best graduate who would achieve academic success.
4. For the Ivy League schools, intellectual achievement is the fairest and highest standard of merit in the best-graduate approach.
5. The goal of Ivy League schools was to search for applicants who could make the greatest achievement in college.

III. Summary:

Complete the summary below. Choose ONLY ONE WORD from the text for each answer.

In 1905, the enrollment policy of Harvard was merely based on _____ achievements.

By 1922, this _____ education system met with a crisis: increasing numbers of _____ students. The administration became aware that the ultimate way to change the current situation was to change the _____ of merit. In 1922, a new admissions system was set up which made efforts to draw details of the applicants _____ life. This new system was used by the Ivy League schools until now. At Harvard, interests and abilities were given priorities as it could improve the school's reputation. By 1960, Harvard's admissions system graded each applicant in four dimensions: personal, academic, athletic and _____. The Ivy League schools chose to adopt the best-graduate approach to admissions. The Ivy Leagues did not want the mediocrities but the _____.

IV. Chart Filling:

Fill in the following chart about the development of Ivy Leagues with only one word.

Year	Enrollment Standards	Talent Types	Students Percentage	Characteristics
1905	test scores	_____ gifted	_____	meritocratic
1908	test scores	_____ gifted	Jews:_____%	meritocratic
1922	intangible qualities	leaders	Jews:_____%	elevation of _____
1960	complex algorithm	ambitious, energetic and _____	Jews: 15%	leaders

V. Critical Questions:

Why does Harvard use integrated standards to evaluate candidates rather than use only academic performance? As far as China is concerned, what can we learn from them?

Unit 2 My Perspectives on Education Between China and America

Text C

Brainstorming

> *Cost of Higher Education:* A number of factors come into play when estimating the cost of a student's higher education. The overall cost will be dependent upon the student's chosen course, institution and household income.
>
> Broadly speaking, the cost of education includes the financial cost and opportunity cost. In accordance with the different educational subjects, the financial costs can be divided into school (or social) cost of inputs and individual input costs; the opportunity cost can be divided into public and personal opportunity cost. In a narrow speaking, the cost of education mainly refers to the school (or society) into the resource costs which can be divided into personnel costs and material costs.

Questions before reading:
Can you calculate how much you have spent studying in the college?

Is College Really Worth the Money?[①]
Tia Ghose

The Real World

Este Griffith had it all figured out. When she graduated from the University of Pittsburgh in April 2001, she had her sights set on one thing: working for a labor union.

The real world had other ideas. Griffith left school with not only a degree, but a boatload of debt. She owed $15,000 in student loans and had racked up $4,000 in credit card debt for books, groceries and other expenses. No labor union job could pay enough to bail her out.

dilema

So Griffith went to work instead for a Washington, D.C., firm that specializes in economic development. Problem solved? Nope. At age 24, she takes home about $1,800 a month, $1,200 of which disappears to pay her rent. Add another $180 a month to retire her student loans and $300 a month to whittle down her credit card balance. "You do the math," she says.

Griffith has practically no money to live on. She brown-bags her lunch and bikes to work. Above all, she fears

---

① Excerpt from "Is College Really Worth the Money?"《双语时代》, March 29, 2008.

she'll never own a house or be able to retire. It's not that she regrets getting her degree. "But they don't tell you that the trade-off is the next ten years of your income," she says.

That's precisely the deal being made by more and more college students: They're mortgaging their futures to meet soaring tuition costs and other college expenses. Like Griffith, they're facing a one-two punch at graduation: hefty student loans and smothering credit card debt—not to mention a job market that, for now anyway, is dismal.

"We are forcing our children to make a choice between two evils," says Elizabeth Warren, a Harvard Law professor and expert on bankruptcy. "Skip college and face a life of diminished opportunity, or go to college and face a life shackled by debt."

Don't think this Catch-22[①] only traps those shelling out big bucks for schools like Harvard or Yale. The eight in ten paying for a public college or university are also in for sticker shock. For the past two decades, tuition at these schools has zoomed far above inflation. Last year, the annual tuition and fees at four-year public colleges averaged $4,081 (room and board added another $5,582). That was a leap from the previous year of 9.6 percent—six times the rate of inflation, then less than 2 percent. This year, the increase at certain schools was even more dramatic. Tuition at the University of Virginia and the University of California rose nearly 30 percent, and at the University of Arizona it jumped by 40 percent.

For some time, colleges have insisted their steep tuition hikes are needed to pay for cutting-edge technologies, faculty and administration salaries, and rising health care costs. Now there's a new culprit: shrinking state support. Caught in a severe budget crunch, many states have sharply scaled back their funding for higher education.

Someone had to make up for those lost dollars. And you can guess who—especially if you live in Massachusetts, which last year hiked its tuition and fees by 24 percent, after funding dropped by 3 percent, or in Missouri, where appropriations fell by 10 percent, but tuition rose at double that rate. About one-third of the states, in fact, have increased tuition and fees by more than 10 percent.

One of those states is California, and Janet Burrell's family is feeling the pain. A bookkeeper in Torrance, Burrell has a daughter at the University of California at Davis. Meanwhile, her sons attend two-year colleges because Burrell can't afford to have all of them in four-year schools at once.

Meanwhile, even with tuition hikes, California's community colleges are so strapped for cash that they dropped thousands of classes last spring. The result: 54,000 fewer students.

---

① *Catch-22* is a satirical, historical novel by the American author Joseph Heller. He began writing it in 1953, and the novel was first published in 1961. It is set during World War II in 1943 and is frequently cited as one of the great literary works of the twentieth century. Resulting from its specific use in the book, the phrase "Catch-22" is common idiomatic usage meaning "a no-win situation" or "a double bind" of any type.

Unit 2 My Perspectives on Education Between China and America

Collapsing Investments

Many families thought they had a surefire plan: Even if tuition kept skyrocketing, they had invested enough money along the way to meet the costs. Then a funny thing happened on the way to Wall Street. Those investments collapsed with the stock market. Among the losers last year: the wildly popular "529" plans[①]—federal tax-exempt college savings plans offered by individual states, which have attracted billions from families around the country. "We hear from many parents that what they had set aside declined in value so much that they now don't have enough to see their students through," says Penn State financial aid director Anna Griswold, who witnessed a 10 percent increase in loan applications last year. Even with a market that may be slowly recovering, it will take time, perhaps several years, for people to recoup their losses.

Nadine Sayegh is among those who didn't have the luxury of waiting for her college nest egg to grow back. Her father had invested money toward her tuition, but a large chunk of it vanished when stocks went south. Nadine was then only partway through college. By graduation, she had taken out at least $10,000 in loans, and her mother had borrowed even more on her behalf. Now 22, Nadine is attending law school, having signed for yet more loans to pay for that. "There wasn't any way to do it differently," she says, "and I'm not happy about it. I've sat down and calculated how long it will take me to pay off everything. I'll be 35 years old." That's if she's very lucky: Nadine based her calculation on landing a job right out of law school that will pay her at least $120,000 a year.

The American Council on Education has its own calculation that shows how students are more and more dependent on loans. In just five years, from 1995 to 2000, the median loan debt at public institutions rose from $10,342 to $15,375. Most of this comes from federal loans, which Congress made more tempting in 1992 by expanding eligibility (home equity no longer counts against your assets) and raising loan limits (a dependent undergraduate can now borrow up to $23,000 from the federal government).

But students aren't stopping there. The College Board estimates that they also borrowed $4.5 billion from private lenders in the 2000—2001 academic year, up from $1.5 billion just five years earlier.

For lots of students, the worst of it isn't even the weight of those direct student loans. It's what they rack up on all those plastic cards in their wallets. As of two years ago, according to a study by lender Nellie Mae, more than eight out of ten undergrads had their own credit cards, with the typical student carrying four. That's no big surprise, given the in-your-face marketing by credit card companies, which set up tables on campus to entice students to sign up. Some colleges ban or restrict this hawking, but

---

[①] "529" plans are named after section 529 of the Internal Revenue Code 26 U.S.C. § 529. While most plans allow investors from out of state, there can be significant state tax advantages and other benefits, such as matching grant and scholarship opportunities, protection from creditors, and exemption from state financial aid calculations for investors who invest in 529 plans in their state of residence.

others give it a boost. You know those credit cards emblazoned with a school's picture or its logo? For sanctioning such a card—a must-have for some students—a college department or association gets payments from the issuer. Meanwhile, from freshman year to graduation, according to the Nellie Mae study, students triple the number of credit cards they own and double their debt on them. As of 2001, they were in the whole an average $2,327.

Soaring Credit Card Debt

Beth Foster's credit card debt was not much better—$1,500—when she graduated last December from the University of Iowa. Her student loans, meanwhile, came to $18,000. Wanting to work for a nonprofit, she was prepared for money to be tight.

But she hadn't factored in a terrible job market. Now, to stay afloat, she's working two together, she takes in about $800 a month, while paying out $600 for rent, utilities and food. What is left barely makes a dent in her debts. "I'm scared out of my mind," says Foster.

She's not the only cash-strapped graduate who's freaking out. Rich Call sees them all the time. As regional vice president for Consumer Credit Counseling Service of the Midwest Inc., Call has witnessed a big switch from a decade ago: His agency is now swamped with recent graduates deeply in hock. What he can do is help them restructure credit card debt. What he can't do anything about are student loans.

If the debt is too far gone, the wisest person to visit may be someone like Jeffrey Freedman. A bankruptcy attorney in Buffalo, N.Y., Freedman says his firm never saw students come through the door a few years ago. "Now, five percent of our clients are college students," he says.

There's plenty of business to go around. According to Harvard's Elizabeth Warren, about 100,000 young people under age 25 declared bankruptcy last year. "A student will graduate believing she can make her debt payments," says Warren. "But she will fall further and further behind, borrow more money on credit cards and finally realize that she has no possible chance of catching up. Those are the people we see in bankruptcy."

Camille Holt, 22, actually filed for Chapter 7 bankruptcy① several weeks before she graduated last spring from the University of North Carolina—ironically, with an economics degree. She was loaded down with about $25,000 in student loans, and nearly $20,000 in credit card debt from clothes, books, food and trips home while in school. Chapter 7 won't wipe clean the student loan debt, but it clears away all the rest. "Before, I worried all the time about my loans," says Holt, who works in a bank's trust division. Her Chapter 7 filing "has been like a sigh of relief".

Still, she may discover her diploma cost her even more than she thinks. For the next

---

① Chapter 7 Bankruptcy: When a troubled business is badly in debt and unable to service that debt or pay its creditors, it may file for bankruptcy in a federal court under Chapter 7. In a Chapter 7 bankruptcy, the individual is allowed to keep certain exempt property.

ten years, Holt's bankruptcy will be a visible part of her financial history. It could well come back to haunt her when she applies for a mortgage or car loan.

In a few tragic cases, the pressure of debt has overwhelmed students before they could see a way out. Sean Moyer was given a full scholarship to attend the University of Texas at Dallas. Soon after his arrival, he was being offered something else: his first credit card from an on-campus vendor. Before long he had signed for another card, and another. Eventually, Moyer was juggling 12 credit cards and owed about $13,000. Trapped by the debt, he moved back home in his junior year, enrolled at the University of Oklahoma, and hoped to figure out how to make ends meet. Moyer wound up taking on two jobs—one at the college library and another manning the night desk at a Holiday Inn. Even those two paychecks weren't enough.

A Wise Choice?

One day, Moyer sat down with his mother, Janne O'Donnell, to talk about his goal of going to law school. Don't count on it, O'Donnell told him. She couldn't afford the cost and Moyer doubted he could get a loan, given how much he owed already. "He said he felt like a failure," O'Donnell recalls. "He didn't know how he had gotten into such a mess."

A week later, the 22-year-old hanged himself in his bedroom, where his mother found him. O'Donnell is convinced the money pressures caused his suicide. "Sean tried to pay his debts off," she says. "And he couldn't take it."

Trisha Johnson underwent an eerily similar tragedy. Her daughter, Mitzi Pool, was a freshman at the University of Central Oklahoma in 1997 when, like Sean Moyer, she loaded up on credit cards. One evening that fall, Pool called her mother, sobbing. She was $2,500 in debt and had just been laid off from her part-time job. "I told her, 'This weekend, we'll go through everything and figure out what to do,'" says Johnson. That was their last conversation. Hours later, Pool hanged herself in her dorm room. There was no note, but her pile of bills and her checkbook were spread out on her bed. "Credit card debt of $2,500 may not sound like much, but to an 18-year-old, it was a mountain," says Johnson.

To be sure, suicides are exceedingly rare. But despair is common—and it sometimes leads students to rethink whether college was worth it. In fact, there are quite a few jobs that don't require a college degree, yet pay fairly well. On average, though, college graduates can expect to earn 80 percent more than those with only a high school diploma. Also, all but two of the 50 highest paying jobs (the exceptions being air traffic controllers and nuclear power reactor operators) require a four-year college degree. So foregoing a college education is often not a wise choice.

Merit Mikhail, who graduated last June from the University of California, Riverside, is glad she borrowed to get through school. But she left Riverside owing $20,000 in student loans and another $7,000 in credit card debt. Now in law school, Merit hopes to become a public-interest attorney, yet she may have to postpone that goal—which bothers her. To handle her debt, she'll probably need to start with a more lucrative legal job.

Like so many other students, Mikhail took out her loans on a kind of blind faith that she could deal with the consequences. "You say to yourself, 'I have to go into debt to make it work, and whatever it takes later, I'll manage.'" Later has now arrived, and Mikhail is finding out the true cost of her college degree.

No Degree? Apply Here: Four years of college may be your best ticket to a high-paying career, but these solid jobs don't require an undergraduate degree:

Profession	Median Annual Earnings
Air traffic controller	$87,930
Nuclear power reactor operator	60,180
Dental hygienist*	54,700
Elevator installer/repairer	51,630
Real estate broker	51,380
Commercial pilot (non-airline)	47,410
Electrical power line installer/repairer	47,210
Locomotive engineer	46,540
Telecom equipment installer/repairer*	46,390
Funeral director*	42,010
Aircraft mechanic*	41,990
Brick mason	41,590
Police officer	40,970
Electrician	40,770
Flight attendant	40,600
Court reporter*	40,410
Real estate appraiser*	38,950

*Requires associate's degree or vocational diploma.

Unit 2 My Perspectives on Education Between China and America

Exercises

I. Reading Comprehension:

There are four suggested answers marked A, B, C and D. Choose the best answer for each question.
1. What is the correct understanding of the sentence "We are forcing our children to make a choice between two evils"?
   A. It is very difficult to make a choice between going to college and skipping the college.
   B. Either choice will follow with bad results.
   C. Going to college is not worthwhile as people generally have expected.
   D. Going to college or skipping the college will have the same results.
2. Which one of the following statements is NOT the reason to the dramatic increase of the cost of public higher education?
   A. Soaring inflation.
   B. Reduced state funding.
   C. Reduced private donations.
   D. Increasing costs of the universities.
3. For most students, the biggest financial problem is _____.
   A. clearing the students' loans
   B. handling the credit card debt
   C. facing the dismal job market
   D. dealing with the increasing tuition fees
4. What is the likely consequences of students in the debts pressures?
   A. Getting more jobs and working extra hours.
   B. Going bankruptcy.
   C. Committing suicides.
   D. All of above.
5. What is the author's attitudes held towards the value of higher education?
   A. Doubtful.   B. Negative.   C. Positive.   D. Ambiguous.

II. Judgments and Implications:

Do the following statements agree with the information given in the passage?
True   if the statement is true according to the passage
False   if the statement contradicts the passage
1. The cost for private universities is very high while the public universities are generally affordable by American students.
2. The annual tuition and fees at four-year public colleges increased over 10% last year.

3. Most universities increased tuitions and fees by more than 10% this year.
4. It is now easy for students in need to get loans in the college.
5. It is extremely difficult to cover the loans and credit card debt while some students would rather to choose to declare bankruptcy.
6. The author believed that going to college is generally not a wise choice for most people.

III. Chart Filling:

Read the section "The Real World" again and find out those words and phrases expressing the movements.

Direction	Verbs/Verb phrase/Nouns
↑	Example: racked up
↓	Example: whittle down

IV. Critical Questions:

Nowadays, due to the economic recession, college graduates meet the toughest job market. Thereby some parents and students even question themselves whether it is a reasonable decision to study in the college. Would you provide your own ideas about this issue?

Learning Skills

Oral Presentation Skills

A good oral presentation is well structured; this makes it easier for the listener to follow.

Basically there are three parts to a typical presentation: the beginning, the middle and the end (or introduction, body and conclusion). We are going to look at each part in turn and present the language needed to express both the structure and the content.

1. The Beginning or the Introduction

The beginning of a presentation is the most important part. It is when you establish a rapport with the audience and when you have its attention.

A. Get the audience's attention and signal the beginning.
Right. / Well. / OK. / Erm. / Let's begin.
Good. / Fine. / Great. / Can we start?

Unit 2 My Perspectives on Education Between China and America

Shall we start? Let's get the ball rolling.
Let's get down to business.

In English-speaking countries it is not uncommon for the speaker to begin with a joke, an anecdote, a statement made to surprise or provoke in order to gain the audience's attention, to make people want to listen, to feel relaxed and even to introduce the subject. This may or may not be appropriate in your country; you are probably the best judge. Certainly humour is difficult to convey and would not be appropriate in all contexts.

A good technique is to try to get your audience involved in your talk either by asking direct or rhetorical questions. Ask for a show of hands for example, in response to a question or, present information in such a way that the audience can identify with it. You can give an anecdote, unusual or surprising facts, or an illustration from real life could be employed here.

B. Greet audience.

It is important to greet the audience by saying something like:
Hello ladies and gentlemen.
Good morning members of the jury.
Good afternoon esteemed guests.
Good evening members of the board.
Fellow colleagues Mr. Chairman/Chairwoman.
Thank you for your kind introduction.

C. Introduce oneself (name, position, and company).

Do this not only to give important information so people can identify you but also to establish your authority on the subject and to allow the audience to see your point of view on the subject.

D. Give title and introduce subject.

What exactly are you going to speak about? Situate the subject in time and
place, in relation to the audience and/or its importance. Give a rough idea or a working definition of the subject.

I plan to speak about...
Today I'm going to talk about...
The subject of my presentation is...
The theme of my talk is...
I've been asked to give you an overview of...

E. Give your objectives (purpose, aim, goals).

The main purpose of an informative speech is to have the audience understand and remember a certain amount of information. You should therefore have two purposes: a general purpose and a specific one. The former is to inform: to give an overview, to present, to summarize, to outline; to discuss the current situation or to explain how to do something or how something is done. The latter is what you want the audience to take away with them after listening to you, what you want them to do, what they should remember.

My purpose in doing this paper is to give you a solid background on the subject of oral presentation skills so that in the future, at the conference or elsewhere, you can deliver a successful speech in front of a group.

What I would like to do today is to explain... / to illustrate... / to give you the essential background information on... / to outline... / to have a look at...

What I want my listeners to get out of my speech is...

If there is one thing I'd like to get across to you today it is that…

F. Announce your outline.

You want to keep the outline simple so 2 or 3 main points are usually enough. Concerning grammar the headings of the outline should be of the same grammatical form.

I have broken my speech down/up into X parts.

I have divided my presentation (up) into Y parts.

In the first part I give a few basic definitions.

In the next section I will explain

In part three, I am going to show...

In the last part I would like/want to give a practical example...

G. Make a transition between the introduction and the body.

You should refer to your transparency or outline.

Now let us turn to point one.

Let us now move on to the second part, which is, as I said earlier....

II. The Middle or the Body

A. Content

What information should you give in your speech? All your information should support your purpose. In most cases you will have to limit the content, as time is usually precious!

B. Quantity

How much information should you give? Enough to clearly develop your ideas. Don't forget to illustrate through examples.

C. Sequencing your ideas

Here are a few possibilities for organizing your ideas:

logical; chronological order; from general to specific; from known to unknown; from accepted to controversial; cause/effect; problem/solution.

Whatever sequencing you choose, the headings should be all of the same grammatical form.

D. Keeping the audience's attention

The beginning and the end or the first and last parts of a talk are what listeners will remember best. Think of ways you can keep the audience's attention throughout the rest of the speech.

Unit 2 My Perspectives on Education Between China and America

E. Signposting or signaling where you are

Just as when you are driving along a road that you don't know very well, you depend on signs to guide you, you need to guide the listener by using expressions to tell him/her where you are going. That is to say, first announce what you are going to say (give an example, reformulate, etc.) and then say what you want to say. This is very like verbal punctuation. Indicate when you have finished one point and then go on to the next one. It is redundant in text but very useful in oral presentations. Experienced presenters will also clearly pause, change their stance and the pitch of their voice as they move from one part of a presentation to another.

F. Listing information

Lists are often a necessary evil. Vary your language whenever possible and avoid reading directly.

There are three things we have to consider: one, two, and three.
Now let us look at the first aspect which is...
First of all,...
In the first place...

III. The End or Conclusion

The end of a talk should never come as a surprise to an audience; it needs special consideration.

A. Content

The end or the conclusion of your talk should include four parts: a brief reminder of what you tried to show in your speech and how you tried to do so, a short conclusion, thanks to the audience for listening, and an invitation to ask questions, make comments or open a discussion.

At the end you should briefly summarize your speech in a few lines to make sure the audience has retained the main points. Alternatives are: to state the point of the speech; give the essential message to retain; list the main points and what you want the audience to remember; review informally or indirectly by using a quote, a comparison or example. Then you should give some kind of conclusion. That is to say you should give a message that logically comes out of the ideas developed in your speech. This could be a commentary, the lessons learned, some recommendations, or the next steps. You could also make a call to action—the audience should have to do something. Thirdly, thank the audience for being there. Finally, ask for questions and comments or invite a discussion. If you choose the former, you put yourself in a superior position compared to the audience and should be considered as an expert. You will need to be very prepared intellectually and psychologically to transfer control to the audience and be able to answer any questions. However, in the case of the latter, you put yourself more or less on equal terms with the audience and do not have to be the expert with all the answers. The audience may have some clear ideas or some practical knowledge about the subject themselves!

Naturally you need to signpost the end of your talk. This may take the form of a recapitulation of the main points.

I'd like to summarize/sum up
At this stage I would like to run through/over the main points...
So, as we have seen today....
As I have tried to explain this morning BT finds itself in....
Or there may be recommendations or proposals that you wish to make;
As a result we suggest that...
In the light of what we have seen today I suggest that...
My first proposal is...

Above all when you conclude do not do it abruptly or as if surprised to get to the end of your talk.

In conclusion I would like to say that...
My final comments concern...
I would like to finish by reminding everyone that...
If there are any questions please feel free to ask.
Thank you very much for your attention and if there are any suggestions or comments.

B. Dealing with difficult questions

a. Make sure you understand the question.
- Ask a question to see if you understand.
- Repeat the question in your own words to check that you have understood. If not, ask the questioner to repeat.

b. In answering:
- delay the answer (ask for time and/or repeat the question).
  Just a minute please. What is a...?
  How can I put it?
  I'm glad you asked that question.
  That's a good question/point/remark.
  Can I answer that question later?
- admit that you are not responsible.
  I saw that in the work of...
- agree but give an alternative point of view.
  I agree with you but there is another way of looking at it.

Unit 2 My Perspectives on Education Between China and America

Group Work Activities

Choose one of the following topics and make comparisons between China and America, and then prepare an oral presentation in a group within 5 to 7 students.

Topics:
    Educational system
    Instruction and pedagogy
    Educational policy
    Culture and philosophy

Self-evaluation Form

What are the main objectives in this unit?
_____
_____
_____

What useful vocabularies and expressions have you learned from this unit?
_____
_____
_____

What key terms and educational knowledge have you learned?
_____
_____
_____

Have you used the learning skills before? Why do you think they are useful or not useful?
_____
_____
_____

If possible, what would you like to add to make learning more interesting and relevant?
_____
_____
_____

Unit 3

Education and Students' Development

Introduction

Student Diversity[1]
Kelvin Seifert

I'll tell you this: There are some people, and then there are others.

Anna Harris was Kelvin Seifert's grandmother as well as a schoolteacher from about 1910 to 1930. She used to make comments, like the one above, that sounded odd but that also contained a grain of wisdom. In this case her remark makes a good theme for this topic—and even for teaching in general. Students do differ in a multitude of ways, both individually and because of memberships in families, communities or cultural groups. Sometimes the differences can make classroom-style teaching more challenging, but other times, as Anna Harris implied, they simply enrich classroom life. To teach students well, we need to understand the important ways that they differ among themselves, and when or how the differences really matter for their education. This chapter offers some of that understanding and suggests how you might use it in order to make learning effective and enjoyable for everyone, including yourself.

For convenience we will make a major distinction between differences among individuals and differences among groups of students. As the term implies, **individual differences** are qualities that are unique; just one person has them at a time. Variation in hair color, for example, is an individual difference; even though some people have nearly the same hair color, no two people are exactly the same. **Group differences** are qualities shared by members of an identifiable group or community, but not shared by everyone in society. An example is gender role: for better or for worse, one portion of society (the males) is perceived differently and expected to behave a bit differently than another portion of society (the females). Notice that distinguishment between individual and group differences is convenient, but a bit arbitrary. Individuals with similar, but nonetheless unique qualities sometimes group themselves together for certain purposes,

---

[1] Excerpt from "Student diversity", *Contemporary Educational Psychology, Wikibooks*, 2014.

and groups unusually contain a lot of individual diversity within them. If you happen to enjoy playing soccer and have some talent for it (an individual quality), for example, you may end up as a member of a soccer team or club (a group defined by members' common desire and ability to play soccer). But though everyone on the team fits a "soccer player's profile" at some level, individual members will probably vary in level of skill and motivation. The group, by its very nature, may obscure these signs of individuality. To begin, then, we look at several differences normally considered to be individually rather than group based. This discussion will necessarily be incomplete simply because individual differences are so numerous and important in teaching that some of them are also discussed in later chapters. Later sections of this chapter deal with three important forms of group diversity: gender differences, cultural differences, and language differences.

Individual Styles of Learning and Thinking

All of us, including our students, have preferred ways of learning. Teachers often refer to these differences as **learning styles**, though this term may imply that students are more consistent across situations than is really the case. One student may like to make diagrams to help remember a reading assignment, whereas another student may prefer to write a sketchy outline instead. Yet in many cases, the students could in principle reverse the strategies and still learn the material: if coaxed (or perhaps required), the diagram-maker could take notes for a change and the note-taker could draw diagrams. Both would still learn, though neither might feel as comfortable as when using the strategies that they prefer. This reality suggests that a balanced, middle-of-the-road approach may be a teacher's best response to students' learning styles. Or put another way, it is good to support students' preferred learning strategies where possible and appropriate, but neither necessary nor desirable to do so all of the time. Most of all, it is neither necessary nor possible to classify or label students according to seemingly fixed learning styles and then allow them to learn only according to those styles. A student may prefer to hear new material rather than see it; he may prefer for you to explain something orally, for example, rather than to see it demonstrated in a video. But he may nonetheless tolerate or sometimes even prefer to see it demonstrated. In the long run, in fact, he may learn it best by encountering the material in both ways, regardless of his habitual preferences.

That said, there is evidence that individuals, including students, do differ in how they habitually think. These differences are more specific than learning styles or preferences, and psychologists sometimes call them **cognitive styles**, meaning typical ways of perceiving and remembering information, and typical ways of solving problems and making decisions. In a style of thinking called **field dependence**, for example, individuals perceive patterns as a whole rather than focus on the parts of the pattern separately. In a complementary tendency, called **field independence**, individuals are more inclined to analyze overall patterns into their parts. Cognitive research from the

1940s to the present has found field dependence/independence differences to be somewhat stable for any given person across situations, though not completely so. Someone who is field dependent (perceives globally or "wholistically") in one situation, tends to a modest extent to perceive things globally or wholistically in other situations. Field dependence and independence can be important in understanding students because the styles affect students' behaviors and preferences in school and classrooms. Field dependent persons tend to work better in groups, it seems, and to prefer "open-ended" fields of study like literature and history. Field independent persons, on the other hand, tend to work better alone and to prefer highly analytic studies like math and science. The differences are only a tendency, however, and there are a lot of students who contradict the trends. As with the broader notion of learning styles, the cognitive styles of field dependence and independence are useful for tailoring instruction to particular students, but their guidance is only approximate. They neither can nor should be used to "lock" students to particular modes of learning or to replace students' own expressed preferences and choices about curriculum.

Another cognitive style is **impulsivity** as compared to **reflectivity**. As the names imply, an impulsive cognitive style is one in which a person reacts quickly, but as a result makes comparatively more errors. A reflective style is the opposite: the person reacts more slowly and therefore makes fewer errors. As you might expect, the reflective style would seem better suited to many academic demands of school. Research has found that this is indeed the case for academic skills that clearly benefit from reflection, such as mathematical problem solving or certain reading tasks. Some classroom or school-related skills, however, may actually develop better if a student is relatively impulsive. Being a good partner in a cooperative learning group, for example, may depend partly on responding spontaneously (*i.e.* just a bit "impulsively") to others' suggestions; and being an effective member of an athletic team may depend on not taking time to reflect carefully on every move that you or your teammates make.

There are two major ways to use knowledge of students' cognitive styles. The first and the more obvious is to build on students' existing style strengths and preferences. A student who is field independent and reflective, for example, can be encouraged to explore tasks and activities that are relatively analytic and that require relatively independent work. One who is field dependent and impulsive, on the other hand, can be encouraged and supported to try tasks and activities that are more social or spontaneous. But a second, less obvious way to use knowledge of cognitive styles is to encourage more balance in cognitive styles for students who need it. A student who lacks field independence, for example, may need explicit help in organizing and analyzing key academic tasks (like organizing a lab report in a science class). One who is already highly reflective may need encouragement to try ideas spontaneously, as in a creative writing lesson.

Multiple Intelligences

For nearly a century, educators and psychologists have debated the nature of intelligence, and more specifically whether intelligence is just one broad ability or can take more than one form. Many classical definitions of the concept have tended to define **intelligence** as a single broad ability that allows a person to solve or complete many sorts of tasks, or at least many academic tasks like reading, knowledge of vocabulary, and the solving of logical problems. There is research evidence of such a global ability, and the idea of general intelligence often fits with society's everyday beliefs about intelligence. Partly for these reasons, an entire mini-industry has grown up around publishing tests of intelligence, academic ability, and academic achievement. Since these tests affect the work of teachers, I return to discussing them later in this book.

But there are also problems with defining intelligence as one general ability. One way of summing up the problems is to say that conceiving of intelligence as something general tends to put it beyond teachers' influence. When viewed as a single, all-purpose ability, students either have a lot of intelligence or they do not, and strengthening their intelligence becomes a major challenge, or perhaps even an impossible one. This conclusion is troubling to some educators, especially in recent years as testing school achievements have become more common and as students have become more diverse.

But alternate views of intelligence also exist that portray intelligence as having multiple forms, whether the forms are subparts of a single broader ability or are multiple "intelligences" in their own right. For various reasons such this perspective has gained in popularity among teachers in recent years, probably because it reflects many teachers' beliefs that students cannot simply be rated along a single scale of ability, but are fundamentally diverse.

One of the most prominent of these models is **Howard Gardner's theory of multiple intelligences**. Gardner proposes that there are eight different forms of intelligence, each of which functions independently of the others. (The eight intelligences are summarized in the following table. Each person has a mix of all eight abilities—more of one and less of another—that helps to constitute that person's individual cognitive profile. Since most tasks—including most tasks in classrooms—require several forms of intelligence and can be completed in more than one way, it is possible for people with various profiles of talents to succeed on a task equally well. In writing an essay, for example, a student with high interpersonal intelligence but rather average verbal intelligence might use his or her interpersonal strength to get a lot of help and advice from classmates and the teacher. A student with the opposite profile might work well alone, but without the benefit of help from others. Both students might end up with essays that are good, but good for different reasons.

Table: Multiple intelligences according to Howard Gardner

Form of intelligence	Examples of activities using the intelligence
Linguistic: verbal skill; ability to use language well	• verbal persuasion • writing a term paper skillfully
Musical: ability to create and understand music	• singing, playing a musical instrument • composing a tune
Logical / Mathematical: logical skill; ability to reason, often using mathematics	• solving mathematical problems easily and accurately • developing and testing hypotheses
Spatial: ability to imagine and manipulate the arrangement of objects in the environment	• completing a difficult jigsaw puzzle • assembling a complex appliance (*e.g.* a bicycle)
Bodily-kinesthetic: sense of balance; coordination in use of one's body	• dancing • gymnastics
Interpersonal: ability to discern others' nonverbal feelings and thoughts	• sensing when to be tactful • sensing a "subtext" or implied message in a person's statements
Intrapersonal: sensitivity to one's own thoughts and feelings	• noticing complex of ambivalent feelings in oneself • identifying true motives for an action in oneself
Naturalist: sensitivity to subtle differences and patterns found in the natural environment	• identifying examples of species of plants or animals • noticing relationships among species and natural processes in the environment

  As evidence for the possibility of multiple intelligences, Gardner cites descriptions of individuals with exceptional talent in one form of intelligence (for example, in playing the piano) but who are neither above nor below average in other areas. He also cites descriptions of individuals with brain damage, some of whom lose one particular form of intelligence (like the ability to talk) but retain other forms. In the opinion of many psychologists, however, the evidence for multiple intelligences is not strong enough to give up the "classical" view of general intelligence. Part of the problem is that the evidence for multiple intelligences relies primarily on anecdotes—examples or descriptions of particular individuals who illustrate the model—rather than on more widespread information or data. Nonetheless, whatever the status of the research evidence, the model itself can be useful as a way for teachers to think about their work.

Unit 3 Education and Students' Development

Multiple intelligences suggest the importance of diversifying instruction in order to honor and to respond to diversity in students' talents and abilities. Viewed like this, whether Gardner's classification scheme is actually accurate is probably less important than the fact there is (or may be) more than one way to be "smart". In the end, as with cognitive and learning styles, it may not be important to label students' talents or intellectual strengths. It may be more important simply to provide important learning and knowledge in several modes or styles, ways that draw on more than one possible form of intelligence or skill. A good example of this principle is your own development in learning to teach. It is well and good to read books about teaching (like this one, perhaps), but it is even better to read books and talk with classmates and educators about teaching and getting actual experience in classrooms. The combination both invites and requires a wide range of your talents and usually proves more effective than any single type of activity, whatever your profile of cognitive styles or intellectual abilities happens to be.

Questions after reading:
　　How can you explain the phenomenon that some students' academic performances are better than other students?

Group work:
　　Topic: The term "students' development" in its most general psychological sense refers to certain changes that occur in human beings' mental and physical growth. In your learning experience, can you list one of the most impressive examples of learning development?
　　Directions: Work as a group and share your ideas with others.

Text A

Brainstorming

Multiple intelligences: Howard Gardner's theory of multiple intelligences is based on studies not only of normal children and adults but also by studies of gifted individuals (including so-called "savants"), of persons who have suffered brain damage, of experts and virtuosos, and of individuals from diverse cultures. This led Gardner to break intelligence down into at least eight different components: logical, linguistic, spatial, musical, kinesthetic, interpersonal, intrapersonal, and naturalist intelligences.

Questions before reading:

What special talents do you have? Do you think that talented people have more advantages than the ordinaries? Why?

MI (Multiple Intelligence), IT (Instructional Technology) and Standards: The Story of Jamie[①]

Walter McKenzie

Consider the story of Jamie, a fourth grader I had in my classroom the year the state of Virginia first counted student Standards of Learning (SOL) test scores. In fourth grade the only test we were responsible for was Virginia History, which actually not only included the state history from 1585 to the present, but civics, economics, anthropology, sociology, geography and current events. Students entered fourth grade with some exposure to Jamestown but little else. For the best and the brightest in my class, passing that state mandated SOL test was going to be a challenge. For Jamie it was going to be a struggle. You see, he came from a disadvantaged home where he had little of the experiences and material advantages of his peers.

From day one Jamie walked into my classroom stirring things up letting it be known "I hate school." I firmly set up expectations for him and followed through with consequences those first few weeks so that he had the structure to get back into the swing of things. With his red hair, freckles and striking blue eyes, Jamie was always a site to behold. Often unkempt and rarely rested upon his morning arrival, Jamie pretty much raised himself and ran the streets.

Anyone who has ever taught probably remembers their own Jamie somewhere along the way. Moreover, Jamie's school records read like the running record of a struggling student: consistently low report grade grades, identified as needing remedial math and reading assistance since first grade, tested but in the "gray area" where he could not be identified for any other special services. Aside from ninety minutes a day when he went for Title I instruction, Jamie was all mine.

Not that I sized up the situation that way at the time. I was much more preoccupied with the daunting task of preparing my students for the Virginia History SOL test. The fourth grade team met several times that August and early September discussing strategies for meeting the challenge head on. Three of my colleagues were simply overwhelmed with the sheer volume of content we had to cover to prepare children for the test. They decided to use the time-tested drill and skill approach in which students would be hit daily with large amounts of information that they would be made responsible for memorizing. Study guide packets and nightly homework to reinforce

---

[①] Excerpt from "MI, IT and Standards: The story of Jamie", *New Horizons for Learning*. Sep, 2002. Retrieved from http://surfaquarium.com/jamie.htm.

information were their plan for reinforcing what was taught.

One other teammate, Ms. Donohue, shared my sentiments that simply focusing on covering such a vast amount of content would not be enough to help these kids pass that test. We wanted to tap into what we knew about how children learn, especially with regard to Gardner's multiple intelligences model of human cognition. We wanted to come up with ways to make the learning experiential, meaningful and memorable. We were all under the gun to have our students pass that test, so we were glad to swap ideas and discuss our options. But as the dust settled it was clear that Ms. Donohue and I would be on our own. We would work together to try and prepare our kids for the SOL test and the other three teachers would work together in a more traditional approach to meeting the state standards.

What I have realized since then, is that the difference between the two of us and our three colleagues was a basic assumption we made. The three teachers opting to drill and skill their students to prepare for the state test were operating under the assumption that in order to successfully pass a pencil and paper assessment, students needed to learn through pencil and paper tasks. This is certainly understandable. It was how we all were taught as students, and on the surface it makes sense.

Ms. Donohue and I, however, were willing to gamble on the fact that in order for our students to master all this material, they were going to need to learn using all their intelligences, and that when the time came to take the standardized test if the students had truly mastered the material through the different paths to learning they would be able to apply their knowledge base and determine the correct answers well enough to at least pass the required 70% mark set by the state. It was indeed a gamble. We were actually frightened to be taking a different tact from our three colleagues. After all, our professional reputation was at stake in making sure these students were ready and able to pass. If we were wrong, our jobs may be in jeopardy.

The one thing Ms. Donohue and I agreed to work on as two combined classes was a weekly SOL Olympics or Solympics as we came to refer to them in which the two classes would compete with one another each Friday in different competitions which tested their mastery of the Virginia History material we were covering. This was a great motivator for the students, as the two groups became very close and they looked forward to the weekly get-togethers. Beyond this, both classes worked individually through projects and units of instruction that involved all the intelligences.

In the early Fall we built a Powhatan wigwam in the classroom and studied the ways of the native people of Virginia. We took on the roles of the English settlers and the Native Americans and held a pow wow in which we danced, sang, played original wood instruments, wore costumes and prepared shellfish and vegetables to share. I remember how excited Jamie got as we prepared for this event and what a leader he was the day of the pow wow. He was so fascinated by the clams and their anatomy, he was eager to share his knowledge of bivalve body systems with anyone who would listen. It was an early turning point for Jamie as he conceded there may be some reasons to come to school after all.

As the Fall continued I assigned each student a research project on a colonial craft and we studied the colonial period Christmas traditions in Virginia as a class using Internet resources. By December we took a field trip to Colonial Williamsburg, and those kids were so primed when they got off that bus they kept out tour guide hopping all day with questions and ideas to share. It was an incredible trip. But the culminating event for this unit was having a colonial Christmas day in our classroom, where we invited other classes, parents and community members to come in and see us in period costume sharing what we each had learned about a specific colonial craft, all in the atmosphere of colonial Christmas customs. There was candle making, woodworking, stitchery, arts crafts, medicine, carolers and so much more all taking place at once as we entertained and informed visitors. It was a magical day and you guessed it. My fondest memory was Jamie teaming up with two other boys demonstrating woodworking. You've never seen a nine year old work harder non-stop all day hammering, sawing and sharing his expertise with onlookers. Jamie was truly finding his niche in school.

At about this time, I remember one Friday's Solympics that was being done in a Jeopardy format. The question was "Why had the colonists on Roanoke Island been left on their own while the ships returned to England, and why did it take three years for the ships to return?" The rule was each class had one chance to answer and then the question was up for grabs. Lisa, a very high functioning young lady in Ms. Donohue's class attempted to answer first, explaining that they had to return to England for supplies. While this was true, it did not explain why it took three years to return. Brittany from my class was then up to try and earn the points for her team, but she too could not recall what caused the delay in leaving the new colonists stranded for three years. So the question was up for grabs.

There was an uncomfortable silence as both classes needed these points to win the game, but no one seemed to have the answer. When suddenly, Jamie's hand shot up with a look of surprise even on his own face. I called on him and he blurted out, "Because Queen Elizabeth needed the ships to help fight a war against the Spanish Armada!" He was right and the class cheered him all the way to lunch. This was the first time it registered in my mind that Jamie was truly retaining information. It wasn't just that he was having fun and finding his place in the classroom. He was soaking up information in the process. I was very pleased for him.

Upon our return from winter break, I wanted to review everything we had studied through the Fall and take a thorough look at Virginia's role in the American Revolution. To accomplish this task, I rewrote the lyrics to songs from the Broadway show 1776 and had the class learn the songs, take on roles, and put on the play for anyone who would attend. It was a hit, and by the time the class was done they knew well of Jefferson's role in writing the Declaration of Independence and Richard Henry Lee's role in getting Virginia to vote for independence.

The Spring rolled on in likewise style. To study Virginia as the mother of presidents, we sponsored an online collaborative project known as the Presidents' Project through which we researched and created a web page about Thomas Jefferson *http://surfaquarium. com/tj.htm* and other classes from around the country researched and created home pages about Presidents from their home states. In learning about Virginia's role in the Civil War (the battles of Fredericksburg, Chancellorsville and Spotsylvania all took place within ten miles of our school), we learned Civil War songs, made an encampment, drilled carrying mop handles, and ate hard tack, salted ham and biscuits to experience the war first hand.

The entire time, mind you, we were reading the approved Virginia history textbook and completing all kinds of tasks to fill in the blanks with names, dates and facts as we worked our way along. We also practiced filling in bubbles on sample standardized test sheets and discussed strategies for figuring out the correct answer on a multiple choice test, using a process of elimination. But if you asked any of those kids what they remember most about that fourth grade year, they'd tell you about the crafts, cooking, singing, dancing, building, performing and competing they did to experience everything they could about Virginia History.

Ms. Donohue and I had no idea how our kids were shaping up as May approached. Certainly we had done everything we felt we could to prepare our students. But all of these different units and projects took time away from rote learning and there was certainly the nagging doubt that we had sold ourselves down the proverbial river by chasing our ideals about what is instructionally best for our children. Our counterparts were no more confident, wondering how much their students would be able to retain and recall when they finally sat in front of that standardized test. In a perfect world we would all come through this unscathed, students would do well regardless of our pedagogy, and we would all feel more secure about how to address these new state standards.

Jamie was a special concern for me, not because he hadn't made many strides socially and personally throughout the year, but because ultimately his weakness was reading and the state test was all text. He may know all kinds of important facts from our many different learning experiences, but would he be able to read well enough to show off his stuff on a standardized test? I hoped against hope that this would be the case; that even Jamie could pull off enough recall to get at least 70% on the test.

The day of testing came and went. Students took it in stride and gave no indication that they felt they did especially well or especially poor. We teachers each pored over the test as our students took it silently; trying to reassure ourselves that yes we had indeed covered all these items in some way, shape or form during the year. At the end of test day, all five of us got together in a panic as we realized one test item on the New River in the far western region of Virginia had been overlooked by all of us. We had covered the Potomac, the James, the Rappahannock, the Shenandoah; but the New River? Who would have guessed? It was a seeming omen to all of us that our worst fears may have been realized that perhaps we had not prepared our students as well as we should have.

What an awful feeling! After all was said and done we all were in the same boat with the same fears. Would any of us be able to say 70% of our kids had passed this test?

June rolled in and along with it came the SOL test results. Personally I couldn't bear to look. But Ms. Donohue wasn't afraid to take the bull by the horns. She spread out those class results in front of her and before I knew it she was in my room whooping and hollering. Two of the five classes passed the test, hers and mine. We both scored above the 70% mark! We were so elated that our students had been able to succeed faced with this seemingly insurmountable load of material to master; it was a true moment of validation for our constructivist approach to standardized testing. For the first time in my career I felt certain about my constructivist beliefs. We had put everything on the line to stick to our guns and it paid off! For the last time in my career I worried about those educators who warned that constructivist teaching could not meet the demands of standardized testing. I now knew better.

Later that day I sat down with all my students' individual test scores to see how they broke down. For student after student there was clear indication that learning had occurred and that they had truly mastered the content they had been taught. I was gratified by their success. It had all been worth it. Then I came to Jamie's scores. I was dumbstruck. Here was my special case, the child who had been struggling to simply be promoted to each new grade level since Kindergarten, and he scored in the 99th percentile on the Virginia History SOL test! He outscored almost every other student in the class, and came through clearly demonstrating that he was able to convert his hands-on learning experiences from across the months into successful recall on the day of the test. Whatever his reading difficulties may have been at that point, he was able to compensate for them and show everyone his best effort. I was so proud of Jamie!

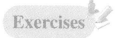

Exercises

I. Reading Comprehension:

There are four suggested answers marked A, B, C and D. Choose the best answer for each question.

1. Why does the author say that "I was much more preoccupied... the Virginia History SOL test" in the third paragraph?

    A. The new standard test is tough and competitive.

    B. The author was filled with uncertainty and dubitation with all the students.

    C. The author was anxious with the teaching job for a test.

    D. The test requirement seems to be an impossible task to complete.

2. In paragraph 6, the author describes "If we were wrong, our jobs may be in jeopardy". It means _____.

    A. they were about to experiment

    B. the result of the experiment is hard to say

Unit 3 Education and Students' Development

   C. if the experiment fails, they may lose their jobs
   D. the way of the experiment needs to be cautious
3. Why does the author describe the question and answering process between other students and Jamie?
   A. Because the author was inclined to show how smart Jamie actually was.
   B. Because the author was really impressed by Jamie's outstanding talents.
   C. Because the author hardly believed the question could be answered by Jamie.
   D. Because the author were more likely to indicate Jamie's progress in the process.
4. The sentence "Who would have guessed? ...as well as we should have" indicates _____.
   A. all the teachers blamed themselves for the question mentioned in the test
   B. all the teachers should be criticized for their irresponsibility in teaching
   C. all the teachers claimed they should not prepare that question in the test
   D. all the teachers prepared the question in the test
5. Through the description of Jamie, the author is more likely to convey _____.
   A. Jamie can make an improvement if the teacher teaches in a right way
   B. Jamie can learn history very well, which reflects his special talent
   C. Jamie's case shows the success of multi-intelligence
   D. Jamie's case means that poor students can make progress when they really enjoy learning

II. Judgments and Implications:
Do the following statements agree with the information given in the passage?
True   if the statement is true according to the passage
False   if the statement contradicts the passage
1. The author and his colleague would try out an untraditional method because they hold a new rationale of teaching.
2. In an outdoor trip, Jamie found his interest and role at school at the first time.
3. The author and his colleague trained students with written exercises and memorization work as well as their counterpart did.
4. I (the author) concerned about Jamie's ability before the exam because of his poor academic background.
5. It was surprised that Jamie scored the highest among all the other students in the test.

III. Chart Filling:
Read the text again and fill in the chart with appropriate activities.

| stories   flashcards   chants   miming |
| work individually on personalized project |

Learner type	Is good at	Learns best by	Activities
Linguistic	reading, writing and stories	saying, hearing and seeing words	trivia quizzes, _____
Logical / mathematical	solving puzzles, exploring patterns, reasoning and logic	asking questions, categorising and working with patterns	puzzles, problem solving _____
Visual / Spatial	drawing, building, arts and crafts	visualising, using the mind's eye	colours, pictures, _____ drawing, project work
Musical	singing, listening to music and playing instruments	using rhythm, with music on	using songs, _____
Bodily-Kinaesthetic	moving around, touching things and body language	moving, touching and doing	action songs, running dictations, _____
Interpersonal	mixing with others, leading groups, understanding others and mediating	co-operating, working in groups and sharing	mingle activities, group work, debates, discussions
Intrapersonal	working alone and pursuing own interests	working alone	
Naturalistic	nature	working outside and observing nature	environmental projects

Unit 3 Education and Students' Development

IV. Critical Questions:

What kind of intelligences did the teacher use to teach students? What actually changed Jamie?

Text B

Brainstorming

Cognition: In science, cognition is a group of mental processes that includes attention, memory, producing and understanding language, learning, reasoning, problem solving, and decision making. Various disciplines, such as psychology, philosophy, linguistics, and computer science all study cognition. However, the term's usage varies across disciplines; for example, in psychology and cognitive science, "cognition" usually refers to an information processing view of an individual's psychological functions.

Questions before reading:

How do you memorize information and what special methods do you employ? How can we use image to facilitate memorization?

The Man Who Couldn't Forget: The Story of Solomon's Memory[①]

Dr Geoff Rolls

The editor was amazed by Solomon's memory, whereas Solomon was amazed that anyone should think his memory was remarkable. Didn't others have equally good memories? He would discover the answer over the coming months and years. Sensing an interesting story, the editor sent Solomon to the local university for some further tests of his memory ability and this is where he met Alexander Romanovich Luria, a Russian professor who was to spend the next 30 years systematically studying the most remarkable memory ever examined.

Luria started the examination by collecting biographical details. Solomon, a Latvian by birth, was in his late twenties. His father owned a bookstore and therefore, not surprisingly, his mother was well read. His father could apparently recall the location of every book in the store and his mother, a devout Jew, could quote long paragraphs from

---

① Excerpt from Part 5 in *Classic Case Studies in Psychology*, 2nd edition. Philadelphia, Pennsylvania: Trans-Atlantic Publications, 2010.

the Torah. His brothers and sisters were well balanced individuals and there was evidence of some musical talent within the family. Indeed, Solomon trained as a violinist until an ear infection put paid to that choice of profession and he turned to journalism instead. Given the suggested link between exceptional ability and mental illness, Luria noted no history of mental illness in the family.

Luria began by giving Solomon a series of tests to ascertain his memory capacity. Words and numbers were presented to him in spoken or written form and he had to replicate them in their original form. Luria started with 10 or 20 items but increased this gradually to 70 items. Solomon recalled all the items perfectly. Solomon occasionally hesitated with his answers, and stared into space, paused, but then continued with word-perfect recall.

Solomon could also report the letters or numbers in reverse order or determine which letter or number followed another in a sequence. This is known as a serial probe technique, whereby a list of letters or numbers is read out and then one item is repeated and the item that follows has to be recalled. This can be conducted as a test of **short-term memory** (recall duration of up to about 30 seconds). Most people find this task extremely difficult, especially with a long sequence of items, but Solomon had no difficulty, providing that the initial presentation of the list was at a pace that he dictated. This pace tended to be fairly slow, which is the exact opposite of so-called "normal" participants who tend to perform slightly better on a serial probe task if the items are presented quickly. This is because with normal participants, the quicker the presentation, the less time the items have to decay in their short-term memory. However, with Solomon it was discovered that he was using a different system for remembering the items—not one based on normal acoustic or sound processing but one which involved images or pictures. This also meant that, once learnt, Solomon would remember the sequence of items indefinitely, whereas most normal participants would have little recall for the items beyond the minutes that the experiment would take.

Luria began to present Solomon with different memory tasks. Most people find meaningful words far easier to recall than nonsense syllables or trigrams (three consonants with no meaning, *e.g.* PQV) but Solomon had no problem with any of them. The same findings occurred with sounds and numbers—all Solomon required was a 3- or 4-second delay between each item to be recalled. In order to test the capacity of memory, researchers have devised a technique developed originally by Jacobs in 1887 called the serial digit span technique. This involves gradually increasing the items to be remembered until the participant becomes confused and can no longer recall the items in the correct order. If you try this, you'll find that the typical digit span is 7, plus or minus 2 items. However, with Solomon it was Luria who became confused, since Solomon appeared to have no limit to his digit span! Indeed, Luria had to give up in the end since there appeared to be no limit to his memory capacity.

Luria arranged for Solomon to return to the university for further tests of his memory. At these sessions, Solomon could recall perfectly all the previous items he had learnt. These results confused Luria even more, since Solomon seemed to have no limit either to the capacity of his memory or to the durability of the traces he retained. As Luria writes, "I soon found myself in a state verging on utter confusion. An increase in the length of a series led to no noticeable increase in difficulty for S., and I simply had to admit that the capacity of his memory had no distinct limits."

Luria couldn't measure either the capacity or duration of Solomon's memory, both of which can usually be tested fairly easily in a laboratory. Indeed, even more amazingly, Luria found out 16 years later that Solomon could recall the items learnt at his original sessions. Luria reports Solomon's saying, "Yes, yes... This was a series you once gave me once when we were in your apartment... You were sitting at the table and I in the rocking chair... You were wearing a gray [sic] suit and you looked at me like this... Now then I can see you saying..." This gives a clue as to how Solomon's memory worked—images were the key to his remarkable memory.

Luria had a problem. He realised that there was no way to measure Solomon's memory, since it seemed to have no capacity limit. A quantitative analysis of his memory was impossible. For the next 30 years, he decided to concentrate on *describing* Solomon's memory: to provide a qualitative account of its structure.

Solomon used one particular mechanism to aid his memory. Regardless of what information in whatever form (words, numbers, sounds, tastes and so on), Solomon always converted these items into visual images. Providing Solomon was given the time to convert the items into images, there was no limit to the capacity or duration of his memories. A table of 50 random numbers would typically take him about three minutes to commit to memory. How was this done? Solomon stated that if numbers were written on paper, then when asked to recall them later, he would recall the image he had of the paper and recall them as though he was still staring at it. If you were to stop reading now and try to recall all that you had seen on this page, after looking up, you would probably recall only a fraction of what you'd actually seen. For Solomon, recall was as though he was still looking at the items to be remembered. Indeed, Solomon could still picture the page in his mind's eye in perfect detail!

Many memory tasks work on the basis of errors made during recall. Such memory experiments are called "**substitution error**" studies. Mistakes that are made during recall often provide a clue as to how the memory works. It would be wrong to give the impression that Solomon never made any mistakes; although they did not occur that often, they were usually of a similar type and give us a further clue as to how his memory worked. For example, Solomon occasionally misread one number for another, especially if the numbers appeared similar, *i.e.* 3 and 8 or 2 and 7. Such errors again suggested that his memory was almost exclusively dependent on visual or so-called orthographic processing.

When given a list of words or numbers to recall, "normal" people often recall the first and last items on the list. Recall of the first items is called the "**primacy**" **effect** and the last is called the "**recency**" **effect**. This pattern of recall is known as the "serial position effect". It is suggested that the first words have been transferred to **long-term memory** through rehearsal and the last items on the list are still held in short-term memory. Once again, as with Solomon's duration and capacity of memory, Luria did not record this phenomenon, since Solomon could recall all the items wherever they appeared on a list! Solomon had the most amazing memory. Indeed, he had memories dating back to childhood that few of us possess. It's suggested that our memories of our first few years aren't recalled because we haven't learnt to encode the material due to a lack of development in terms of memory and/or speech. However, Solomon encoded his memories in a different way and, since this ability was innate, he possessed it at a very early age. Solomon reported memories from lying in his cot as an infant when his mother picked him up: "I was very young then... not even a year old perhaps... What comes to mind most clearly is the furniture in the room... I remember that the wallpaper in the room was brown and the bed white... I can see my mother taking me in her arms..." He even recalls his smallpox vaccination: "I remember a mass of fog, then of colours. I know this means there was noise, most likely conversation... But I don't feel any pain." Of course, it's impossible to discover the accuracy of these memories but their vividness certainly suggests an element of truth.

With such an amazing memory, Solomon was brilliant at spotting contradictions in stories, often pointing out things that the writers had failed to notice. He reports a character in the Chekhov story entitled "Fat and Thin" who takes off his cap, where earlier he is described as not having worn a cap. Given his precise ability, one might have imagined Solomon becoming a detective or lawyer. Solomon could "see" every detail and could not fail to spot any contradictions.

Exercises

I. Reading Comprehension:

There are four suggested answers marked A, B, C and D. Choose the best answer for each question.

1. The very first sentence of the passage means _____.
    A. not everyone agrees that Solomon's memory is more distinctive than other people
    B. even Solomon himself has realized that his capacity of memory is out of ordinary
    C. it is amazed that Solomon owns super memory
    D. everyone who has noticed Solomon surprised at his remarkable memory except himself

2. The main idea of this passage is to indicate _____.
    A. Solomon's extraordinary memory to memorize details
    B. the ways in which editors attempt to find out the truth of his remarkable memory
    C. the ways how Solomon memorizes things differently from ordinary people
    D. Solomon as an innate gifted man who is able to memorize numbers in large quantity

3. Solomon used his memory differently from ordinary people, because it can be witnessed that _____.
   A. his capacity of memory can not be measured
   B. his memory can not be tested by quantitative method
   C. Solomon would remember the sequence of items indefinitely
   D. Solomon would remember things in visual pictures and retain the items
4. The type of this passage is _____.
   A. narration
   B. exposition
   C. argumentation
   D. poem

II. Judgments and Implications:

Do the following statements agree with the information given in the passage?
True   if the statement is true according to the passage
False   if the statement contradicts the passage

1. Solomon as an innate genius inherited his capacities biologically from his parents.
2. For normal participants, the quicker the presentation, the less time the items have to decay in their short-term memory.
3. Luria was confused that Solomon would recall all information whatever the forms are.
4. From the details of Solomon's memory, it can be concluded that what he recalled are always true.
5. Solomon's capacity enables him to identify details easily than detectives or lawyers do.

III. Summary:

Complete the summary by using the appropriate forms of the words in the table below.

| temporarily | retaining | sensory | process |
| immediate | recycle | retrieve | network |

A flow chart is a useful tool for illustrating the relationship between the different stages in a _____. It shows the stages involved in creating short and long term memory. Short-term memory is a way of storing information for _____ use. On the other hand, long-term memory is a system for _____ information we need to _____ over extended periods of time. In the first stage of the process, the brain receives information through _____ stimuli. Then this information is stored _____ in a _____ of neural connections which constitute short-term memory. Before it can be transferred to the long-term memory, the information must be "rehearsed" or _____ in the short-term memory system. At the end of the process, it is stored in the long-term memory.

IV. Critical Questions:

PC (Personal computer) is similar to human beings' brain, which performs the function from input, processing to output. Look at the following picture and categorize them into different categories.

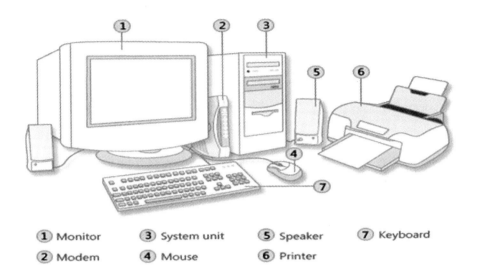

① Monitor ③ System unit ⑤ Speaker ⑦ Keyboard
② Modem   ④ Mouse   ⑥ Printer

Input hardware:

Output hardware:

The similarities between PC and brain have been listed below. Can you describe some differences?

Similarities:

A computer consists of many many parts, including a motherboard(which itself is made up of many parts), the disk drives, the processor, graphic cards and many more ... all of which have their own roles in the computer's processes.

Like a computer, the brain is formed out of parts. Besides having the left and right brain, there are also parts of the brain that take care of emotions, mathematical calculations, body co-ordinations and many other tasks needed for our daily activities.

Unit 3 Education and Students' Development

Text C

Brainstorming

Individual Differences: Individual differences are essential whenever we wish to explain how individuals differ in their behavior. In any study, significant variation exists between individuals. Reaction time, preferences, values, and health linked behaviors are just a few examples. Individual differences in factors such as personality, intelligence, memory, or physical factors such as body size, sex, age, and other factors can be studied and used in understanding this large source of variance.

Special Education (or special needs education) is the practice of educating students with special needs in a way that addresses their individual differences and needs. Ideally, this process involves the individually planned and systematically monitored arrangement of teaching procedures, adapted equipment and materials, accessible settings, and other interventions designed to help learners with special needs achieve a higher level of personal self-sufficiency and success in school and community than would be available if the student were only given access to a typical classroom education.

Questions before reading:
   How would you define problem students? Can you describe a case of problem students and provide a solution?

The Boy Who Needed to Play: The Story of Dibs[①]
Dr Geoff Rolls

"No go home"

The story of Dibs begins at school. Unlike most children of his age, Dibs appeared to hate school. In fact, he appeared to hate life. He often stood for minutes on end with his head buried in his arms leaning against a wall. He sometimes sat in the same place all morning, not moving and not saying a word. He would sometimes snuggle up in a ball and lie there till it was time to go home. Outside in the playground, he usually sought out a far corner, crouched down and scratched the dirt with a stick. He was a silent, withdrawn and unhappy child. Despite this strange behaviour, the teachers recognised that he actually liked school. When it was time to leave, his chauffeur would appear and

---

① Excerpt from Part 4 in *Classic Case Studies in Psychology*, 2nd edition. Philadelphia, Pennsylvania: Trans-Atlantic Publications, 2010.

Dibs would shout and scream, bite and kick and shout *"No go home"*, over and over again. These temper tantrums never occurred on his way into school.

Dibs never spoke to anyone who addressed him and he never made eye contact with anyone. He was an unhappy child, alone, in what seemed to him an unfriendly world. Despite this behaviour, his teachers had a genuine fondness for him. The force of his personality had touched them all. His behaviour was certainly erratic—most often he appeared to be mentally retarded, but occasionally he would do something that suggested a ready intelligence. He loved books and always accepted them when offered and during story time would often lurk under a table near enough to hear what was being said.

The school received many complaints about Dibs' disruptive and aggressive behaviour and the staff arranged for him to have some psychological tests. The psychologists failed to assess him, since he refused to participate in any of their tests. Was he mentally retarded? Was he autistic? Did he have some mental illness? After two years of this behaviour, when Dibs was five years old, his teachers called in a clinical psychologist. This is how Dibs first met Virginia Axline. She was to provide the stimulation and prompting necessary for Dibs to overcome his problems.

The door begins to open

Dibs' mother agreed to let him attend a series of play therapy sessions with Axline. These consisted of a one-hour session every Thursday. Play therapy is a specific form of psychotherapy for children. It uses the therapeutic powers of play to help children prevent or resolve various psychological difficulties. Children are given the chance to express or act out their experiences, feelings and problems by playing with dolls, toys and other play materials under the guidance or observation of a trained therapist. Through such a process children can, sometimes, be helped to achieve their full potential. Play therapists believe that play can be a means of acting out "blocked" feelings and emotions. It can also help address self-esteem issues, anger management, feelings of inadequacy and allow for emotional release.

There are two broad types of play therapy. Non-directive therapy involves allowing the child a free rein in the playroom. They can play with anything that interests them. The therapist listens or records all the behaviour. This is often done on video from behind a one-way mirror. The therapist uses factual comments on the behaviour, such as *"So, you're going to play with the father doll today"*, to allow the play to develop. The therapist is a supportive presence but does not become too involved in the play process. This is the method that Axline favoured with Dibs. It is also commonly referred to as client-centred therapy, for obvious reasons.

Directive therapy, on the other hand, involves the therapist taking a more active role in the play. Often they will make suggestions as to appropriate games to play and will use the sessions for specific diagnostic purposes. Therapists will often set up role-playing scenarios which might symbolise the child's own life experiences and then work on possible solutions. For example, animal glove puppets may be used in play fights that symbolise arguments between parents that a child might have witnessed.

Since five-year-olds lack the cognitive maturity to benefit from talking through their problems, it was felt that play could give Dibs a necessary sense of empowerment. Dibs was given the chance to take charge of the sessions and direct the play activities himself. Through play, Dibs would be given the opportunity to overcome any negative feelings and symbolically triumph over the upsets and traumas that had stolen his sense of well-being. Furthermore, he could do this in his own safe and accepting environment. But the question remained: How would Dibs cope with this new situation? The key to this healing process would be his own imagination and creativity.

The play therapy room used by Axline contained a doll's house with numerous dolls, toy cars, a sand pit, watercolour and finger paints, drawing paper and materials, and an inflatable doll that bounced upright when hit. During his first session, Dibs merely walked around the room naming each toy in a monotone voice. Axline encouraged this vocalization by confirming what each object was. On reaching the doll's house, Dibs sobbed urgently, "no lock doors... no lock doors." He repeated this over and over again. The therapeutic process was beginning.

"The rapy"

On one visit, Dibs noticed a sign on the door to the playroom. He recognized and read aloud "play" and looked at the other word. He was trying to work out what this unfamiliar word was. "*The rapy*," he said.

During the play sessions, Dibs frequently chose to play with the doll's house and the sandpit. He often asked for the doll's house doors to be locked up. As part of the therapy, Axline merely prompted Dibs to carry out his own suggestions. For instance, when Dibs asked for the house to be locked up, Axline would ask whether he wanted the house locked up. If he said that that was his wish, she would suggest that he did it, not her. When Dibs declared that the house was locked, she would congratulate him on his success.

Axline tried to avoid asking direct or probing questions of Dibs. This helped to avoid any suggestion of confrontation and helped his feelings of security. She recognised her desire to ask straightforward questions but believed that no-one ever answered them accurately during therapy and thus considered them to be of limited use. Instead, Axline always tried to ask open questions that allowed Dibs to express himself further. She often rephrased what he had said to give him more time to identify his thoughts. For example, when Dibs offered to give her a painting he'd done, rather than accept it with a simple thank you, she would ask, "*Oh, you want to give it to me, do you?*" This technique allowed her to keep open the communication and allowed Dibs to add more if he wished. It also helped to slow down the process and not impose her standards of behaviour on the interaction. Using such subtle techniques, Dibs was gradually coming out of his shell. He was beginning to reveal his true self. He was taking control and beginning to enjoy his new-found confidence and freedom. He started to make eye contact with Axline and, more frequently, a smile could be found framed by his curly, black hair.

Every week has a Thursday

Axline felt that Dibs was making progress. She had little contact with his parents or, indeed, his school, and so was unsure whether this progress was evident beyond the play therapy room. Nevertheless, Dibs continued to have profound difficulties. When upset, he would often pick up a baby's bottle and suck on it, seemingly using it as a method of reassurance. Axline also noticed that Dibs used one of two defensive strategies whenever he discussed his emotions and feelings. Sometimes his language would become very basic and rudimentary, and on other occasions he would change the subject by demonstrating his undoubted intellectual ability in writing, reading, counting and so forth. Axline recognised that Dibs felt the need to disguise his true feelings and emotions. Axline believed that Dibs was more comfortable demonstrating his intellectual abilities. Perhaps he also hid his true ability on occasions because he felt upset that people placed too high a value on them.

One day during a session, Dibs picked up a soldier and identified it as "Papa". He stood it up, standing, as he put it, "*so stiff and straight like an old iron railing from a fence*," and then proceeded to knock it down. He repeated this several times and then buried it in the sand. Dibs left it there for the week. Axline noticed the obvious message in the play and, at the same time, was amazed by his creative and impressive use of language. Given time and space, Dibs would work through his feelings for his father.

It is easy to see the symbolic significance of much of Dibs' play. For example, the locked doll's house could represent all the locked doors that he had faced in his short life—the locked door of his playroom at home and the locked door to his parents' love. Such interpretations were never suggested to Dibs and were not a required part of the therapy, but it seems reasonable to suggest that they may have represented such things. Only Dibs could know for sure.

As each week went by, it became obvious that Dibs was enjoying the sessions. He would rush to the playroom and enter with a ready smile. He told Axline how much he enjoyed the sessions. He told her, "*I come with gladness into this room and I leave it with sadness.*" He appeared to count the days till his next session. He worked out which day next Thursday was, whether it be George Washington's birthday or the day after the Fourth of July. He always knew what date Thursday was. Wednesday always seemed a long day before his session with "Miss A", as he liked to called her.

"Mother, I love you"

Over the coming weeks Dibs became more confident and relaxed. He reported how much he liked himself. He told of happy day-trips out to the seaside with his parents.

Dibs still withheld his speech when he wanted to. He knew how much it upset his father and it was his way of coping with any criticisms that came his way. One day after a therapy session, he ran down the corridor and jumped into his mother's arms shouting, "*Oh mother, I love you.*" His mother left in floods of tears.

Dibs was looking forward to the summer holidays with his family. He seemed to recognise that the therapy had run its course. He was happy and content. His mother visited Axline once more. This time she came to thank her for her efforts. She also confided in her that she always knew that Dibs wasn't retarded. She was sure that Dibs could read at the age of two. She had systematically taught him from a remarkably early age. She reported that, at the age of six, he could recognise hundreds of classical symphonies and that his drawings had an amazing sense of perspective. She had painstakingly pressured him to achieve. She thought she was helping him, developing his innate abilities, but this was at the expense of his emotional well-being. Perhaps his mother was unsure about how to relate to Dibs and had concentrated on the areas she felt comfortable with—the intellectual side—to hide her inability to become emotionally close to her son.

At his last session, Dibs was relaxed, outgoing and happy. All his behaviour was spontaneous. He said a final goodbye to "*the lady of the wonderful playroom*". A week later, a clinical psychologist administered an intelligence (IQ) test to Dibs. This is a standardised test, used to establish an intelligence level rating by measuring a person's ability to form concepts, solve problems, acquire information, reason and perform other intellectual operations. The average IQ score of the general population is 100. Dibs had an astoundingly high IQ of 168. Less than one person in a thousand would score as high. He did not finish the reading test since he grew bored, but he had already achieved a score far in advance of his years. He was an intellectually gifted individual who was thriving in all respects. Dibs had come to terms with himself and so had his parents.

It is very difficult to evaluate the success of play therapy. After all, what kind of measure of success might be employed? The therapy with Dibs certainly appeared successful, but what were the ingredients that brought this about? Was it the play activities, the toys, the warm relationship with Axline, the one-to-one contact or merely developmental maturation that helped Dibs? It may indeed have been some subtle combination of them all. This is one of the criticisms of play therapy: that it lacks experimental rigour. After all, it would be impossible to take another child with exactly the same problems and deny them therapy merely to try to determine whether they would have shown any improvement over the same time.

Exercises

I. Reading Comprehension:

There are four suggested answers marked A, B, C and D. Choose the best answer for each question.

1. From reading the section of "No go home", it can be inferred that _____.
   A. Dibs was an erratic child
   B. he was an unhappy child
   C. his destructive behaviors occurred at school were caused by offenses
   D. his destructive behaviors occurred at school were caused by family

2. Which one of the following situation is NOT true about directive therapy?
   A. It can help children to achieve their full potential.
   B. It is carried out under the guidance of a trained therapist.
   C. It is a client-centered therapy with the therapist's active participation.
   D. Directive therapy did not fit Dibs' case as the boy preferred to direct the play activities himself.

3. What is Dibs's mother's major mistreatment with Dibs?
   A. She knew the real problems with Dibs.
   B. She had started to systematically teach Dibs from the age two.
   C. She made great efforts to teach Dibs to achieve in many aspects.
   D. She developed Dibs, intellectual ability while ignored his emotional needs.

4. Which one of the following techniques is NOT adopted by Axline?
   A. Axline always tried to ask open questions that allowed Dibs to express himself further.
   B. Axline often rephrased what he had said to give him more time to identify his thoughts.
   C. Axline often encouraged Dibs to do things himself and praised his achievements.
   D. Axline set good example by herself for Dibs to follow.

II. Judgments and Implications:

Do the following statements agree with the information given in the passage?

True   if the statement is true according to the passage
False   if the statement contradicts the passage

1. Dibs, stranger and aggressive behavior in school suggested that he disliked school and studies.
2. Although the teachers had a warm affection for Dibs, they found him mentally abnormal and retarded.
3. Axline found the directive therapy most suitable with Dibs as it allowed Dibs the freedom to direct the play himself.

Unit 3 Education and Students' Development

4. Axline discovered that Dibs disguised his true feelings, emotions and true ability when he felt upset and in confident.
5. Dibs enjoyed in the play process and made significant progress in controlling emotions and making communications.

III. Matching:

Read the following sentences and pay attention to the underlined words. Choose an appropriate use of word which shares the similar contextual meaning with the original sentence.

1. His behavior was certainly erratic—most often he appeared to be mentally retarded, but occasionally he would do something that suggested a ready intelligence.
    A. The erratic fluctuation of market prices is in consequence of unstable economy.
    B. The old man had always been cranky and erratic.
2. The school received many complaints about Dibs' disruptive and aggressive behavior and the staff arranged for him to have some psychological tests.
    A. If you want to succeed in business you must be aggressive.
    B. He gets aggressive when he's drunk.
3. Axline merely prompted Dibs to carry out his own suggestions.
    A. Japan's recession has prompted consumers to cut back on buying cars.
    B. Our discussions prompted some questions worthy of consideration.
4. She often rephrased what he had said to give him more time to identify his thoughts.
    A. A small baby can identify its mother by her voice.
    B. Some people identify happiness with health.
5. Using such subtle techniques, Dibs was gradually coming out of his shell.
    A. She was, after long experience, wary of her uncle's selfishness, sometimes blatant, sometimes subtle.
    B. More discerning eyes could see subtle signs of weakness in the economy, apart from the dangerous stock market boom.
6. Axline recognized that Dibs felt the need to disguise his true feelings and emotions.
    A. We can not disguise the fact that business is bad.
    B. He disguised himself by wearing a false beard.

IV. Critical Questions:

Common special needs include learning disabilities, communication disabilities, emotional and behavioral disorders, physical disabilities, and developmental disabilities. What methods can be used to help students with special needs?

Learning Skills

Academic Report Skills I

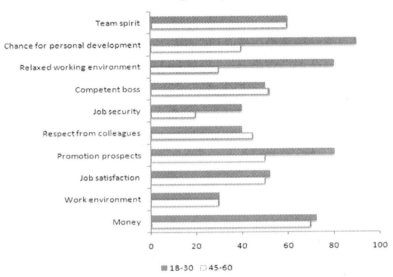

Questions:
Read the above graph and try to answer the following questions:
- How many different variables can you see in the graph and what categories can you classify them into?
- What outstanding statistic features can you identify from the graph?

The purposes to write an academic report:
- Present information, not an argument
- Use short, concise ways to demonstrate (short paragraphs and graphics)
- Cater for academic staff such as lecturers and professors
- Consider important facts more than format (no references and bibliography)

Structure of academic report:
Introduction
- Give enough background information to provide a context for the report
- State the purpose of the report. (indicate the topic or theme)

Body
The content of the body depends on the purpose of the report, a report would include:
- Demonstrate findings or results
- Generalize the changes and trends from the data, describe facts and data.

Unit 3 Education and Students' Development

Conclusion

Sum up the main points of the report. The conclusion should clearly relate to the objectives of your report.

Samples of introduction:

Which one is more suitable? Why?
A. The bar chart below shows the results of a survey conducted by a personnel department at a major company. The survey was carried out on two groups of workers: those aged from 18—30 and those aged 45—60, and shows factors affecting their work performance.
B. The bar chart indicates a survey on two different age groups on the factors contributing to make their environment pleasant for working.

Useful words and expressions:

In writing body of an academic report, some words are essential to be used to describe:

Expressing movement: nouns and verbs

For each trend there are a number of verbs and nouns to express the movement. We can use a verb of change, for example:

Verbs	Nouns
rose (to)	a rise
increased (to)	an increase
went up (to)	growth
climbed (to)	an upward trend
boomed	a boom (a dramatic rise)
fell (to)	
declined (to)	a decrease
decreased (to)	a decline
dipped (to)	a fall
dropped (to)	a drop
went down (to)	a slump (a dramatic fall)
slumped (to)	a reduction
reduced (to)	
levelled out (at)	
did not change	
remained stable (at)	a levelling out
remained steady (at)	no change
stayed constant (at)	
maintained the same level	

fluctuated (around)	a fluctuation
peaked (at) plateaued (at) stood at (we use this phrase to focus on a particular point, before we mention the movement, for example: in the first year, unemployment stood at ...)	reached a peak (of) reached at plateau (at)

Describing the movement: adjectives and adverbs

Sometimes we need to give more information about a trend as follows:

There has been a **slight** increase in the value of the dollar. (degree of change)
Unemployment fell **rapidly** last year. (the speed of change)

Remember that we modify a noun with an adjective (a slight increase) and a verb with an adverb (to increase slightly).

Describing the degree of change

Adjectives	Adverbs
dramatic	dramatically
sharp	sharply
huge	
enormous	enormously
steep	steeply
substantial	substantially
considerable	considerably
significant	significantly
marked	markedly
moderate	moderately
slight	slightly
small	
minimal	minimally

Unit 3 Education and Students' Development

Describing the speed of change

Adjectives	Adverbs
rapid	rapidly
quick	quickly
swift	swiftly
sudden	suddenly
steady	steadily
gradual	gradually
slow	slowly

Using prepositions:
Complete the following sample report by putting a preposition in each space.

Student expenditure (aged under 26 in higher education) in United Kingdom

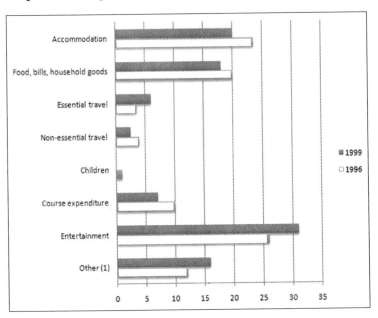

Percentage of total expenditure

  The chart shows the changes which took place _____ student spending in the United Kingdom _____ the three-year period from 1996 to 1999.

  Students spent 3% less on accommodation, which fell _____ 23% 20% of total expenditure, and there was a 2% decrease _____ spending on food, bills and household goods, which fell from 20% to 18%. At the same time course expenditure went down _____ 3% from 10% to 7%. Children, who constituted 1% _____ students' expenditure in 1996, are not represented in 1999.

On the other hand, there was a 5% growth _____ spending on entertainment, which stood _____ 26% of total expenditure in 1996 but rose _____ 31% in 1999. Spending on other non-essential items and credit repayments grew _____ 4% to make _____ 16% of total expenditure. Spending on essential travel went up _____ 3% while non-essential travel underwent a 1% fall.

Overall, with the exception of expenditure _____ travel, the most significant general change was a shift _____ spending on essential items _____ spending on non-essential items.

Complete the answer by filling the gaps with an adverb or adjective from the box below.

| dramatic | dramatically | impressive | impressively | slight | slightly |
| steady | steadily | sharp | sharply | steep | steeply |

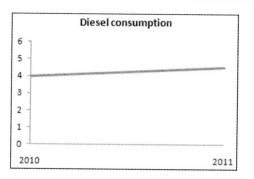

Diesel consumption showed a _____ increase between 2010 and 2011.
Diesel consumption increased _____ between 2010 and 2011.

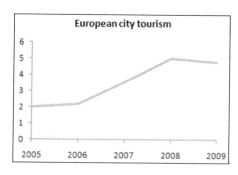

European city tourism showed an _____ growth of 50% for three consecutive years from 2006 to 2008.

Unit 3　Education and Students' Development

European city tourism grew _____ by 50% for three consecutive years from 2006 to 2008.

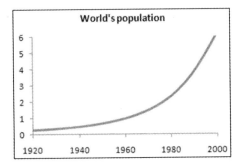

The world's population grew _____ between 1960 and 2000.
The world's population experienced a _____ growth between 1960 and 2000.

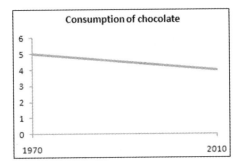

Consumption of chocolate fell _____ between 1970 and 2010.
There was a _____ fall in consumption of chocolate between 1970 and 2010.

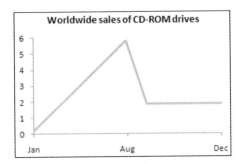

Worldwide sales of CD-ROM drives climbed _____ during the first half of the year before falling _____ in August.
There was a _____ climb in worldwide sales of CD-ROM drives during the first half of the year before a _____ fall in August.

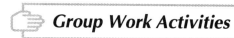

Group Work Activities

Work in groups to complete the following two tasks:

Task 1: Exercises

A. How can you change the following words in the introduction paragraph?

	other words can be used
show	Sample: display
diagram	Sample: table

B. Read the direction of the academic report and introductions from two students, which sample is better and why?

The bar chart shows the percentage of the total workforce in different employment sectors in three different countries.

Introduction:

Sample 1:

The bar chart illustrates the proportion of the total workforce in different employment sectors in three different countries.

Sample 2:

The bar chart compares the proportion of the workers employed in the service, agriculture and industrial sectors in Japan, India and Australia.

C. Questions to be discussed:

1. What do we have to write in the body of the report?
2. What details do we have to describe?
3. What orders do we have to follow to describe?
4. Read the following table to identify the most distinctive feature.

The table below shows the average band scores for students from different language groups taking the IELTS General Test in 2010.

	Listening	Reading	Writing	Speaking	Overall
German	6.8	6.3	6.6	6.9	6.7
French	6.3	6.1	6.5	6.6	6.5
Indonesian	6.3	6.1	6.1	6.7	6.3
Malay	6.2	6.4	6.0	6.6	6.4

Task 2: Writing

Would you please write an introduction and body based on the table above?

Self-evaluation Form

What are the main objectives in this unit?
_____
_____
_____

What useful vocabularies and expressions have you learned from this unit?
_____
_____
_____

What key terms and educational knowledge have you learned?
_____
_____
_____

Have you used the learning skills before? Why do you think they are useful or not useful?
_____
_____
_____

If possible, what would you like to add to make learning more interesting and relevant?
_____
_____
_____

Unit 4

English Language and Learning

Introduction

Learning English[1]
David Graddol

The EFL Tradition

EFL, as we know it today, is a largely 19th century creation, though drawing on centuries of experience in teaching the classical languages. EFL tends to highlight the importance of learning about the culture and society of native speakers; it stresses the centrality of methodology in discussions of effective learning; and emphasises the importance of emulating native speakers' language behaviour. EFL approaches, like all foreign languages teaching, positions the learner as an outsider, as a foreigner; one who struggles to attain acceptance by the target community.

The target language is always someone else's mother tongue. The learner is constructed as a linguistic tourist—allowed to visit, but without rights of residence and required always to respect the superior authority of native speakers.

Designed to Produce Failure

Modern foreign languages, English amongst them, have traditionally belonged to the secondary school curriculum, with learners rarely starting study before the age of 11 or 12. They have focused on the language as a timetabled subject, with stress on such things as grammatical accuracy, native speaker-like pronunciation, and literature. When measured against the standard of a native speaker, few EFL learners will be perfect. Within traditional EFL methodology there is an inbuilt ideological positioning of the student as outsider and failure—however proficient they become. Although EFL has become technologised, and has been transformed over the years by communicative methods, these have led only to a modest improvement in attainment by learners.

The model, in the totality of its pedagogic practices, may even have historically evolved to produce perceived failure. Foreign languages, in many countries, were largely learned to display social position and to indicate that your family was wealthy enough to

---

[1] Excerpt from Part 2, Section 2 in *English Next*, British Council, 2006.

have travelled to other countries. Even if you do not accept the argument that the tradition is ideologically designed as a gate keeping device which will help the formation of elites, it is nevertheless true that the practice of EFL can and does tolerate high levels of failure. In those countries where passing English exams has been made a condition of promotion or graduation, it has often led to considerable stress and resentment by learners, rather than significantly enhanced levels of proficiency. In recent years, several developments in the practice of ELT have started to take EFL in new directions. The European "language portfolio", for example, attempts to record a learner's experience and achievement in non-traditional ways. The Common European Framework of Reference for languages (CEFR) which attempts to provide a uniform approach to attainment levels across all languages, employs the concept of "can do" statements rather than focusing on aspects of failure. Such developments illustrate the way that ELT practices are evolving to meet new social, political and economic expectations and I believe significantly depart from the traditional EFL model, even where that term is still employed.

English as a Second Language

In contrast to EFL, one of the defining features of teaching English as a second language is that it recognizes the role of English in the society in which it is taught. Historically, there have been two major strands of development in ESL, both dating from the 19th century. The first kind of ESL arose from the needs of the British Empire to teach local people sufficient English to allow the administration of large areas of the world with a relatively small number of British civil servants and troops. The imperial strategy typically involved the identification of an existing social elite who would be offered a curriculum designed to cultivate not just language skills but also a taste for British—and more generally western—culture and values. Literature became an important strand in such a curriculum and a literary canon was created which taught Christian values through English poetry and prose. Such an approach to ESL helped widen existing divisions within colonial society through the means of English. In postcolonial contexts today, the use of English is still often surrounded by complex cultural politics and it is proving surprisingly difficult to broaden the social base of English speaking even where English is used as the language of the educated middle classes. For many decades, no more than 5% of Indians, for example, were estimated to speak English, even though it plays an important role in Indian society. In colonial times there was no strong need to impose a metropolitan spoken standard and many local varieties of English emerged—the so-called "New Englishes"—from contact with local languages. Many new Englishes have since flourished, and have developed literatures and even grammar books and dictionaries.

In ESL countries, children usually learn some English informally before they enter school, so that the role of the classroom is often to extend their knowledge of the language. Where there exists a local, vernacular variety of English, a major role of the classroom is teaching learners a more formal and standard variety.

The ecology of English in such countries is a multilingual one where English is associated with particular domains, functions and social elites. A related characteristic of ESL societies is code-switching: speakers will often switch between English and other languages, even within a single sentence. Knowledge of code-switching norms is an essential part of communicative competence in such societies. A quite different approach to ESL arose in the USA and, later, in countries such as Canada, Australia and New Zealand where generations of immigrants had to be assimilated and equipped with a new national identity. In the UK, ESL did not become fully institutionalised until the 1960s. ESL is often nowadays referred to as ESOL (English for Speakers of Other Languages).

ESL in such contexts must also address issues of identity and bilingualism. Some learners—even in the USA and the UK—will not be quite as immersed in an English speaking world as might be imagined. Many live in ethnic communities in which many of the necessities of daily life can be conducted within the community language. Furthermore, in most such communities standard English is only one of the varieties of English which learners need to command. Often, there exist local as well as ethnic varieties of English—such as Indian or Jamaican English in London. In such communities, the communicative competence required by an ESL learner includes a knowledge of the community norms of code-switching. The learning of English for ESL students is often a family matter, with different generations speaking with different levels of competence—even different varieties of English—and acting as interpreters as necessary for less-skilled family and community members.

Translation and interpreting are important skills for ESL users, though not always well recognised by education providers. Where ESL is taught to immigrants entering English-speaking countries it is not surprising that a key component in the curriculum is often "citizenship": ensuring that learners are aware of the rights and obligations as permanent residents in English speaking countries. Citizenship rarely figured in the traditional EFL curriculum.

Questions after reading:

What are the differences between EFL and ESL? What are the two different contexts described in the ESL society?

Group work:

Topic: English we have learned from school is a simplified version of standard English which domains mainly in daily communications. However, authentic Englishes can be varied from pronunciation, grammar to meanings as language changes all the time.

Directions: Identify a variety of different Englishes with relevant examples to illustrate the features and explain the reasons for the differences.

Unit 4 English Language and Learning

Text A

Brainstorming

Mother Tongue is the language(s) a person has learned from birth or within the critical period, or that a person speaks the best and so is often the basis for sociolinguistic identity. By contrast, a second language is any language that one speaks other than one's first language.

Cultural Assimilation: The term assimilation is often used when referring to immigrants and various ethnic groups settling in a new land. New customs and attitudes are acquired through contact and communication. Each group of immigrants contributes some of its own cultural traits to the new society. Assimilation usually involves a gradual change and takes place in varying degrees; full assimilation occurs when new members of a society become indistinguishable from older members.

Questions before reading:

In what way does your mother tongue influence your English learning? Can you show some examples?

Mother Tongue[①]
Amy Tan

I am not a scholar of English or literature. I cannot give you much more than personal opinions on the English language and its variations in this country or others.

I am a writer. And by that definition, I am someone who has always loved language. I am fascinated by language in daily life. I spend a great deal of my time thinking about the power of language—the way it can evoke an emotion, a visual image, a complex idea, or a simple truth. Language is the tool of my trade. And I use them all—all the Englishes I grew up with.

Recently, I was made keenly aware of the different Englishes I do use. I was giving a talk to a large group of people, the same talk I had already given to half a dozen other groups. The nature of the talk was about my writing, my life, and my book, *The Joy Luck Club*. The talk was going along well enough, until I remembered one major difference that made the whole talk sound wrong. My mother was in the room. And it was perhaps the first time she had heard me give a lengthy speech, using the kind of English I have never used with her. I was saying things like, "The intersection of memory upon

---

① Excerpt from "Mother Tongue", *Threepenny Review*, 1990.

imagination" and "There is an aspect of my fiction that relates to thus-and-thus"—a speech filled with carefully wrought grammatical phrases, burdened, it suddenly seemed to me, with nominalized forms, past perfect tenses, conditional phrases, all the forms of standard English that I had learned in school and through books, the forms of English I did not use at home with my mother.

Just last week, I was walking down the street with my mother, and I again found myself conscious of the English I was using, the English I do use with her. We were talking about the price of new and used furniture and I heard myself saying this: "Not waste money that way." My husband was with us as well, and he didn't notice any switch in my English. And then I realized why. It's because over the twenty years we've been together I've often used that same kind of English with him, and sometimes he even uses it with me. It has become our language of intimacy, a different sort of English that relates to family talk, the language I grew up with.

So you'll have some idea of what this family talk I heard sounds like, I'll quote what my mother said during a recent conversation which I videotaped and then transcribed. During this conversation, my mother was talking about a political gangster in Shanghai who had the same last name as her family's, Du, and how the gangster in his early years wanted to be adopted by her family, which was rich by comparison. Later, the gangster became more powerful, far richer than my mother's family, and one day showed up at my mother's wedding to pay his respects. Here's what she said in part:

"Du Yusong having business like fruit stand. Like off the street kind. He is Du like Du Zong—but not Tsung-ming Island people. The local people call putong, the river east side, he belong to that side local people. That man want to ask Du Zong father take him in like become own family. Du Zong father wasn't look down on him, but didn't take seriously, until that man big like become a mafia. Now important person, very hard to inviting him. Chinese way, came only to show respect, don't stay for dinner. Respect for making big celebration, he shows up. Mean gives lots of respect. Chinese custom. Chinese social life that way. If too important won't have to stay too long. He come to my wedding. I didn't see, I heard it. I gone to boy's side, they have YMCA dinner. Chinese age I was nineteen."

You should know that my mother's expressive command of English belies how much she actually understands. She reads the *Forbes* report, listens to *Wall Street Week*, converses daily with her stockbroker, reads all of Shirley MacLaine's books with ease—all kinds of things I can't begin to understand. Yet some of my friends tell me they understand 50 percent of what my mother says. Some say they understand 80 to 90 percent. Some say they understand none of it, as if she were speaking pure Chinese. But to me, my mother's English is perfectly clear, perfectly natural. It's my mother tongue. Her language, as I hear it, is vivid, direct, full of observation and imagery. That was the language that helped shape the way I saw things, expressed things, made sense of the world.

Lately, I've been giving more thought to the kind of English my mother speaks.

Unit 4 English Language and Learning

Amy Tan

Like others, I have described it to people as "broken" or "fractured" English. But I wince when I say that, it has always bothered me that I can think of no way to describe it other than "broken", as if it were damaged and needed to be fixed, as if it lacked a certain wholeness and soundness. I've heard other terms used, "limited English", for example. But they seem just as bad, as if everything is limited, including people's perceptions of the limited English speaker.

I know this for a fact, because when I was growing up, my mother's "limited" English limited my perception of her. I was ashamed of her English. I believed that her English reflected the quality of what she had to say. That is, because she expressed them imperfectly her thoughts were imperfect. And I had plenty of empirical evidence to support me: the fact that people in department stores, at banks, and at restaurants did not take her seriously, did not give her good service, pretended not to understand her, or even acted as if they did not hear her.

My mother has long realized the limitations of her English as well. When I was fifteen, she used to have me call people on the phone to pretend I was she. In this guise, I was forced to ask for information or even to complain and yell at people who had been rude to her. One time it was a call to her stockbroker in New York. She had cashed out her small portfolio and it just so happened we were going to go to New York the next week, our very first trip outside California. I had to get on the phone and say in an adolescent voice that was not very convincing, "This is Mrs. Tan."

And my mother was standing in the back whispering loudly, "Why he don't send me check, already two weeks late. So mad he lie to me, losing me money."

And then I said in perfect English, "Yes, I'm getting rather concerned. You had agreed to send the check two weeks ago, but it hasn't arrived."

Then she began to talk more loudly. "What he want, I come to New York tell him front of his boss, you cheating me?" And I was trying to calm her down, make her be quiet, while telling the stockbroker, "I can't tolerate any more excuses. If I don't receive the check immediately, I am going to have to speak to your manager when I'm in New York next week." And sure enough, the following week there we were in front of this astonished stockbroker, and I was sitting there red-faced and quiet, and my mother, the real Mrs. Tan, was shouting at his boss in her impeccable broken English.

We used a similar routine just five days ago, for a situation that was far less humorous. My mother had gone to the hospital for an appointment, to find out about a benign brain tumor a CAT scan had revealed a month ago. She said she had spoken very good English, her best English, no mistakes. Still, she said, the hospital did not apologize when they said they had lost the CAT scan and she had come for nothing. She said they did not seem to have any sympathy when she told them she was anxious to know the exact diagnosis, since her husband and son had both died of brain tumors. She said they would not give her any more information until the next time and she would have to make another appointment for that. So she said she would not leave until the doctor called her daughter. She wouldn't budge. And when the doctor finally called her daughter, me, who spoke in perfect English—lo and behold—we had assurances the CAT scan would be found, promises that a conference call on Monday would be held, and apologies for any suffering my mother had gone through for a most regrettable mistake.

  I think my mother's English almost had an effect on limiting my possibilities in life as well. Sociologists and linguists probably will tell you that a person's developing language skills are more influenced by peers. But I do think that the language spoken in the family, especially in immigrant families which are more insular, plays a large role in shaping the language of the child. And I believe that it affected my results on achievement tests, I.Q. tests, and the SAT. While my English skills were never judged as poor, compared to math, English could not be considered my strong suit. In grade school I did moderately well, getting perhaps B's, sometimes B-pluses, in English and scoring perhaps in the sixtieth or seventieth percentile on achievement tests. But those scores were not good enough to override the opinion that my true abilities lay in math and science, because in those areas I achieved A's and scored in the ninetieth percentile or higher.

  This was understandable. Math is precise; there is only one correct answer. Whereas, for me at least, the answers on English tests were always a judgment call, a matter of opinion and personal experience. Those tests were constructed around items like fill-in-the-blank sentence completion, such as, "Even though Tom was ____, Mary thought he was ____". And the correct answer always seemed to be the most bland combinations of thoughts, for example, "Even though Tom was shy, Mary thought he was charming." with the grammatical structure "even though" limiting the correct answer to some sort of semantic opposites, so you wouldn't get answers like, "Even though Tom was foolish, Mary thought he was ridiculous." Well, according to my mother, there were very few limitations as to what Tom could have been and what Mary might have thought of him. So I never did well on tests like that.

  The same was true with word analogies, pairs of words in which you were supposed to find some sort of logical, semantic relationship—for example, "Sunset is to nightfall as is to." And here you would be presented with a list of four possible pairs, one of which showed the same kind of relationship: red is to stoplight, bus is to arrival, chills is to fever, yawn is to boring: Well, I could never think that way. I knew what the tests were asking, but I could not block out of my mind the images already created by the first pair, "sunset is to nightfall"—and I would see a burst of colors against a darkening sky, the moon rising, the lowering of a curtain of stars. And all the other pairs of words —red, bus, stoplight, boring—just threw up a mass of confusing images, making it impossible for me to sort out something as logical as saying: "A sunset precedes nightfall." is the same as "A chill precedes a fever." The only way I would have gotten that answer right would have been to imagine an associative situation, for example, my being disobedient and staying out past sunset, catching a chill at night, which turns into feverish pneumonia as punishment, which indeed did happen to me.

I have been thinking about all this lately, about my mother's English, about achievement tests. Because lately I've been asked, as a writer, why there are not more Asian Americans represented in American literature. Why are there few Asian Americans enrolled in creative writing programs? Why do so many Chinese students go into engineering! Well, these are broad sociological questions I can't begin to answer. But I have noticed in surveys—in fact, just last week—that Asian students, as a whole, always do significantly better on math achievement tests than in English. And this makes me think that there are other Asian-American students whose English spoken in the home might also be described as "broken" or "limited". And perhaps they also have teachers who are steering them away from writing and into math and science, which is what happened to me.

Fortunately, I happen to be rebellious in nature and enjoy the challenge of disproving assumptions made about me. I became an English major my first year in college, after being enrolled as pre-med. I started writing nonfiction as a freelancer the week after I was told by my former boss that writing was my worst skill and I should hone my talents toward account management.

But it wasn't until 1985 that I finally began to write fiction. And at first I wrote using what I thought to be wittily crafted sentences, sentences that would finally prove I had mastery over the English language. Here's an example from the first draft of a story that later made its way into *The Joy Luck Club*, but without this line: "That was my mental quandary in its nascent state." A terrible line, which I can barely pronounce.

Fortunately, for reasons I won't get into today, I later decided I should envision a reader for the stories I would write. And the reader I decided upon was my mother, because these were stories about mothers. So with this reader in mind—and in fact she did read my early drafts—I began to write stories using all the Englishes I grew up with: the English I spoke to my mother, which for lack of a better term might be described as "simple"; the English she used with me, which for lack of a better term might be described as "broken"; my translation of her Chinese, which could certainly be described as "watered down"; and what I imagined to be her translation of her Chinese if she could speak in perfect English, her internal language, and for that I sought to preserve the essence, but neither an English nor a Chinese structure. I wanted to capture what language ability tests can never reveal: her intent, her passion, her imagery, the rhythms of her speech and the nature of her thoughts.

Apart from what any critic had to say about my writing, I knew I had succeeded where it counted when my mother finished reading my book and gave me her verdict: "So easy to read."

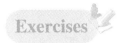

Exercises

I. Reading Comprehension:

There are four suggested answers marked A, B, C and D. Choose the best answer for each question.

1. Why did the author choose to major in English?
   A. She was good at English.
   B. English was her favorite subject.
   C. She wanted to challenge her ability in English and to change people's assumptions.
   D. Her mother encountered indifferences and humiliations using English and she urged her daughter to study English well.

2. In paragraph 4, the author spoke "Not waste money that way", why did she speak English in this way?
   A. Because the price of furniture is too expensive.
   B. Because it is the English she used to speak.
   C. Because she spoke to her mother in that way.
   D. Because her husband had got used to it.

3. Why does the author score higher in math and science?
   A. Because the evaluating system of English is more subjective than that of math.
   B. Because she has talents for math.
   C. Because she did not like studying English.
   D. Because her mother told her to study hard at math.

4. From reading this article, it can be inferred that the author's mother _____.
   A. speaks limited English
   B. hasn't learned English grammar or vocabulary well enough
   C. has no courage to complain over phone
   D. fails to account herself in most cases

5. What kind of English did Amy Tan use in her writing?
   A. Complicated standard English.   B. Simplified English.
   C. Grammatically wrong English.   D. All of the above.

6. Which of the following statements could NOT be concluded from the text?
   A. The immigrants in America with language barriers would be prejudiced in many social occasions.
   B. It was more suitable for the Asian immigrants to study science than to study English.
   C. Amy Tan was an influential writer in America.
   D. Amy Tan didn't meet any prejudices thanks to her good English ability.

II. Judgments and Implications:

Do the following statements agree with the information given in the passage?
True   if the statement is true according to the passage

Unit 4 English Language and Learning

False   if the statement contradicts the passage
1. Amy Tan's mother was not aware of the limitation of her English.
2. Amy Tan's comprehensive ability was much better than that of her mother's.
3. Amy Tan's mother could read and understand English fairly well.
4. The American society was not friendly towards the Chinese immigrants.
5. Amy Tan's mother called the stockbroker directly to get the check from him.
6. Asian students usually get higher marks in math than in English because their analytical ability was strong.

III. Matching:

Read the following sentences and pay attention to the underlined words. Choose an appropriate use of word which shares the similar contextual meaning with the original sentence.

1. You should know that my mother's expressive command of English belies how much she actually understands.
   A. What he does belies his commitments.
   B. War belied hopes for peace.
2. She had cashed out her small stock portfolio and it just so happened we were going to go to New York the next week, our very first trip outside California
   A. His newly bought portfolio is of sound brand and of good quality.
   B. He went mad when the bad news came about the failure of his portfolio in the stock market.

IV. Critical Questions:

How does language reflect one's personal, cultural, social, and political identity? What is the connection among language, culture, and identity?

Text B

Brainstorming

Second Language Acquisition (SLA) is the process by which people learn a second language. That is, it is the process of learning an additional language by someone who has already learned a native language or multiple native languages.

Questions before reading:
What factors or reasons drive you to learn English? How does that motivation influence your learning?

Identity, Motivation and Autonomy in Second Language Acquisition from the Perspective of Complex Adaptive System[①]

Veralucia Menezes de Oliveira e Paiva

In this world, nothing is permanent except change.

——American Proverb

Identity

Learning a language is also a process of identity construction. Norton defines identity as, "how a person understands his or her relationship to the world, how that relationship is constructed across time and space, and how the person understands possibilities for the future." As explained by Wenger:

An identity is not an abstract idea or a label, such as a title, an ethnic category, or a personality trait. It is a lived experience of belonging (or not belonging). A strong identity involves deep connections with others through shared histories and experiences, reciprocity, affection, and mutual commitments.

However, identity is not a unified experience of belonging, but an array of multiple memberships in a fractal dimension. Sade explains that in a fractal "no matter the number of internal fragmentations, the parts are interconnected into a whole which is self-similar to the parts". Identity is a complex system that displays a fractalized process of expansion as it is open to new experiences. In SLA, this expansion occurs through one's engagement in diverse linguistic social practices, with which one identifies.

Motivation

Motivation has been traditionally understood as either an integrative or instrumental orientation, as proposed by Gardner and Lambert. They define integrative motivation as "a willingness to become a member of another ethno linguistic group", while the instrumental orientation is "characterized by a desire to gain social recognition or economic advantage through knowledge of a foreign language". Later on, Deci and Ryan developed "the self-determination theory" and added to the field two other notions of motivation "intrinsic motivation, which refers to doing something because it is inherently interesting or enjoyable, and extrinsic motivation, which refers to doing something because it leads to a separable outcome". By separable outcome, they refer to the instrumental characteristic of extrinsic motivation and exemplify with a hypothetical student who does his work just to avoid parental sanctions and another who studies because she believes it is important for her future career.

[①] Excerpt from *Identity, Motivation and Autonomy in Language*, Short Run Press, Ltd., 2011.

Autonomy

In Paiva, I argue that autonomy is a socio-cognitive system nested in the SLA system. It involves not only the individual's mental states and processes, but also political, social and economic dimensions. It is not a state, but a non-linear process, which undergoes periods of instability, variability and adaptability. It is an essential element in SLA because it triggers the learning process through learners' agency and leads the system beyond the classroom. Autonomous learners take advantage of the linguistic affordances in their environment and act by engaging themselves in second language social practices. They also reflect about their learning and use effective learning strategies.

As human beings are different, so are their contexts and so are their SLA processes, which are mediated by different human agents and cultural artifacts. As a consequence, unequal learning experiences may occur in very similar situations. When we turn our observation to language teaching practices, we see that no matter how much teachers plan and develop their classes, students will react in different ways and unforeseen events will inevitably be part of their learning experiences. The seemingly orderly world of acquisition is, in fact, chaotic and chaos seems to be fundamental in such a process. SLA consists of a dynamic interaction among different individual and social factors put into movement by inner and social processes. The random interaction among all the elements of the acquisition system yields the changes responsible for acquisition. The rate of change is not predictable and varies according to the nature of the interactions among all the elements of the system. A live acquisition system is always in movement and never reaches equilibrium, although it undergoes periods of more or less stability.

The Connections Among Identity, Motivation and Autonomy

For the sake of textual organization, identity, motivation and autonomy will be discussed in separate subsections, but I am aware that they represent interconnected elements in the SLA complex system.

Identity

Learning a language involves coping with fractal dimensions of the identity complex system. Besides being a learner, one has other identities, such as gender and social class identities, and additional ones can arise along the SLA process. For example, it is the identity of Michael Jackson's fan that urges a Brazilian learner to learn English. Listen to her: "I've started to study English by myself, when I was about 15, because of Michael Jackson. He's been my idol since 1991, and I really wanted to understand him and his music since I was a child." Another one took advantage of her identity of waitress to improve her English. All of them demonstrated in their ELLHs that they were highly motivated autonomous learners.

A good example of gender identity is found in the Japanese corpus. Being a female implies certain constraints in Japanese society. One narrator remarks that she worked in a trade company that used to send employees to study abroad, but females were not included in that policy. Others were housewives and mothers and those identities demanded, for instance, taking care of children, which interfered with their studies or even interrupted the flow of their SLA processes. Nevertheless, as chaotic systems exhibit unpredictable and irregular dynamics, it is the very identity of a Japanese housewife that moved one learner's SLA system. According to that narrator, she hated English in school and almost died of boredom, but something unexpected happened and she felt motivated and restarted learning English. She explains:

It was spring at my age of twenty-eight. As my youngest child went up to kindergarten, I began thinking about my own life which had had no free time. I desired strongly that I could have something special providing me a sense of fulfillment. Whatever it was, I would be OK if it gave me satisfaction at that time. One day in those days, my husband once said to me: "I will take you to Hawaii some day." As I heard from him, I thought that's it. It was what I wanted to do. The idea of going shopping with fluent English in Hawaii suddenly popped in my mind. But at the same time I thought the English I would take must be practical, not useless. Now I come to think of my choice then, it was too childish, wasn't it?

That choice worked as a butterfly effect. The metaphor "the flapping of a butterfly's wing in Brazil can cause a tornado in Japan" can explain what happened to that student's SLA system. The promise "I will take you to Hawaii some day," in her own words "was a direct trigger to make me her restart it." The SLA system, which was temporarily at rest, was moved by sudden motivation and consequent autonomy as the learner took control of her SLA process.

She started following a radio language program, on NHK (Nippon Hoso Kyokai), the Japan Broadcasting Corporation, which broadcasts various language lessons on its international shortwave Radio Japan service. But again, her identity of mother was responsible for experiences of engagement in two different communities of practice. Let us listen to her again:

One and half years later after I chose it, a new cute girl from America enrolled in the kindergarten where my youngest child had been. The America girl and my daughter became good friends and both families became very close. Thanks to this relationship, my poor English was getting better little by little. I was lucky I could have the opportunity to use English. Necessity helped motivate me to brush up my skill. They returned to the US after their five-year stay in Japan. During their stay, I got a job introduced by her father and worked for a while using English.

We can see that new identities emerged: friend of an American family and worker. Not only had her SLA system changed, but also her identity system, which increased its complexity with the addition of new identities: autonomous language learner, friend and worker. She realized that she had changed: "I know myself that relearning English made me change. I have come to care about my own life. I have become a little bit more outgoing than I used to be." This remark is a good example of how interrelated complex systems are. Acquiring a language is interrelated with the complexity of identity construction, social life and family complex systems.

Motivation

It has been revealed that motivation is not a linear phenomenon and small changes in the student's experiences can yield an enormous change in motivation, as we saw in the case of the Japanese housewife. On the other hand, motivation may disappear in the face of monotonous activities in the classroom, but can revive if the learner meets a new teacher, a new school or interesting experiences outside school. An example is the Brazilian student who said that "the only thing she learned was to hate the language" in junior high school. She lost her motivation in high school, but it came back with a rewarding experience when she attended private lessons. She says, "the teacher taught me not only there was not to be scared of, but also to love the language." Then she started her major in English and motivation vanished, she hated the course and dropped out. Later on she traveled to Canada, lived there for six months, and when she returned to Brazil, she went to another university to get her degree as an English teacher. English culture, especially music and literature, seems to be a source of extrinsic motivation. In both corpora, some learners register in their histories that they wanted to learn the language to understand the lyrics. The Brazilians say: "I always liked foreign songs"; "The music was my motivation to study English"; "I was a big fan of a rock 'n' roll band called Guns 'n' Roses (certainly you know about them) and I really wanted to understand what those guys were saying in their songs"; "I've started to study English by myself, when I was about 15, because of Michael Jackson. He's been my idol since 1991, and I really wanted to understand him and his music since I was a child". The Japanese also talk about their affiliation to Western culture: "I love Western music"; "I was a lover of English poetry, especially Shakespeare, Wordsworth, Milton and so on".

Motivation is also a changing phenomenon, it can grow or decrease and it can differ depending on the school or social experiences. One Brazilian girl mentioned she hated repeating dialogues, but loved listening to music. Several narrators confessed their fear of speaking in public, but said they wanted to interact with foreigners. A Japanese learner claimed she was always willing to participate in class, but others did not feel motivated in high school. A Japanese narrator confessed that, when she was in high school, she was shy and did not want to learn more than she already knew, but that changed and her fear of speaking disappeared during a two-month home stay in the USA. It is interesting to see that motivation varies from student to student and so does the degree of motivation in similar situations.

Autonomy

Identity, motivation and autonomy are interconnected elements in an SLA complex system as we can see if we go back to the Brazilian girl who was a fan of Michael Jackson. Her fan identity motivated her to learn English in order to understand her idol's discourse and she demonstrates she was a very autonomous learner in order to achieve her goals. Let us listen to her:

I used to use a Dictionary in order to find the meaning of each word in songs or in texts written by him. (. . .) One thing that I can say is that I started learning English through comparing patterns and observing the language structure, comparing it to Portuguese and trying to memorize rules, and I used to make lists of words in order to memorize them and their meanings. Another thing that helped me a lot was the fact that I would spend hours studying and memorizing every rule I could notice, the uses, tenses, etc. of the words. After having a good vocabulary, I started working on pronunciation, which was the hardest part of the process for me, because the only source I had was music, although I used a Pronunciation Dictionary, too.

This student is the only one who talks about comparing structures and using a dictionary and translating. The other students in the Brazilian group mentioned practicing the language alone and monitoring pronunciation; listening to music and radio; repeating song lines; reading books; watching TV; looking for opportunities to communicate; and volunteering in a school. The Japanese learners also talked about similar strategies, which prove that learners autonomously create opportunities to use the language.

Exercises

I. Reading Comprehension:

There are four suggested answers marked A, B, C and D. Choose the best answer for each question.

1. Which one of the following cases does NOT have the extrinsic orientation?
   A. A student is motivated to study English as he's fascinated by English culture, especially music and literature.
   B. A student works hard and he says he really enjoys others' admirations.
   C. A student does his work just to avoid parental sanctions.
   D. A student studies because she believes it is important for her future career.

2. Which identity could appear during SLA process?
   A. Learner identity.   B. Gender identity.
   C. Social class identity.   D. All of the above.

3. What is the correct understanding of this sentence "That choice worked as a butterfly effect"?
   A. The flapping of a butterfly's wing in Brazil can cause a tornado in Japan.
   B. Her husband's promise to take her to Hawaii serves as a direct trigger to make her restart learning English.
   C. Her husband's promise to take her to Hawaii really makes her feel worried about the future trip because of her poor English.
   D. She had long being waiting for this Hawaii trip.

II. Judgments and Implications:

Do the following statements agree with the information given in the passage?
True   if the statement is true according to the passage

False   if the statement contradicts the passage
1. According to Gardner and Lambert, motivation has either integrative or instrumental orientation, or either the intrinsic orientation or the extrinsic orientation.
2. Learning a language is also a process of identity construction which undergoes periods of instability, variability and adaptability.
3. SLA is an orderly world of acquisition and autonomous learner reflect about their learning and use effective learning strategies.
4. Autonomy is a movement system which never reaches equilibrium and never undergoes stability.
5. Identity, motivation and autonomy are interconnected elements in an SLA complex system.

III. Chart Filling:

Reflect on your own SLA experiences and list the intrinsic motivations and extrinsic motivations.

	SLA Experiences	Intrinsic Orientations	Extrinsic Orientations
1.			
2.			
3.			

IV. Critical Questions:

As autonomous learning is proved to be an effective way in language learning, how can you apply it in the Chinese classroom?

Text C

Brainstorming

The critical period hypothesis is the subject of a long-standing debate in linguistics and language acquisition over the extent to which the ability to acquire language is biologically linked to age. The hypothesis claims that there is an ideal time window to acquire language in a linguistically rich environment, after which further language acquisition becomes much more difficult and effortful.

The critical period hypothesis states that the first few years of life is the crucial time in which an individual can acquire a first language if presented with adequate stimuli. If language input doesn't occur until after this time, the individual will never achieve a full command of language—especially grammatical systems.

Questions before reading:

How would you define a child's development? Which aspects would you emphasize and why?

Development: Some General Principles[1]
Anita E Woolfolk-Hoy

The term **development** in its most general psychological sense refers to certain changes that occur in human beings (or animals) between conception and death. The term is not applied to all changes, but rather to those that appear in orderly ways and remain for a reasonably long period of time. A temporary change caused by a brief illness, for example, is not considered a part of development. Psychologists also make a value judgment in determining which changes qualify as development. The changes—at least those that occur early in life—are generally assumed to be for the better and to result in behavior that is more adaptive, more organized, more effective, and more complex. Human development can be divided into a number of different aspects. **Physical development**, as you might guess, deals with changes in the body. **Personal development** is the term generally used for changes in an individual's personality. **Social development** refers to changes in the way an individual relates to others. And **cognitive development** refers to changes in thinking. Many changes during development are simply matters of growth and maturation. **Maturation** refers to changes that occur naturally and spontaneously and that are, to a large extent, genetically programmed. Such changes emerge over time and are relatively unaffected by environment, except in cases of malnutrition or severe illness. Much of a person's physical development falls into this category. Other changes are brought about through learning, as individuals interact with their environment. Such changes make up a large part of a person's social development. But what about the development of thinking and personality? Most psychologists agree that in these areas, both maturation and interaction with the environment (or nature and nurture, as they are sometimes called) are important, but they disagree about the amount of emphasis to place on each. Although there is disagreement about both what is involved in development and the way it takes place, there are a few general principles almost all theorists would support.

1. *People develop at different rates.* In your own classroom, you will have a whole range of examples of different developmental rates. Some students will be larger, better coordinated, or more mature in their thinking and social relationships. Others will be much slower to mature in these areas. Except in rare cases of very rapid or very slow development, such differences are normal and should be expected in any large group of students.

---

[1] Excerpt from *Educatinal Psychology*, 9/e, ACTIVE LEARNING EDITION. Longman, 2005.

2. *Development is relatively orderly.* People develop abilities in a logical order. In infancy, they sit before they walk, babble before they talk, and see the world through their own eyes before they can begin to imagine how others see it. In school, they will master addition before algebra, Bambi before Shakespeare, and so on. Theorists may disagree on exactly what comes before what, but they all seem to find a relatively logical progression.

3. *Development takes place gradually.* Very rarely do changes appear overnight. A student who cannot manipulate a pencil or answer a hypothetical question may well develop this ability, but the change is likely to take time.

The Development of Language

All children in every culture master the complicated system of their native language, unless severe deprivation or physical problems interfere. This knowledge is remarkable.

At the least, sounds, meanings, words and sequences of words, volume, voice tone, inflection, and turn-taking rules must all be coordinated before a child can communicate effectively in conversations.

It is likely that many factors—biological and experiential—play a role in language development. We saw earlier that culture plays a major role by determining what language tools are necessary in the life of the people. The important point is that children develop language as they develop other cognitive abilities by actively trying to make sense of what they hear and by looking for patterns and making up rules to put together the jigsaw puzzle of language. In this process, humans may have built in biases, rules, and constraints about language that restrict the number of possibilities considered. For example, young children seem to have a constraint specifying that a new label refers to a whole object, not just a part. Another built-in bias leads children to assume that the label refers to a class of similar objects. So the child learning about the rabbit is equipped naturally to assume that rabbit refers to the whole animal (not just its ears) and that other similar-looking animals are also rabbits. Reward and correction play a role in helping children learn correct language use, but the child's thinking in putting together the parts of this complicated system is very important.

Language Development in the School Years

By about age 5 or 6, most children have mastered the basics of their native language. What remains for the school-age child to accomplish?

Pronunciation. The majority of 1st graders have mastered most of the sounds of their native language, but a few may remain unconquered. The *j, v, th,* and *zh* sounds are the last to develop. About 10% of 8-year-olds still have some trouble with *s, z, v*.

Syntax. Children master the basics of word order, or syntax, in their native language early. But the more complicated forms, such as the passive voice ("The car was hit by the truck"), take longer to master. By early elementary school, many children can understand the meaning of passive sentences, yet they do not use such constructions in their normal conversations. Other accomplishments during elementary school include first understanding and then using complex grammatical structures such as extra clauses, qualifiers, and conjunctions.

Vocabulary and Meaning. The average 6-year-old has a vocabulary of 8,000 to 14,000 words, growing to about 40,000 by age 11. In fact, some researchers estimate that students in the early grades learn up to 20 words a day. School-age children enjoy language games and jokes that play on words. In the early elementary years, some children may have trouble with abstract words such as justice or economy. They also may not understand the subjunctive case ("If I were a butterfly...") because they lack the cognitive ability to reason about things that are not true ("But you aren't a butterfly..."). They may take statements literally and thus misunderstand sarcasm or metaphor. Fairy tales are understood concretely simply as stories instead of as moral lessons, for example. Many children are in their preadolescent years before they are able to distinguish being kidded from being taunted or before they know that a sarcastic remark is not meant to be taken literally.

Pragmatics. Pragmatics involves the appropriate use of language to communicate. For instance, children must learn the rules of turn-taking in conversation. Young children may appear to take turns in conversations, but if you listen in, you realize that they are not exchanging information, only talk time. In later elementary school, children's conversations start to sound like conversations. Contributions are usually on the same topic. Also, by middle childhood, students understand that an observation can be a command, as in "I see too many children at the pencil sharpener." By adolescence, individuals are very adept at varying their language style to fit the situation. So they can talk to their peers in slang that makes little sense to adults, but marks the adolescent as a member of the group. Yet these same students can speak politely to adults (especially when making requests) and write persuasively about a topic in history.

Metalinguistic Awareness. Around the age of 5, students begin to develop metalinguistic awareness. This means their understanding about language and how it works becomes explicit. They have knowledge about language itself. They are ready to study and extend the rules that have been implicit—understood but not consciously expressed. This process continues throughout life, as we all become better able to manipulate and comprehend language. One goal of schooling is the development of language and literacy.

Partnerships with Families. Especially in the early years, the students' home experiences are central in the development of language and literacy. In homes that promote literacy, parents and other adults value reading as a source of pleasure, and there are books and other printed materials everywhere. The more proficient speakers are in their first language, the faster they will learn a second language. Parents read to their children, take them to bookstores and libraries, limit the amount of television everyone watches, and encourage literacy-related play such as setting up a pretend school or writing "letters". Of course, not all homes provide this literacy-rich environment, but teachers can help, as you can see in the Family and Community Partnerships Guidelines.

Family and Community Partnerships

Communicate with families about the goals and activities of your program.
Examples:

1. At the beginning of school, send home a description of the goals to be achieved in your class—make sure it is in a clear and readable format.

2. As you start each unit, send home a newsletter describing what students will be studying—give suggestions for home activities that support the learning.

Involve families in decisions about curriculum.
Examples:

1. Have planning workshops at times family members can attend—provide child care for younger siblings, but let children and families work together on projects.

2. Invite parents to come to class to read to students, take dictation of stories, tell stories, record or bind books, and demonstrate skills.

Provide home activities to be shared with family members.
Examples:

1. Encourage family members to work with children to read and follow simple recipes, play language games, keep diaries or journals for the family, and visit the library. Get feedback from families or students about the activities.

2. Give families feedback sheets and ask them to help evaluate the child's school work.

3. Provide lists of good children's literature available locally—work with libraries, clubs, and churches to identify sources.

Exercises

I. Reading Comprehension:

There are four suggested answers marked A, B, C and D. Choose the best answer for each question.

1. Which one of the following statements is Not true?
   A. Some people may develop rapidly while some may develop slowly.
   B. Development is an orderly process which can not be reversed.
   C. Development of human beings is based on a complex collection of system.
   D. Development takes time and can not be achieved overnight.

2. According to the text, which one of the factors below plays a decisive role in language development?
   A. biological, cultural and historical factors
   B. biological, experiential and social factors
   C. cultural, biological and experiential factors
   D. physical, personal and mental factors
3. Around the age of 6 or 7, some children may have trouble understanding abstract words, metaphors, or difficult sentence structures because _____.
   A. They lack the cognitive ability to analyze something nonexistent.
   B. They could not understand the implied meanings.
   C. They take statements literally and misunderstand.
   D. They lack the imagination to build meanings.
4. From around age 5 or 6, it could be inferred that children develop _____ and continues throughout life.
   A. syntax
   B. vocabulary and meaning
   C. C. pragmatics
   D. D. meta-linguistics
5. This article is more possibly to be read from _____
   A. Newspaper report.
   B. Academic journal.
   C. Specialist magazine.
   D. Novel story.

II. Judgments and Implications:

Do the following statements agree with the information given in the passage?
True   if the statement is true according to the passage
False   if the statement contradicts the passage

1. According to the theories of developmental principles, people vary differences in developmental rates and order.
2. It is generally agreed that people have different developmental rates, which indicate such differences of development can be observed in any age groups of human beings.
3. Every child has the ability to master the complicated system of their native language unless being isolated from social interactions or suffered from innate disabilities.
4. The more complicated structure of syntax means the more difficult task for students to acquire.
5. The sentence "I see too many children at the pencil sharpener." shows the good observation of the speaker.

Unit 4 English Language and Learning

III. Matching:

Find the appropriate explanation of the terms in Column A with the explanations in Column B.

Column A

1. Personal development
2. Social development
3. Syntax
4. Pragmatics
5. Metalinguistic awareness

Column B

A. changes over time in the ways we relate to others
B. changes in personality that take place as one grows
C. gradual orderly changes by which mental processes become more complex and sophisticated
D. understanding about one's own use of language
E. rules for when and how to use language to be an effective communicator in a particular context
F. the order of words in phrases or sentences

IV. Critical Questions:

Restate or exemplify two definitions in the text with your own understanding. What teaching implications can you suggest for English teaching?

Learning Skills

Academic Report Skills II

I. Read the following directions and choose an appropriate text:

The chart below shows the number of men and women in further education in Britain in three periods and whether they were studying full-time or part-time. Write a report for a university lecturer describing the information shown below.

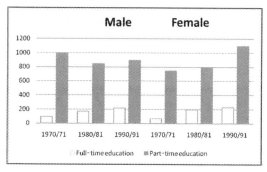

The following two sample texts have been written on the basis of the above graph. Would you read and compare the advantages and disadvantages of two samples?

Sample 1

This is a bar chart of the number of men and women in further education in Britain in three periods. In 1980, most of men were studying part-time. But from 1980, studying full-time was increased and in 1990, it was twice as many students as in 1970. On the other hand, women studying full-time were increased and not only full-time, part-time also were increased. In 1990, studying full-time was three times as many students as in 1970. If compare, men and women, as you see, in 1970, men were studying more than women in both full-time and part-time study, but it changed from 1980 and later in 1990. Women were studying part-time more than men and studying full-time was the same number. It shows you women have a high education now.

Sample 2

According to the graph, the number of men and women in further education in Britain shows the following pattern.

In the case of male, the number of male has declined slightly from about 1000 thousands in 1970 to about 850 in 1990. However, the figure rose back to about 850 in 1990 from about 830 in 1980. The proportion of full-time education has declined during period. However, the proportion of part-time education has increased dramatically.

On the other hand, in the case of female, the number of total full-time and part-time education has increased during the period. From about 700 thousands in 1970, these figures rose to about 820 thousands in 1980, to about 1100 in 1990.

In terms of full-time education, figure rose by about 260 to about 900 in 1990. On the other hand, with respect to part-time education, this figure rose dramatically between 1980 and 1970, but it rose slightly between 1980 and 1990.

Work in groups to discuss the strengths and weaknesses of each text above.

II. Useful language in writing academic report:

Introducing the topic
- The graph shows... /The table reveals...
- The chart displays... /The diagram illustrates...
- Some interesting facts concerning... are revealed in the diagram.
- Several key trends are revealed by the graph showing...

Introducing the first set of data
- Beginning with the...
- To begin with the...

Introducing the second set of data
- Meanwhile, the... shows that...
- As for the..., it shows that...
- Turning to the..., it can be seen that...

Introducing the first major trend
- First of all, it is clear that...
- Most noticeably of all, it can be seen that...
- The first result worth pointing out is that...

Introducing lesser trends
- Another trend that can be observed is that...
- It is also worth pointing out that...
- Also worth noting is that...

Exceptions to the main trend
- However, this was not always the case.
- However, it should be pointed out that...
- There was one noticeable exception, however.

Comparing and contrasting
- Similarly, ... / By contrast, ...
- A similar trend can be observed in...
- The results for... , however, reveal a markedly different trend.

Adding figures
- The figures were X and Y respectively.
- ..., at X. / ..., with Y. (Usage note: use "at" when you mean "the figure was"; use "with" when you mean "something had")
- ..., at/with X and Y respectively.

Concluding and summarizing
- To sum up, ... / In summary, ... / In short, ...
- Overall, ... / On the whole, ...
- The main thing that can be observed here is that...

While writing academic report, the introduction paragraph always needs to be paraphrased, and you might use the following structures to paraphrase sentences.

| how many...   what proportions of...   how...changed...   the process of... |

1. The diagrams show the life cycle of the silk worm and the stages in the production of silk. (how the silk worm changed...)
2. The charts show the proportions of the world's oil resources held in different areas, together with the proportions consumed annually in the same areas.
3. The graph below shows the number of complaints made about noise to Environmental Health authorities in the city of Newtown between 1980 and 1996.
4. The three pie charts show the changes in annual spending by a particular UK school in 1981, 1991 and 2001.
5. The graph shows the quantities of goods transported in the UK between 1974 and 2002 by four different modes of transport.
6. The table gives information about changes in modes of travel in England between 1985 and 2000.

III. The chart below shows the number of girls per 100 boys enrolled in different levels of school education.

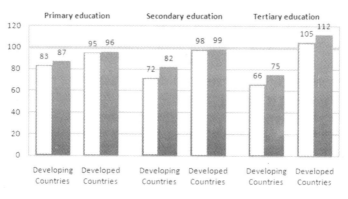

Use the following words to complete the report.

| on average | shows | moreover | regarding tertiary education |
| however | balance | discrepancy | even |

The chart _____ the number of female students per 100 male students in primary, secondary and tertiary education between developing and developed nations.

_____, more boys than girls were enrolled in school both in 1990 and 1998 in all the countries, except in tertiary education in developed countries. The number of girls per 100 boys was bigger in 1998 than in 1990 in the two country groups and in all the educational stages.

_____, there were more boys than girls in primary and secondary education. As can be seen, developing countries saw a bigger _____ between the numbers of male and female students than developed countries, with the number of girls per 100 boys at 83 in 1990 and 87 in 1998 in primary education.

_____, in developed countries, the _____ of the two was much closer to the ideal, particularly in secondary education, with 98 girls per 100 boys in 1990 and 99 in 1998.

_____, the balance was _____ worse than in any other levels of education in developing countries with 66 girls enrolled for every 100 boys in 1990 and 75 in 1998. On the other hand, in developing countries, the number of girls overtook that of boys at 105 per 100 boys in 1990 and 112 in 1998.

Unit 4　English Language and Learning

Group Work Activities

Work in groups to complete the following two tasks:
Task 1: Exercises
　　A. Read the two conclusions below and decide which one is better? Why?
Sample 1:
　　To sum up, the data clearly indicates that economies of Japan and Australia have a dissimilar distribution of workforce compared to that of India, which has a higher proportion employed in the agricultural sector.
Sample 2:
　　Overall, it is clear that Japan and Australia have a more advanced workforce as a high proportion of workers are employed in the service and industrial sector. However, the workforce in India has much less income to spend as a consequence the service sector is less than that of both Japan and Australia.

　　B. Questions to be discussed.
　　What makes a good academic report?
　　While discussing the question, can you complete the following table?

Content	Coherence & cohesion	Lexical resource	Grammatical range & accuracy
presents a clear overview of main trends, differences or stages			
	uses a range of cohesive devices appropriately	uses less common lexical items with some awareness of style and collocation	rare minor errors occur only as "slips"

Task 2: Writing
　　You should spend about 20 minutes on this task.
　　The bar chart below gives information about the number of students studying Computer Science at a UK university between 2010 and 2012.
　　Summarize the information by selecting and reporting the main features, and make comparisons where relevant. Write at least 150 words.

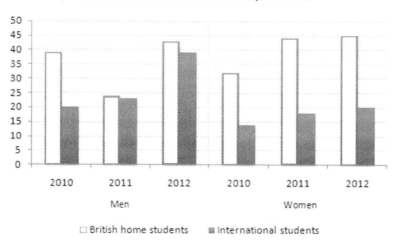

Self-evaluation Form

What are the main objectives in this unit?
_____
_____
_____

What useful vocabularies and expressions have you learned from this unit?
_____
_____
_____

What key terms and educational knowledge have you learned?
_____
_____
_____

Unit 4 English Language and Learning

Have you used the learning skills before? Why do you think they are useful or not useful?
_____
_____
_____
_____

If possible, what would you like to add to make learning more interesting and relevant?
_____
_____
_____
_____

Unit 5

Learning Model-cooperative Learning

Introduction

What Is Happening to Cooperative Learning?[1]

Any former student who was ever assigned a group project knows the difficulty in group work: more often than not, the bulk of the responsibilities falls on one or two students while the others quietly tag along. Cooperative learning is a highly structured educational model where each member is not only responsible for learning an individual concept, but also for educating other group members about it. While the theory has really gained traction in recent years, cooperative learning was first developed in the early 90s—it began as an approach intended to be equally applicable in traditional classrooms and in business settings.

It's based on the premise that all group members succeed or fail together. A commonly used iteration of this model is called a jigsaw activity. Each member is required to take ownership of an idea, or puzzle piece, and gain an understanding of it. Then all other group members share their knowledge of other puzzle pieces to fellow group members. When each puzzle piece is understood and assembled, the group successfully grasps a new concept.

There are three styles of cooperative learning groups: formal, informal, and cooperative. Formal groups are very common in classrooms today; educators structure out a particular study method and then designate a strict list of activities, built around a clearly defined subject, all of which is finished over a short period of time. Informal learning is somewhat off-the-cuff and is often used to break up lectures with group exercises. Cooperative-based groups are designed to exist over a longer period of time; group members support each other by meeting regularly and holding each other accountable for their contributions.

The Five Fundamental Concepts of Cooperative Learning

All cooperative learning is distinguished by the presence of five key elements:

---

[1] From *Education News*, Wednesday, April 3rd, 2013.

positive interdependence, face-to-face interaction, accountability, interpersonal skills and group processing. True cooperative learning study design incorporates all five of these concepts for each member to successfully learn. Student motivation is crucial to the entire process; as group members move through an assignment, momentum should be generated by each member's desire to share information so that the entire group succeeds.

Positive Interdependence: Students must understand that they essentially sink or swim together. Each member of the group must participate fully, or the entire group will fail. Each participant is assigned a distinct role without which other group members will not complete the assignment. Groups may be assigned to develop a solid understanding of a complex idea, to develop a product that has multiple interdependent components or perform peer review of scholarly literature to reach a consensual opinion. The idea here is to use the division of labor to accomplish a mutual goal. Carefully structured design creates an atmosphere that is far superior to seating several students in a group and simply instructing them to discuss an idea. The project outcome, whether it be a grade, a paper or a product, is judged equally among all participants, so all group members have a stake in the success of the project. Educators can create this interdependence in a variety of ways. The group may have a common goal or incentive; the group's progress may be dependent on each participant's contribution; groups might compete against other groups; or group work can be bound to a designated physical space. Written lab work, research projects, case study review and interactive role play can all serve to foster this interdependence.

Face-to-Face Interaction: Sometimes referred to as promotive interaction, this element of cooperative learning relies on group dynamics to exchange ideas and collaborate effectively. Instructors strive to create as much oral discussion as possible; this is accomplished via classroom message boards like Blackboard or pre-scheduled online chats. These interactions underscore the idea that participants are dependent on one another for success, which ultimately ends up building up the group's trust. Cognitive learning is reinforced when students share data and resources, problem-solve, and support one another's group roles. Educators should consider this an opportunity to challenge traditional societal roles; group facilitators can also use these interactions to observe individual skills or competencies in group members and ensure that each member's talents are put to the best use. Incorporating spontaneous face-to-face encounters often help group members get to know one another in a non-threatening environment, which can strengthen a group's personal commitment to success.

Accountability: Individual and group accountability is really what makes cooperative learning different from the days when lazy participants could get away with little to no contributions. Educators design projects so that accountability is built into the process at both expected and random times. Formative assessment occurs while the project is ongoing and serves to provide feedback to group facilitators and students.

Summative assessment takes place at the completion of the activity, and evaluates individual participation instead of evaluating the whole group. Educators, members of a particular group and the other participating groups can all provide accountability feedback. Teachers may assign roles like secretary or recorder; these individuals must be able to give a current report on the group status at all times, thus requiring good communication among participants. Teachers may also request unscheduled oral reports or administer pop quizzes to test the group's participation; group participants also benefit from this as it's a chance for them to refine their extemporaneous speaking and writing skills. Students may assess one another's participation during and after the project is completed. Anonymous ratings sheets can be used for this purpose. Other groups may assess the group's accountability by evaluating the finished product or quizzing various group members during project presentations. Students may be required to teach other students or groups what was produced or learned during a project.

Interpersonal and Small Group Skills: The social skills that are required for effective group collaboration are learned skills that students often need to be taught. As group participants learn to function as part of a team while they accomplished a defined task, this cooperative learning increases cognitive development. Social nuances such as leadership, trust, confidence, good communication and conflict management skills are all required to function in a group; educators anticipate this in project design and focus on this aspect of learning just as much as the task at hand. Over time, students should be able to appreciate other group member's strengths and weaknesses, and then learn to articulate questions and answers about projects.

Group Processing: This fifth component of cooperative learning is absolutely essential, though it is the step most likely to be rushed at the end of a project or class. During group processing, participants reflect individually and collectively on what worked and what didn't. Helpful and unhelpful behaviors are identified; ideally, decisions are made about the next time the group works together. This important phase adds much to students' comprehension of the material. In a best case scenario, all students give and receive positive feedback on individual contributions; this positivity will drive momentum in future group work. Students reflect on that feedback and then set goals for improvement. For example, a participant may choose a social skill that he or she would like to improve, or a group can decide to ask more questions of one another in the future. Finally, participants should have a celebration of some sort that marks the end of the project; this will also motivate positive cooperative learning experiences in the future.

Advantages to Cooperative Learning Models

Cooperative learning is of enormous benefit to schoolchildren. Academically, group participants gain a better comprehension of the course material when all five elements of cooperative learning are instituted. Students work with participants who have different learning styles; teaching a peer not only reinforces cognitive comprehension, but is likely to be better understood by the other student. When working in groups, lower-performing students will work harder to keep up with high-performing peers. Since group grading provides more students with an opportunity to "win" in the somewhat competitive school atmosphere, there is additional incentive to achieve. Socially, learning in a group model exposes children to different learning styles, cultural or ethnic backgrounds and varying levels of enthusiasm. Cooperative learning allows educators to reinforce concepts of equality in the classroom, using a group environment to discount stereotypes. Sharing is implicit in this teaching model, enforcing the idea that knowledge is for everyone. Children who receive recognition for taking risks become more comfortable in doing so. Students also enjoy classes that require participation more than a traditional lecture class; in fact, they are more likely to attend and complete these courses. Perhaps most importantly, cooperative learning teaches necessary life skills. Working as a group to reach a common goal demonstrates the value of teamwork, for example. Some group participants will emerge as natural leaders, allowing them an early opportunity to develop effective leadership habits. The ability to communicate ideas well, obviously a cornerstone life skill, is necessary for successful cooperative learning. Conflict can unfortunately be part of any collaboration effort, and conflict management skills cannot be taught too early. Learning to make decisions within a group also prepares students for a productive career.

What Is in Store for Cooperative Learning?

This learning model also has economic ramifications. Because participants work in groups and share materials, fewer supplies must be purchased. This is good news for budget-strapped school systems in the U.S. As the planet's conventional resources are depleted, less consumption means less waste and less damage to the planet. The societal shift to digital resources meshes well with cooperative learning styles. On a larger scale, cooperative learning techniques—like conflict resolution and effective communication—better prepare participants for a global society. Corporations today, ever more global in scope, are leaning on interdisciplinary teams that consist of different cultural influences and specialized skill sets. The original cooperative learning model, which looked much like informal study groups in a dorm lounge, will become a more structured part of classroom curricula. Continued advances in technology will only augment this learning model, since learning blended with technology is already a large part of many schools' curricula. Cooperative learning models have been proven to enforce cognitive learning better than class lectures; it is reasonable to expect that advances in technology will continue to drive a more collaborative classroom that shares knowledge across a broader scope.

Questions after reading:

What are the main advantages of cooperative learning? Which element would you stress in cooperative learning?

Group work:

Topic: Before we further study cooperative learning, it is helpful to learn its history, rationale or development in all round ways. As a group, search for articles, books or online resources to enrich your understanding of cooperative learning and share your ideas with other members in the group.

Directions: Work as a group and share your ideas with others.

Text A

Brainstorming

Social Interdependence Theory: Social interdependence exists when the outcomes of individuals are affected by their own and others' actions. There are two types of social interdependence: positive (when the actions of individuals promote the achievement of joint goals) and negative (when the actions of individuals obstruct the achievement of each other's goals.) Social interdependence may be differentiated from social dependence, independence, and helplessness.

Formal cooperative learning: it is structured, facilitated, and monitored by the educator over time and is used to achieve group goals in task work (e.g. completing a unit). Any course material or assignment can be adapted to this type of learning, and groups can vary from 2-6 people with discussions lasting from a few minutes up to an entire period. Types of formal cooperative learning strategies include:

1. The jigsaw technique
2. Assignments that involve group problem solving and decision making
3. Laboratory or experiment assignments
4. Peer review work (e.g. editing writing assignments)

Questions before reading:

Do you know what is cooperative learning and how does it contribute to learning?

Have you had any experience of team work? Can you describe the procedure? Is that efficient, why or why not?

Unit 5 Learning Model-cooperative Learning

Cooperative Learning: What Makes Groupwork Work?[1]

Robert E. Slavin

Robert Slavin reviews the substantial body of studies of cooperative learning in schools, in particular those using control groups being taught with more traditional methods. There are two main categories—"Structured Team Learning" and "Informal Group Learning Methods"—each reviewed and illustrated. As regards affective outcomes, cooperative learning overwhelmingly shows beneficial results. For achievement outcomes, positive results depend heavily on two key factors. One is the presence of group goals (the learner groups are working towards a goal or to gain reward or recognition), the other is individual accountability (the success of the group depends on the individual learning of every member). The chapter presents alternative perspectives to explain the benefits of cooperative learning—whether it acts via motivations, social cohesion, cognitive development, or cognitive elaboration. Despite the very robust evidence base of positive outcomes, cooperative learning "remains at the edge of school policy" and is often poorly implemented.

There was once a time when it was taken for granted that a quiet class was a learning class, when principals walked down the hall expecting to be able to hear a pin drop. In more recent times, however, teachers are more likely to encourage students to interact with each other in co-operative learning groups. Yet having students work in groups can be enormously beneficial or it can be of little value. How can teachers make best use of this powerful tool?

Cooperative learning has been suggested as the solution for wide array of educational problems. It is often cited as a means of emphasising thinking skills and increasing higher-order learning; as an alternative to ability grouping, remediation, or special education; as a means of improving race relations; and as a way to prepare students for an increasingly collaborative work force. How many of these claims are justified? What effects do the various collaborative learning methods have on student achievement and other outcomes? Which forms of cooperative learning are most effective, and what components must be in place for cooperative learning to work? To answer these questions, this chapter reviews the findings of studies of cooperative learning in elementary and secondary schools that have compared cooperative learning with control groups studying the same objectives but taught using traditional methods.

Cooperative Learning Methods

There are many quite different forms of co-operative learning, but all of them

---

[1] Excerpt from "Cooperative Learning: What Makes Groupwork Work?" *The Nature of Learning Using Research to Inspire Practice*, OECD Publications, 2010.

involve having students work in small groups or teams to help one another learn academic material. Cooperative learning usually supplements the teacher's instruction by giving students an opportunity to discuss information or practise skills originally presented by the teacher. Sometimes cooperative methods require students to find or discover information on their own. Cooperative learning has been used and investigated in every subject at all grade levels.

What Makes Cooperative Learning Work?

Cooperative learning methods are among the most extensively evaluated alternatives to traditional instruction in use today. Use of cooperative learning almost always improves affective outcomes. Students love to work in groups and they feel more successful and like subjects taught cooperatively. They have more friends of different ethnic groups and are more accepting of others different from themselves. Regarding achievement, however, outcomes depend a great deal on how cooperative learning is used. In general, two elements must be present if cooperative learning is to be effective: **group goals** and **individual accountability**. That is, groups must be working to achieve some goal or to earn rewards or recognition, and the success of the group must depend on the individual learning of every group member.

Why are group goals and individual accountability so important? To understand this, consider the alternatives. In some forms of cooperative learning, students work together to complete a single worksheet or to solve a problem together. In such methods, there is little reason for more able students to take time to explain what is going on to their less able group-mates or to ask their opinions. When the group task is to do something, rather than to learn something, the participation of less able students may be seen as interference rather than help. It may be easier in this circumstance for students to give each other answers than to explain concepts or skills to one another. In contrast, when the group's task is to ensure that every group member learns something, it is in the interests of every group member to spend time explaining concepts to his or her group-mates. Studies of student behavior within cooperative groups have consistently found that the students who gain most from cooperative work are those who give and receive elaborated explanations; in fact, giving and receiving answers without explanations were negatively related to achievement gain in these studies. Group goals and individual accountability motivate students to give explanations and to take one another's learning seriously, instead of simply giving answers.

Theoretical Perspectives on Cooperative Learning

While there is a general consensus among researchers about the positive effects of co-operative learning on student achievement, there remains a controversy about why and how they affect achievement and, most importantly, under what conditions they have these effects. Different groups of researchers investigating cooperative learning effects on achievement begin with different assumptions and conclude by explaining the effects in terms that are substantially unrelated or conflicting. In earlier work, Slavin identified *motivationalist, social cohesion, cognitive-developmental* and *cognitive-elaboration* as the four major theoretical perspectives held by different researchers on the achievement effects of co-operative learning.

The motivationalist perspective presumes that task motivation has the greatest impact on the learning process, and that the other processes (such as planning and helping) are driven by individuals' motivated self interest. Motivationalist scholars focus especially on the reward or goal structure under which students operate. By contrast, the social cohesion perspective (also called "social interdependence theory") suggests that the effects of cooperative learning are largely dependent on the cohesiveness of the group. In this perspective, students help each other to learn because they care about the group and its members and come to derive the benefits of self-identity from group membership.

The two cognitive perspectives focus on the interactions among groups of students, holding that these interactions themselves lead to better learning and thus better achievement. The cognitive developmentalists attribute these effects to processes outlined by scholars such as Piaget and Vygotsky. The cognitive elaboration perspective instead asserts that learners must engage in some manner of cognitive restructuring (elaboration) of new materials in order to learn them; cooperative learning is seen to facilitate that process.

Slavin *et al.* have proposed a theoretical model intended to acknowledge the contributions of each of the major theoretical perspectives and the likely role that each plays in cooperative learning processes. They explore conditions under which each may operate, and suggest research and development needed to advance cooperative learning scholarship so that educational practice may truly benefit the lessons of thirty years of research.

The different perspectives on cooperative learning may be seen as complementary, not as exclusive alternatives. For example, motivational theorists would not argue that the cognitive theories are unnecessary but instead assert that motivation drives cognitive process, which in turn produces learning. They would argue that it is unlikely that over the long haul students would engage in the kind of elaborated explanations found by Webb to be essential to profiting from cooperative activity, without a goal structure designed to enhance motivation. Similarly, social cohesion theorists might identify the utility of extrinsic incentives to lie in their contribution to group cohesiveness, caring and pro-social norms among group members, which in turn affects cognitive processes. A model of how cooperative learning might improve learning, adapted from Slavin, is shown in Figure below, depicting the main components of group learning interaction and representing the functional relationships among the different theoretical approaches.

Figure Different factors that influence the effectiveness of co-operative learning

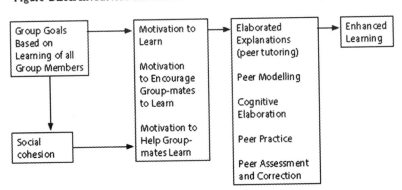

This diagram of the interdependent relationships among the components begins with a focus on group goals or incentives based on the individual learning of all group members. It assumes that motivation to learn and to encourage and help others to do so activates co-operative behaviours that will result in learning. This includes both task motivation and motivation to interact in the group. In this model, motivation to succeed leads directly to learning, and it also drives the behaviour and attitudes that foster group cohesion, which in turn facilitates the types of group interactions—peer modelling, equilibration and cognitive elaboration—that yield enhanced learning and academic achievement.

Cooperative Learning in Learning Environment for the 21st Century

Learning environment for the 21st century must be ones in which students are actively engaged with learning tasks and with each other. Today, teachers are in competition with television, computer games, and all sorts of engaging technology, and the expectation that children will learn passively is becoming increasingly unrealistic. Cooperative learning offers a proven, practical means of creating exciting social and engaging classroom environments to help students to master traditional skills and knowledge as well as develop the creative and interactive skills needed in today's economy and society. Cooperative learning itself is being reshaped for the 21st century, particularly in partnership with developments in technology.

Cooperative learning has established itself as a practical alternative to traditional teaching, and has proven its effectiveness in hundreds of studies throughout the world. Surveys find that a substantial proportion of teachers claim to use it regularly. Yet observational studies find that most use of cooperative learning is informal, and does not incorporate the group goals and individual accountability that research has identified to be essential. Clearly, cooperative learning can be a powerful strategy for increasing students' achievement, but fulfilling this potential depends on the provision of professional development for teachers that is focused on the approaches most likely to make a difference.

Training in effective forms of co-operative learning is readily available, such as from the *Success for All Foundation* in the United States and the United Kingdom (*www.successforall.org*), as well as the US-based *Peer-Assisted Learning Strategies (www.peerassistedlearningstrategies.net)* and *Kagan Publishing and Professional Development (www.kaganonline.com)*.Training should include not only workshops, but also follow-up into teachers' classes by knowledgeable coaches, who can give feedback, do demonstrations and provide support.

In comparison with schooling practices that are often supported by governments—such as tutoring, technology use and school restructuring—cooperative learning is relatively inexpensive and easily adopted. Yet, thirty years after much of the foundational research was completed, it remains at the edge of school policy. This does not have to remain the case: as governments come to support the larger concept of evidence-based reform, the strong evidence base for cooperative learning may lead to a greater focus on this set of approaches at the core of instructional practice. In the learning environment of the 21st century, cooperative learning should play a central role.

Exercises

I. Brainstorming a project:
Complete the chart below to make sure the procedures.

A. Search for information from library books, journals and online resources.
B. Identify main information of research question by doing intensive and extensive reading.
C. Improve the project by raising critical questions in terms of both content and format.
D. Generalize the key point and sequence answers logically.
E. Organize group work, discussion and research activities.
F. Demonstrate the group work by designing a good quality speech.

II. Refining a question:

The following research questions are all under the topic of Lincoln's personality. Can you read them carefully to find any inappropriateness?

Why are these following questions inappropriate?

1. What are the impacts of his personality to the civil war?
   Answers:
   Both impacts and personality are not specific, we have no ideas what characteristic of his personality is going to be discussed or what impacts you are going to focus on, e.g. reunification of USA or economic impacts...

2. Is his personality conducive to the great achievements?
   Answers:
   The question itself is too broad either from the perspective of personality or achievement, besides, the format of the question should be changed in another way so that more ideas can be presented.

3. How did Emancipation Proclamation and Civil War influence his personality?
   Answers:
   If a question contains many objectives, it takes risks of being misled by the question itself. So the best way is to focus on one target in a question.

4. What problems did he confront during the war, and how did he overcome them?
   Answers:
   While the question seems to be quite ambitious, it needs to argue whether it matters the topic "Personality" or not?

Text B

Brainstorming

The American Civil War also known as the War Between the States or simply the Civil War (see naming), was a civil war fought from 1861 to 1865 in the United States after several Southern slave states declared their secession and formed the Confederate States of America (the "Confederacy" or the "South").

The states that remained were known as the "Union" or the "North". The war had its origin in the fractious issue of slavery, especially the extension of slavery into the Western territories. Foreign powers did not intervene. After four years of bloody combat that left over 600,000 soldiers dead and destroyed much of the South's infrastructure, the Confederacy collapsed, slavery was abolished, and the difficult reconstruction process of restoring national unity and guaranteeing rights to the freed slaves began.

Questions before reading:

Do you know anything about Abraham Lincoln? Under what circumstances was he first elected as president of the United States?

Have you ever read Abraham Lincoln's first inaugural address? In what ways are you encouraged by his speech?

"The Union Is Unbroken" March 4, 1861①

Louise Chipley Slavicek

MONDAY, MARCH 4, 1861, began gray and chilly but by noon, when Abraham Lincoln, dressed in a black suit, black boots, and fashionable black stovepipe hat, emerged from Willard's Hotel in Washington, D.C., and stepped into the carriage that would bear him to his inauguration, the sun shone brightly. As the open carriage lurched over cobblestoned Pennsylvania Avenue toward Capitol Hill, almost anywhere the president-elect looked he would have seen armed soldiers. Double files of infantry, guns at the ready, marched close behind and on either side of the carriage, and cavalry with drawn swords patrolled every intersection. If Lincoln had happened to glance upward, he would have observed sharpshooters crouching on the rooftops of the buildings lining the parade route. When the presidential carriage finally reached the Capitol, Lincoln could not have helped but notice the two batteries of

On Inauguration Day, March 4, 1861, crowds assemble beneath the U.S. Capitol, whose old wooden dome was in the process of being replaced by a new cast-iron one. Lincoln, viewing the construction project as a "sign we intend the Union to go on", insisted that the work on the dome continue during the war.

---

① Excerpt from Chapter 1 in *Abraham Lincoln*, Chelsea House Publishers, 2004.

artillery stationed on a nearby hill.

Never in the history of the United States had there been such an inauguration day: The measures taken by army General in Chief Winfield Scott to protect Abraham Lincoln were truly extraordinary. But then, these were extraordinary times. Fearing that the election of a Northerner committed to halting the spread of slavery into the territories signaled the beginning of the end for slavery everywhere in the nation, seven Southern slave states had seceded (withdrawn) from the Union since Lincoln's victory at the polls in November, and seven others appeared poised to follow suit. In Montgomery, Alabama, just two weeks before Lincoln's inauguration day, Jefferson Davis of Mississippi had been sworn in as president of the newly created Confederate States of America. As March 4 approached, rumors of Southern assassination plots against the president-elect and even an all-out Southern assault on Washington, D.C., ran rampant in the capital city. Under the circumstances, General Scott was not about to take any chances.

In keeping with Scott's orders, at the Capitol guards shepherded Lincoln through a covered passageway specially constructed to protect him on his way to the inaugural platform by the building's east portico. Positioning himself behind a small table at the front of the platform, Lincoln placed a pair of steel-rimmed eyeglasses on his nose, took the manuscript of his inaugural address from his coat pocket, and carefully unrolled it. The huge crowd jamming the plaza below listened attentively as Lincoln began to read in a firm voice that "rang out over the acres of people before him with surprising distinctness," according to one eyewitness.

Despite recent events in the South, "the Union is unbroken," Lincoln declared, for according to the Constitution, the "Union of these States is perpetual" (everlasting) and no state had the right to secede from it. To permit states to pull out of the Union at will, he insisted, was "the essence of anarchy".

Although hopeful that "a peaceful solution of the national troubles" was still possible, Lincoln delivered a stern warning to the secessionists: "In *your* hands... is the momentous issue of civil war.... *You* can have no conflict, without being yourselves the aggressors. You have no oath registered in Heaven to destroy the government, while I shall have the most solemn one to 'preserve, protect and defend' it."

"We are not enemies but friends," Lincoln continued, telling his Southern compatriots in closing, "Though passion may have strained, it must not break our bonds of affection." Calling up shared memories of patriotic forefathers and Revolutionary battlefields, Lincoln eloquently appealed to "the better angels of our nature" to bring Northerners and Southerners together, to "swell the chorus of the Union". With that he was finished. Lincoln had made it abundantly clear to his thousands of listeners at the Capitol—and to the millions more who would soon read his address in print—that he intended to be chief executive of the *whole* Union, the South as well as the North. Little could he have imagined on March 4, 1861, the terrible price that he—and the entire nation—would have to pay over the next four years to achieve that goal. Yet throughout the bitter civil war that would consume his entire presidency, Lincoln held firm to what he told the American people on the day he first took the oath of office: The Union was eternal. It was, and must forever remain, "unbroken".

Exercises

I. Sample project:

Read this sample project carefully and try to make your own schedule.

1. Begin with a topic and a question
   a) A thesis is a question about the topic you have chosen.
      Example Topic:
      Lincoln Assassination
      Questions:
      How was the assassination planned?
      What was John Wilkes Booth's state of mind on the fateful night?
      Why did John Wilkes Booth assassinate Lincoln?
   b) Think about the size of your project.
      Short project: a more specific question is needed in order to answer the question in a shortened amount of space.
      Longer project: a more general question may be asked since you will have more space in which to answer the question.

2. Research on a broad scale and then narrow it down
   a) Just as you narrow down to a specific question you want to narrow down your search on the web.
   b) You may want to begin with an online encyclopedia such as:
      Wikipedia
      Encyclopedia.com
      Britannica.com
   c) Once you have acquired a background on your topic you can go to sources that will have more specifics on your topic. This will include secondary sources such as:
      websites specifically addressing your question
      books/E-books
      online journal articles
   d) Look for primary resources. The best way to present new data is going to the original documents from that time period, such as:
      letters
      photos
      newspaper articles
      diaries

oral histories
music
These can all be found on sites such as:
National Archives
Library of Congress

3. Be aware of where you are getting information

You need to make sure that you are gathering information from credible sources. Look on:
University websites
library sites
museum sites
government websites
suggested sites by your teacher or professor
Personal web pages may not have accurate information.

II. Choosing a topic:

Select one theme from the following topics and refine it to a research question.

Causes of the American Civil War
Emancipation
Life at War
Battles
Effects of the War
Important Figures

Text C

Brainstorming

Presidential election of 1860: The United States presidential election of 1860 was the 19th quadrennial presidential election. The election was held on Tuesday, November 6, 1860 and served as the immediate impetus for the outbreak of the American Civil War. The United States had been divided during the 1850s on questions surrounding the expansion of slavery and the rights of slave owners. In 1860, these issues broke the Democratic Party into Northern and Southern factions, and a new Constitutional Union Party appeared. In the face of a divided opposition, the Republican Party, dominant in the North, secured a majority of the electoral votes, putting Abraham Lincoln in the White House with almost no support from the South.

Before Lincoln's inauguration, seven Southern states declared their secession and later formed the Confederacy. Secessionists from four additional Border states joined them when Lincoln's call to restore federal property in the South forced them to take sides, and two states, Kentucky and Missouri, attempted to remain neutral. At the 1864 election, the Union had admitted Kansas, West Virginia, and Nevada as free-soil states, while the Civil War disrupted the entire electoral process in the South, as that no electoral votes were cast by any of the eleven states that had joined the Confederacy.

Questions before reading:

Do you know anything about Emancipation Proclamation? How does it contribute to the development of the U.S.A.?

Under what situations did Abraham Lincoln pass Emancipation Proclamation?

To Save the Union: 1861—1863 Moving Toward Emancipation[1]

Louise Chipley Slavicek

Lincoln had been under pressure to outlaw slavery in the states as well as the territories since the beginning of his presidency. Some of this pressure originated outside the country: All of Europe was appalled by the continuation of slavery in the United States. Lincoln had reason to be particularly concerned about the opinion of England, the chief European power. Antislavery sentiment ran high in England, but because its textile mills used massive quantities of Southern cotton, Lincoln still worried that British leaders might support the Confederacy. In the Trent Affair in 1861, Lincoln even intervened in foreign affairs—an area he usually left to Secretary of State Seward—in order to appease the British. The Trent Affair began when a Union naval officer forcibly removed two Confederate envoys from a British ship. To placate the offended British government, Lincoln personally ordered the Confederates' release. Nonetheless, though Lincoln realized that taking decisive action against slavery could only improve the Union's standing in England and throughout Europe, he was determined to approach emancipation cautiously.

The new president had to resist even more pressure from within the United States to act quickly against slavery. Most of it came from Congress, specifically from the radical antislavery wing of Lincoln's own party (generally known as the Radicals). On issues

---

[1] Excerpt from Chapter 4 in *Abraham Lincoln*, Chelsea House Publishers, 2004.

concerning the economy, Lincoln stuck firmly to the Whig tradition that Congress, not the president, should shape legislation, and promptly signed congressional bills to create a national banking system and currency and to provide assistance to poor Easterners seeking to settle in the West with the Homestead Act. On anything concerning war policy, however, he stubbornly resisted Congress's efforts to tell him what to do. Viewing the issue of slavery as closely linked to his war policy, Lincoln also refused to let Congress dictate to him regarding emancipation.

Lincoln's determination to retain control over when— if at all—the slaves would be freed was tied to his concerns regarding Kentucky, Missouri, and Maryland, where pro-Confederate sentiment remained strong. He worried that any action by the federal government against slavery might drive these wavering border slave states right out of the Union. If that happened, he believed, the Union cause was as good as dead.

In March 1862, the president took some tentative steps toward emancipation by asking the states to consider a plan for gradual emancipation in which slave-owners would receive compensation from the government for their slaves and freed slaves would be encouraged to settle in Central America or Africa. (Lincoln's colonization scheme was nothing new—over the years, many leaders, including Thomas Jefferson, Andrew Jackson, and Henry Clay, had suggested settling freed slaves outside the United States.) Yet as conservative and mild as Lincoln's plan was, not a single border state representative would back it, and leading black Americans such as abolitionist Frederick Douglass were deeply offended by the proposal's emphasis on sending freedmen abroad.

A few months later, impatient congressional Radicals sought to take emancipation into their own hands by passing legislation to confiscate and free the slaves of anyone who supported the Confederacy. Still deeply worried about the border states, Lincoln hesitated to enforce the act. This infuriated antislavery editor Horace Greeley, who publicly criticized the president for dragging his feet on emancipation in Greeley's newspaper *The New York Tribune*. In his reply to Greeley, Lincoln emphasized that although he wished all people could be free, he could not allow his public policy to be determined by his private feelings. Whatever he decided to do—or not do—regarding emancipation would be done to "save the Union", because he firmly believed that restoring the Union was his most important duty as president. What Lincoln chose not reveal to Greeley was that by the time his letter was written in August, he had already committed himself to pushing ahead with emancipation.

By the summer of 1862, Lincoln had concluded that his gradual and voluntary emancipation plan of the previous spring was going nowhere. On July 22, therefore, Lincoln presented a draft for an emancipation proclamation to his cabinet. Secretary Seward persuaded Lincoln to wait for a military victory before issuing the decree; otherwise, he warned, it might appear as an act of desperation in the wake of a string of Union defeats. Victory finally came at Antietam and five days later, on September 22, Lincoln introduced his new emancipation plan to the nation.

Lincoln's Preliminary Emancipation Proclamation announced that in 100 days he would free the slaves within any state still in rebellion against the U.S. government. On January 1, 1863, as promised, Lincoln issued his final Emancipation Proclamation, signing it in the presence of his entire cabinet. One important change had been made in the document since September: The final proclamation stipulated that for the first time, former slaves would be permitted to join the federal army. By the end of the war, nearly 180,000 black Americans were serving in the Union forces.

Lincoln had long acknowledged that the Constitution did not permit the federal government to interfere with slavery in the states. In the Emancipation Proclamation, he got around this difficulty by basing his authority to free the slaves on his war powers as commander in chief, which included the right to seize a military opponent's "property". Because the proclamation was grounded on the president's war powers, it was only valid in those areas of the country actually controlled by the Confederates, and not in slave states still within the Union (in other words, the worrisome border states) or in those parts of the Confederacy occupied by Union troops. Consequently, when it was issued on January 1, the proclamation actually liberated few slaves. Nonetheless, it was immensely important as a symbol: It showed that the federal government was no longer only fighting for reunion; it was also fighting against slavery.

The Emancipation Proclamation fell far short of the expectations of the Radicals and of some Europeans, but because it redefined the war as a struggle for freedom, most antislavery Americans lauded the document. On the other hand, because it left slavery alone in the loyal border states, the proclamation did not alienate the citizens of those strategically critical areas at a time when the final outcome of the war was still in doubt. Most historians today agree that the Emancipation Proclamation was a document of remarkable political insight, ingeniously suited to the particular circumstances and challenges of the time at which it was written.

Exercises

I. Reminders:

When you are about to complete the project:
Jobs for Summarizer & reflector:
How many questions have you decided? What are they?
Why did you choose those topics or questions?0
How many times have you met to discuss?
How many people have been involved in your group meeting?
How much time did you take in each meeting?
What did you do in your group session?
How many references have you used? What are they?
What is the biggest problem in your cooperation?
How did you solve the problem?

Are you satisfied with your performance?
What better suggestions do you have?

To be more critical...
Can you find any questions inappropriate before or after the discussion of questions? And why?
Can you find any references reasonable or unreasonable? And why?
Can you find any connections between research questions and true realities? And why?
Can you find any connections between a team work and an individual work? And why?
Can you find any connections between the project and your prior knowledge? And why?

II. Group evaluation form:

Learning Evaluation Form: (Based on group work)

Class: _____   Date: _____

1. Research Questions/Objectives: (For students use)
   Responsibilities of members:
   Member A (name) _____
   Role as
   Member B (name) _____
   Role as
   Member C (name) _____
   Role as
   Member D (name) _____
   Role as
   Member E (name) _____
   Role as
   Member F (name) _____
   Role as

2. Assessment of group work: (For teacher use)
   Group Participation (leader): 1(very bad), 2(bad), 3(general), 4(good), 5(very good)
   Quality of Questions (group): 1(very bad), 2(bad), 3(general), 4(good), 5(very good)
   Quality of language work (group): 1(very bad), 2(bad), 3(general), 4(good), 5(very good)
   Quality of information (investigator): 1(very bad), 2(bad), 3(general), 4(good), 5 (very good)
   Quality of summary (summarizer): 1(very bad), 2(bad), 3(general), 4(good), 5(very good)
   Quality of references (scanner): 1(very bad), 2(bad), 3(general), 4(good), 5(very good)

Quality of reflection (reflector): 1(very bad), 2(bad), 3(general), 4(good), 5(very good)
3. Assessment of final product: oral/written product (For teacher use)
   Oral presentation: (Presenter)
   1(very bad), 2(bad), 3(general), 4(good), 5(very good)
   or
   Written work: (assignment/essay/reading report)
   1(very bad), 2(bad), 3(general), 4(good), 5(very good)
4. Do you like this group-work activity? (For students use)
   A. like it very much B. like C. neither like nor dislike D. dislike E. dislike it at all
   What suggestions would you make to improve this activity? (Reflector)

Learning Skills

Cooperative Learning Skills

Elements of Cooperative Learning

It is only under certain conditions that cooperative efforts may be expected to be more productive than competitive and individualistic efforts. Those conditions are:

1. **Positive Interdependence** (sink or swim together) Each group member's efforts are required and indispensable for group success. Each group member has a unique contribution to make to the joint effort because of his or her resources and/or role and task responsibilities.	
2. **Face-to-Face Interaction** (promote each other's success) Orally explaining how to solve problems. Checking for understanding. Discussing concepts being learned. Connecting present with past learning.	

3. **Individual & Group Accountability**

(no hitchhiking! no social loafing)

Keeping the size of the group small. The smaller the size of the group, the greater the individual accountability may be.

Randomly examining students orally by calling on one student to present his or her group's work to the teacher (in the presence of the group) or to the entire class.

Observing each group and recording the frequency with which each member—contributes to the group's work.

Assigning one student in each group the role of checker. The checker asks other group members to explain the reasoning and rationale underlying group answers.

4. **Interpersonal & Small-Group Skills**

Social skills must be taught:
- Leadership
- Decision-making
- Trust-building
- Communication
- Conflict-management skills

5. **Group Processing**

Group members discuss how well they are achieving their goals and maintaining effective working relationships.

Describe what member actions are helpful and not helpful.

Make decisions about what behaviors to continue or change.

Unit 5　Learning Model-cooperative Learning

Introducing the Role Sheets and Literature Circle Routines

Leader
Write questions for your group to discuss. The questions should have to do with the section of the unit. Be sure your questions are critical and open-ended so everyone will be able to answer it in their own way.

Investigator
Collect information of the main topic based on all available resources, such as books, journals, magazines, online information or multi-media resources. All the information identified should be circled the main topic or closely related to it.

Scanner
It requires both literal understanding and content learning in reading. Thus, it needs to identify difficult vocabulary and sentences, and discover content information and the background in text.

Connector
It requires the reflection that reading itself can be connected with the real world beyond the text. Examples or cases similar to the topic in reading have to be discovered to illustrate the main theme.

Presenter
Illustrate what you have achieved in your group work and present the product either in written or oral forms in the class. Organize and manage your presentation if more members will demonstrate.

Summarizer
Write a summary that describes what you have learned in this unit. Be sure you write in complete sentences and include lots of details. Your writing should fill most (or all) of the lines below.

A flow chart demonstration of literature circle
Remember the responsibility of each member and all the cooperative work in the group contribute to the final success!

Specific Tasks in the Group Cooperation

	Accountabilities
Leader (Manager)	Make decisions in research questions
	Organize and manage activities
Investigator (Researcher)	Collect target information
	Search for topic-related resources
Scanner (Reader)	Read literatures from investigator
	Select useful content and key elements
Connector (Reflector)	Review what have learned so far
	Build relationships between the topic and reality
Summarizer (Writer)	Summarize what have been acquired after the group work
	Reflect the strengths and weaknesses in the group work
Presenter (Performer)	Present the final product in both oral and written form

Directions to Complete the Group Cooperation

Step 1: Leaders hold a discussion with group members to decide one of the following questions:

● What might be the causes of American Civil War? (Westward Movement or the conflicts between Northern economic system and Southern economic system. You can explain it from the angles of economy, politics, social realities or anything related.)

- Describe the steps of Lincoln's issuing the Emancipation Proclamation and tell Lincoln's attitude toward the outlawing of slavery. Why was Lincoln hesitating at first? Was it wise under such particular circumstance? Why?
- What made Lincoln finally decide to resort war to solve the problem he was facing? What might be possible reasons why the Union won the war? If the Southerners won the war what the America might be? Was the American Civil War inevitable? If not, in what ways?
- Why can Lincoln become one of the most famous American presidents as a not so good-looking man who did not have prominent family background? (Try to explain it from the perspectives of his influences in American Civil War and his great deeds in American history.)
- What are the details of Homestead Law and Emancipation Proclamation? What were their influences at such a specific period of time? Do you think they were the turning point of American Civil War? In what ways they helped the Northern victory of the war?

Step 2: With regard to the questions you have decided, investigators have to learn what information have to be searched for, thus you need to make a list of all the potential content for answering question and possible resources.

Step 3: Scanners need to identify key ideas and answers from a variety of references, so extensive reading is required to complete this task and even proper cooperation with investigator is also needed.

Step 4: Connectors working as a critical thinker mainly deal with the relation between what have been learned and what have been found, that is to say, they have to think and build the connections between theory and practice or past and present, for example, What are the similarities and differences between the American Civil War and the civil war of China?

Step 5: Summarizers write what key points have been made or learned after your group work, as well as those strengths and weaknesses during the cooperation, because it can provide feedbacks for both teachers, evaluation and your learning the next time.

Step 6: Presenter is the performer to display what you have done in your group cooperation. Whatever it is a written work or oral work, they have to be presented in certain forms to audience, as they are also counted in evaluation. Examples of product can be presentation, report, essay, or other exercises.

Group Work Activities

Work in groups as literature circles and complete the following tasks:

1. Select one of the themes from below or choose a theme according to your own interest of the unit, and then narrow down it into a specific topic or question.

> The personality of Abraham Lincoln
> The imbedded conflicts of American Civil War
> The emancipation of black people
> The battles in the war
> The life of the ordinaries in the war

2. Each member in a group has to select a role as a leader, an investigator, a scanner, a connector, a summarizer or a presenter.

3. The final product of the group work has to be presented in the format of a portfolio, including a report, an oral presentation (with PowerPoint), and numbers of collected materials of references.

4. All the required documents have been attached at the end of the unit.

Group Work Report

Class: _____   Date: _____

1. Group Work Questions/Objectives: (For students use)

Responsibilities of members:

Member A_____
Role as
Member B_____
Role as
Member C_____
Role as
Member D_____
Role as
Member E_____
Role as
Member F_____
Role as

2. **Assessment of group work: (For teacher use)**
   Group Participation: 1(very bad), 2(bad), 3(general), 4(good), 5(very good)
   Quality of Questions: 1(very bad), 2(bad), 3(general), 4(good), 5(very good)
   Quality of language work: 1(very bad), 2(bad), 3(general), 4(good), 5(very good)
   Quality of information: 1(very bad), 2(bad), 3(general), 4(good), 5(very good)
   Quality of summary: 1(very bad), 2(bad), 3(general), 4(good), 5(very good)

3. **Assessment of final product: oral/written product (For teacher use)**
   Oral presentation:
   1(very bad), 2(bad), 3(general), 4(good), 5(very good)
   Written work: (assignment/essay)
   1(very bad), 2(bad), 3(general), 4(good), 5(very good)

4. **Do you like this group work activity? (For students use)**
   A. Like it very much.
   B. Like.
   C. Neither like nor dislike.
   D. Dislike.
   E. Dislike it at all.
   What suggestions would you make to improve this activity?

References

List of references
Books_____ (in numbers)
E-books_____(in numbers)
Journals_____(in numbers)
Others_____(in numbers)

Details of references
Library book & E-book
Title:_____
Author: _____
Date of Publication: _____

Journal
Title of article: _____
Author :_____
Title of journal: _____

Date of issue:_____
Volume number:_____ Issue Number:_____ Page article begins:_____

Websites
Topic/Title:_____
Author:_____
Valid date:_____
Retrieved from:_____
Is it clear who wrote the material?_____
Are the author's qualifications stated?_____
Is there a phone or address of the sponsoring organization?_____

Self-evaluation Form

What are the main objectives in this unit?
_____
_____
_____
_____

What useful vocabularies and expressions have you learned from this unit?
_____
_____
_____
_____

What key terms and educational knowledge have you learned?
_____
_____
_____
_____

Have you used the learning skills before? Why do you think they are useful or not useful?
_____
_____
_____
_____

Unit 5 Learning Model-cooperative Learning

If possible, what would you like to add to make learning more interesting and relevant?

下 篇

Unit 6

Educators Philosophies and Teaching Theories

Introduction

Early Teaching Models

Over one hundred years ago theories of teaching were at what might be called the pre-operational level whereby it was assumed that through repeated association, learning would follow. Repeated association imbues the recipient with moral qualities; culture was transmitted by learning works of writers by heart such as *Mort d' Arthur and Hiawatha;* and the skills of reading, writing and arithmetic were taught by rote methods taking up most of each day. Special activities such as sewing, washing and cooking for girls, and woodwork, drawing or gardening for boys were studied on two afternoons per week. Able children were placed with older children whilst the less able repeated the same work year after year.

In more recent years the curriculum widened beyond the basic skills and exercise in general knowledge to encompass a wider range of subject areas and contents. The methods of teaching these new subjects also became more sophisticated, although retaining the elements of telling, writing, rehearsal and recall. Three models have been elaborated to describe, post hoc, some of the changes which have taken place in teaching methods.

The *Behavior Control Model* emphasizes the role of the teacher as an efficient manager of the pupil's learning and controller of his behavior. It is an application of the principles of behavior modification such as the role of reinforcement in learning, and the elaboration of a theory of instruction generalized from the principles of programmed learning. Critics of this approach, such as Ausubel et al, suggest that understanding, thinking and appreciation cannot be reduced to observable student responses, and methods of the psychological laboratory with its experimental controls do not transfer to the classroom.

Others have espoused the *Discovery–Learning Model* in an attempt to give psychological respectability to the methods by which some teachers inspire enthusiasm and interest and help their pupils gain insight. The early origins of this model are found in the writings of Rousseau and Montessori, whilst modern writers such as Bruner advocate it as a means of replacing rote methods. The discovery, as opposed to the expository approach, adopted in the Nuffield science curriculum projects, focused attention and research upon this model; but what has become clear is that these methods cannot be used in every situation, can be time-consuming, and when used may still not lead to meaningful learning and understanding in terms of the learner's own cognitive structures.

The third model is the *Rational–logical Model* derived from analytic philosophy in which it is asserted that rationality implies a manner in which a pupil should be treated. It is argued that thinking and language are essentially human characteristics and that language should play a key role in teaching. Hirst, in fact, has argued that the central function of Education is to bring about thinking by means of language.

This model is couched in terms which have not yet lent themselves either to demonstration of the principles in practice or to evaluation in terms of traditional research methodology. Alongside these advances are the practices in teaching involving knowledge of learning theories, and the long history of attempts to introduce what is seen as the developmentalist's approach. Developmentalists, most often practitioners, advocate that education should be child-centred, suitable to the child's level of development and cannot always appeal to rationality. These teachers are concerned for individual needs, interests, learning abilities and difficulties. Lately this had been constructed as an example of the teacher-centred versus child-centred dichotomy and others have related it to the progressive approach, whilst critics label it "soft-centred" rather than child-centred.

In my view, central to a modern theory of teaching should be the notion that one is developing thinking abilities and teaching thinking skills enabling the pupil to think efficiently and at the same helping him to communicate these thoughts coherently through various modes (speech, drama, writing, music and pictures). One must, of course, have something to think about, and the development of these abilities can only take place in relation to the study of fields and forms of knowledge, that is, through those subjects normally found in the school curriculum and in relation to the body of skills considered necessary such as reading, writing, movement.

Questions after reading:

What do three teaching models emphasize? Could you provide some teaching activities reflecting these teaching models?

Group work:

Topic: While discussing teaching models, we have to mention learning theories in educational psychology, such as Behaviorism, Cognitivism, Constructivism and Humanistic Psychology. Can you describe the similarities between learning theories and teaching models?

Directions: Work as a group and share your ideas with others.

Unit 6 Educators Philosophies and Teaching Theories

Text A

Brainstorming

John Dewey

The Philosophy of Education is a field of applied philosophy that examines the aims, forms, methods, and results of education as both a process and a field of study. It is influenced both by developments within philosophy, especially questions of ethics and epistemology, and by concerns arising from instructional practice.

Pragmatism is a philosophical movement that includes those who claim that an ideology or proposition can be said to be true if and only if it works satisfactorily, that the meaning of a proposition is to be found in the practical consequences of accepting it, and that impractical ideas are to be rejected.

Experiential learning is the process of making meaning from direct experience. Experiential learning focuses on the learning process for the individual.

Questions before reading:

Do you know any great educators? Can you give some examples and tell something about their lives, works and theories or anything you know about them?

Do you know who is Jerome Bruner or John Dewey, and what are their contributions to psychology and education?

My Pedagogic Creed[1]
John Dewey

What Education Is

A. I believe that all education proceeds by the participation of the individual in the social consciousness of the race. This process begins unconsciously almost at birth, and is continually shaping the individual's powers, saturating his consciousness, forming his habits, training his ideas, and arousing his feelings and emotions. Through this unconscious education the individual gradually comes to share in the intellectual and

---

[1] From John Dewey's famous declaration concerning education, first published in *The School Journal*, Volume LIV, Number 3 (January 16, 1897), ARTICLE I, pp.77—80.

moral resources which humanity has succeeded in getting together. He becomes an inheritor of the funded capital of civilization. The most formal and technical education in the world cannot safely depart from this general process. It can only organize it; or differentiate it in some particular direction.

B. I believe that the only true education comes through the stimulation of the child's powers by the demands of the social situations in which he finds himself. Through these demands he is stimulated to act as a member of a unity, to emerge from his original narrowness of action and feeling and to conceive of himself from the standpoint of the welfare of the group to which he belongs. Through the responses which others make to his own activities he comes to know what these mean in social terms. The value which they have is reflected back into them. For instance, through the response which is made to the child's instinctive babblings the child comes to know what those babblings mean; they are transformed into articulate language and thus the child is introduced into the consolidated wealth of ideas and emotions which are now summed up in language.

C. I believe that this educational process has two sides—one psychological and one sociological; and that neither can be subordinated to the other or neglected without evil results following. Of these two sides, the psychological is the basis. The child's own instincts and powers furnish the material and give the starting point for all education. Save as the efforts of the educator connect with some activity which the child is carrying on of his own initiative independent of the educator, education becomes reduced to a pressure from without. It may, indeed, give certain external results but cannot truly be called educative. Without insight into the psychological structure and activities of the individual, the educative process will, therefore, be haphazard and arbitrary. If it chances to coincide with the child's activity it will get a leverage; if it does not, it will result in friction, or disintegration, or arrest of the child nature.

D. I believe that knowledge of social conditions, of the present state of civilization, is necessary in order properly to interpret the child's powers. The child has his own instincts and tendencies, but we do not know what these mean until we can translate them into their social equivalents. We must be able to carry them back into a social past and see them as the inheritance of previous race activities. We must also be able to project them into the future to see what their outcome and end will be. In the illustration just used, it is the ability to see in the child's babblings the promise and potency of a future social intercourse and conversation which enables one to deal in the proper way with that instinct.

E. I believe that the psychological and social sides are organically related and that education cannot be regarded as a compromise between the two, or a superimposition of one upon the other. We are told that the psychological definition of education is barren and formal—that it gives us only the idea of a development of all the mental powers without giving us any idea of the use to which these powers are put. On the other hand, it is urged that the social definition of education, as getting adjusted to civilization, makes of it a forced and external process, and results in subordinating the freedom of the individual to a preconceived social and political status.

F. I believe each of these objections is true when urged against one side isolated from the other. In order to know what a power really is we must know what its end, use, or function is; and this we cannot know save as we conceive of the individual as active in social relationships. But, on the other hand, the only possible adjustment which we can give to the child under existing conditions, is that which arises through putting him in complete possession of all his powers. With the advent of democracy and modern industrial conditions, it is impossible to foretell definitely just what civilization will be twenty years from now. Hence it is impossible to prepare the child for any precise set of conditions. To prepare him for the future life means to give him command of himself; it means so to train him that he will have the full and ready use of all his capacities; that his eye and ear and hand may be tools ready to command, that his judgment may be capable of grasping the conditions under which it has to work, and the executive forces be trained to act economically and efficiently. It is impossible to reach this sort of adjustment save as constant regard is had to the individual's own powers, tastes, and interests—say, that is, as education is continually converted into psychological terms.

In sum, I believe that the individual who is to be educated is a social individual and that society is an organic union of individuals. If we eliminate the social factor from the child we are left only with an abstraction; if we eliminate the individual factor from society, we are left only with an inert and lifeless mass. Education, therefore, must begin with a psychological insight into the child's capacities, interests, and habits. It must be controlled at every point by reference to these same considerations. These powers, interests, and habits must be continually interpreted—we must know what they mean. They must be translated into terms of their social equivalents—into terms of what they are capable of in the way of social service.

The Nature of Method

I believe that the question of method is ultimately reducible to the question of the order of development of the child's powers and interests. The law for presenting and treating material is the law implicit within the child's own nature. Because this is so I believe the following statements are of supreme importance as determining the spirit in which education is carried on:

1. I believe that the active side precedes the passive in the development of the child nature; that expression comes before conscious impression; that the muscular development precedes the sensory; that movements come before conscious sensations; I believe that consciousness is essentially motor or impulsive; that conscious states tend to project themselves in action.

I believe that the neglect of this principle is the cause of a large part of the waste of time and strength in school work. The child is thrown into a passive, receptive or absorbing attitude. The conditions are such that he is not permitted to follow the law of his nature; the result is friction and waste.

I believe that ideas (intellectual and rational processes) also result from action and devolve for the sake of the better control of action. What we term reason is primarily the law of orderly or effective action. To attempt to develop the reasoning powers, the powers of judgment, without reference to the selection and arrangement of means in action, is the fundamental fallacy in our present methods of dealing with this matter. As a result we present the child with arbitrary symbols. Symbols are a necessity in mental development, but they have their place as tools for economizing effort; presented by themselves they are a mass of meaningless and arbitrary ideas imposed from without.

2. I believe that the image is the great instrument of instruction. What a child gets out of any subject presented to him is simply the images which he himself forms with regard to it.

I believe that if nine-tenths of the energy at present directed towards making the child learn certain things, were spent in seeing to it that the child was forming proper images, the work of instruction would be indefinitely facilitated.

I believe that much of the time and attention now given to the preparation and presentation of lessons might be more wisely and profitably expended in training the child's power of imagery and in seeing to it that he was continually forming definite, vivid, and growing images of the various subjects with which he comes in contact in his experience.

3. I believe that interests are the signs and symptoms of growing power. I believe that they represent dawning capacities. Accordingly the constant and careful observation of interests is of the utmost importance for the educator.

I believe that these interests are to be observed as showing the state of development which the child has reached.

I believe that they prophesy the stage upon which he is about to enter.

I believe that only through the continual and sympathetic observation of childhood's interests can the adult enter into the child's life and see what it is ready for, and upon what material it could work most readily and fruitfully.

I believe that these interests are neither to be humored nor repressed. To repress interest is to substitute the adult for the child, and so to weaken intellectual curiosity and alertness, to suppress initiative, and to deaden interest. To humor the interests is to substitute the transient for the permanent. The interest is always the sign of some power below; the important thing is to discover this power. To humor the interest is to fail to penetrate below the surface and its sure result is to substitute caprice and whim for genuine interest.

4. I believe that the emotions are the reflex of actions.

I believe that to endeavor to stimulate or arouse the emotions apart from their corresponding activities, is to introduce an unhealthy and morbid state of mind.

I believe that if we can only secure right habits of action and thought, with reference to the good, the true, and the beautiful, the emotions will for the most part take care of themselves.

Unit 6 Educators Philosophies and Teaching Theories

I believe that next to deadness and dullness, formalism and routine, our education is threatened with no greater evil than sentimentalism.

I believe that this sentimentalism is the necessary result of the attempt to divorce feeling from action.

Exercises

I. Reading Comprehension:

Read "What Education Is" again and choose the correct heading for each section from A to F. There are more headings than sections, so you will not use them all.

Example: Paragraph C Heading 5

Headings

1. The discussion of the two sides of education.
2. Individual interest v.s. group interest.
3. Each individual's engagement in socialization is an unconsious process of Education.
4. The essence of education is to activate motivation to seek for meaningful social existence.
5. Psychological matters play a leading role in the development of education.
6. Psychological education is rather abstract than social education.
7. Education requires participation in society.
8. The correlated relations and balanced development between psychological and socialogical sides.
9. Social knowledge forms child's capabilities.

Paragraph A
Paragraph B
Paragraph C
Paragraph D
Paragraph E
Paragraph F

II. Vocabulary:

Choose an appropriate answer from the following definitions of the word which indicate the contextual meaning of the passage.

Leverage:
A. The action of a lever.

B. Power or ability to act or to influence people, events, decisions, etc.

C. The use of a small initial investment, credit, or borrowed funds to gain a very high return in relation to one's investment.

Potency

A. The state or quality of being potent.

B. Efficacy; effectiveness; strength.

C. A person or thing exerting power or influence.

Fallacy

A. A deceptive, misleading, or false notion, belief, etc.

B. A misleading or unsound argument.

C. Logic, any of various types of erroneous reasoning that render arguments logically unsound.

Prophesy

A. To indicate beforehand.

B. To declare or foretell by or as if by divine inspiration.

C. To utter in prophecy or as a prophet.

III. Judgments and Implications:

Do the following statements agree with the information given in the passage?

True   if the statement is true according to the passage

False   if the statement contradicts the passage

1. Active side comes before the passive one in the progress of the child's nature, so expression precedes the sensory.
2. Action could lead to ideas (intellectual and rational progresses), and ideas are to take better charge of action.
3. The majority of our energy now has been used to make children learn by images.
4. The greatest important thing for the educators to do is to cultivate interest.
5. Once we want to stimulate the emotions, we should also consider its relevant activities.

IV. Critical Questions:

What is John Dewey's philosophy of education and what does he stress in pedagogy? What values do his thoughts serve for current education?

Text B

Brainstorming

Cognitive psychology: It is the study of mental processes such as "attention, language use, memory, perception, problem solving, creativity and thinking". Cognitive psychology has been used to explain learning to oppose behaviorists who claimed mainly that learning is a connection between stimuli and response. However, cognitivism focuses on the inner mental activities — opening the "black box" of the human mind is valuable and necessary for understanding how people learn. Mental processes such as thinking, memory, knowing, and problem-solving need to be explored. Knowledge can be seen as schema or symbolic mental constructions. Learning is defined as change in a learner's schemata.

Schema: A Schema is a structured cluster of concepts, it can be used to represent objects, scenarios or sequences of events or relations. The original idea was proposed by philosopher Immanuel Kant as innate structures used to help us perceive the world.

A schema (pl. schemata) is the mental framework that is created as children interact with their physical and social environments. For example, many 3-year-olds insist that the sun is alive because it comes up in the morning and goes down at night. According to Piaget, these children are operating based on a simple cognitive schema that things that move are alive. At any age, children rely on their current cognitive structures to understand the world around them. Moreover, younger and older children may often interpret and respond to the same objects and events in very different ways because cognitive structures take different forms at different ages.

Questions before reading:

Can you show some similarities between Piaget and Dewey? What are the characteristics of child development?

Jerome Bruner: The Lesson of the Story[①]

John Crace

The richest learning experience comes from narrative, the groundbreaking psychologist tells.

It's easy to forget that, 50 years ago, early years education was an afterthought in

---

① Excerpt from *The Guardian*, Monday, 26 March, 2007.

policy and funding. It was the universities that were considered worth spending money on, and if they tended to be filled with the middle-classes, then that's just the way things were. The better-off simply happened to have brighter children. Thanks to Jerome Bruner and the other pioneers of cognitive development, views like these have long been gathering dust. But Bruner at all no longer get the recognition they deserve. The idea that children go through developmental stages of learning has pretty much been absorbed into mainstream public debate and can seem uncontroversial, even plain obvious. There may be some scraps to argue over, but it's no longer cutting-edge stuff; neurology is the modern academic battleground. Old-timers such as Bruner are sidelined, because there are few takers for what they offer in a 21st-century psychology department.

But Bruner has no intention of changing his line of work. At 91, he's still going strong, teaching in the law department at New York University. At a ceremony in Oxford only this month, at which a building in the education department was named in his honour, he lectured on his recent theories of story-telling as a vital learning tool.

"Why are we so intellectually dismissive towards narrative?" he asks. "Why are we inclined to treat it as rather a trashy, if entertaining, way of thinking about and talking about what we do with our minds? Storytelling performs the dual cultural functions of making the strange familiar and ourselves private and distinctive. If pupils are encouraged to think about the different outcomes that could have resulted from a set of circumstances, they are demonstrating usability of knowledge about a subject. Rather than just retaining knowledge and facts, they go beyond them to use their imaginations to think about other outcomes, as they don't need the completion of a logical argument to understand a story. This helps them to think about facing the future, and it stimulates the teacher too."

Context and culture has underpinned all Bruner's work, dating back to his undergraduate years at Duke University in the 1930s, where he was taught by the distinguished British psychologist William McDougall. "Psychology was dominated by the behaviourists at that time", he says, "and McDougall encouraged me to think of simple 'stimulus and response' as an extremely limited, atavistic model. It was clear to me that it was the interaction—the context in which, the how, a thing is learned—that is key to a person's understanding and development, rather than the mere fact that knowledge is acquired. Take punishment, for example. Not everyone interprets it in the same way; it's what any given action represents to a person that determines whether it is seen as a punishment or not."

McDougall's parting words to Bruner were: "Don't go on to Harvard whatever you do; they're much too positive in their views." So, naturally, that's where he went. And it was there that he developed many of his ideas on the importance of pre-school learning and created a parallel, more interactive model of Piaget's theory of reasoning and childhood development. His work brought him to national attention and John F Kennedy invited him to head a presidential scientific advisory board, where he was instrumental in diverting government cash away from higher education and into pre-school learning.

Bureaucracy of Politics

Lyndon Johnson invited him to run the National Institute of Child Health and Development. "Johnson was a very underrated president," says Bruner. "He had a persuasive Texan drawl and I was tempted. But I had become frustrated with the bureaucracy of politics; I wanted to be free from the pressure of putting details into operation. So I declined—something I rather regret in hindsight."

Bruner was also getting fed up with Harvard, which he began to see as increasingly stuffy. "It was the late 60s, and many of the students were getting involved in the civil rights and anti-war movements. The old sacred cows were being challenged," he explains. "They also wanted more say in how the university was run, and that seemed utterly reasonable to me. Saying that students were old enough to go to war but not old enough to be involved in the administration of their academic life was just a nonsense. But I was made to feel like a rebellious outsider by the Harvard authorities for voicing my support so, when Isaiah Berlin invited me to teach at Oxford, I leapt at the opportunity."

Was Oxford really so much more liberal than Harvard in 1968? Bruner smiles. "I don't suppose so," he says, "but I didn't know any better. I just thought anything must be an improvement on Harvard."

His method of arrival in England—"I think I'm the only academic in the university's history to take up his chair by sailing his boat across the Atlantic"—was as unorthodox as his teaching and research.

He counts his 10 years at Oxford as one of the most productive periods of his life. "There was a wonderfully talented group of academics and tutors that worked flat out, challenging and developing each others' research in a way that was unusual in Britain at the time," he says. "And we produced some great work, highlighting the fact that those who were missing out on the important family interactions were those who were failing in fifth grade. That was taken up by Lady Plowden [who delivered a groundbreaking report on early years education in 1967 in her battles with the then minister for education, Margaret Thatcher]."

Though he was now well into his 60s, Bruner had no thought of retiring. He has just kept on going and, even in his 80s, was still making regular trips to the Italian village of Reggio Emilia, the epi-centre of liberal education in action. He has not kept on working out of a desire to preserve his place in history, but because he loves what he does. He constantly acknowledges the work of those who have collaborated with him and hardly bothers to conceal his pleasure at the misfortunes of those who have got up his nose. He might need a stick to get about these days, but his mind is as lively as ever and he oozes a boyish enthusiasm and curiosity.

Bruner was born blind and only regained his sight after an operation to remove the cataracts when he was two years old. Does he have any recollection of those early years? "Not really," he says, "but there must have been a lasting effect. It's not the worst thing in the world only to have a vision of your parents that you have created for yourself, but there is still a large sensory deprivation. There must have been a longing for attachment that went partially unfulfilled."

Shy and Geeky

Bruner grew up on the south shore of Long Island and was mainly looked after by his mother, while his father ran the family watch-making firm. He spent a lot of time by the sea. "I was quite a shy, geeky boy," he says. "Not at all like my older sister, Alice, who was much more confident and outgoing. I had one or two close friends, and we would go out rowing or sailing together, creating our own fantasies in which no one else had ever done what we were then doing. We were the fastest oarsmen, the best sailors ... This attraction for the water has never left me. Somehow it's the perfect metaphor for your ability to establish your authority over the world while maintaining your own untouchable separation from it."

Everything changed when Bruner was 12. "My father died of liver cancer and my mother never really came to terms with it," he says. "She went into a period of prolonged wandering. We moved from place to place, and I went from school to school. It's hard to say what sense I made of it. On one level, I just took it to be normal and got on with my life but on another, subconscious level, I think I understood she was overwhelmed by grief. What I think I did learn, though, was the importance of context in communication. It's not so much the words and syntax we use, but the way we interact that defines how we understand something."

As with many families in which one parent dies prematurely, Bruner's never fully regained its former intimacy and, with his sister Alice getting married young, he learned to make a virtue of his self-sufficiency. "My mother's real legacy was to make me rebellious and autonomous," he says, "though I'm not sure how my father would have felt about my leftwing political leanings. He was an old-fashioned kind of tough guy, who worshipped Theodore Roosevelt. I loved and respected him, but I suspect we might have fallen out if he had lived."

No one could accuse Bruner of not walking the walk. "I tried to sign up for the Republicans in the Spanish Civil War, and even went along to the Chinese consulate to enlist in the Sixth Army in their struggle against Japan. I can still remember my shame at being told, 'Mr Bruner, we Chinese do not have manpower problems'."

At the start of the second world war, he tried to join the US military, but was turned down because of his poor eyesight and conscripted instead into the Office for Strategic Studies, the equivalent of MI5[①]. "We began by studying foreign radio broadcasts," he remembers, "but our main task came in 1944 when we were sent in behind the invasion force on D-Day[②] to determine whether liberated French villages could be trusted. It was a

---

① MI5: The Security Service commonly known as MI5 (Military Intelligence, Section 5), is the United Kingdom's counter-intelligence and security agency.

② D-day: D-Day is a term often used in military parlance to denote the day on which a combat attack or operation is to be initiated. The best known D-Day is June 6, 1944 — the day of the Normandy landings.

Unit 6   Educators Philosophies and Teaching Theories

tricky time; there were still Vichy sympathisers but the Free French hated the idea that some Yanks were interrogating their people. Still, it was a useful lesson in learning that people don't always mean what they say."

Once the war was over, Bruner's academic life proceded more smoothly than his personal one. He divorced his first wife after his return from Europe and has been married twice since. "You know," he sighs, "you think you meet people by chance, but when you look back on your life you realise there was nothing random going on at all. We're all just trying to resolve our lives as best we can." He pauses. "And that's all I want to say on that."

And regrets? "My critics have always accused me of ignoring potentially interesting areas of research," he says. "And they've got a point. The whole field of cognitive development was just so new, so exciting, and so open when we started that you could only do so much at any one time, and you just headed off in the directions that seemed most interesting. So, undoubtedly, there are bits I would like to go back and look at more thoroughly."

Exercises

I. Reading Comprehension:

There are four suggested answers marked A, B, C and D. Choose the best answer for each question.

1. In the section "Bureaucracy of politics", the sentence "His method of arrival in England ... was as unorthodox as his teaching and research." implies _____.
   A. Brunner was a rather brilliant psychologist in America
   B. few experts from Harvard went to Oxford
   C. he is a scholar with an unusual characteristic
   D. Oxford attached importance to the invitation of Brunner

2. In the section "Bureaucracy of politics", the sentence "And we produced some great work...those who were failing in fifth grade." refers to _____.
   A. the disharmonious relations in some families
   B. a fact between family life and school achievement
   C. a fact of research findings of those who failed in the fifth grade
   D. a comparative finding and relation between home communication and school achievement

3. In the section "Bureaucracy of politics", the sentence "He constantly acknowledges the work ... misfortunes of those who have got up his nose." reflects that _____.
   A. he is an optimistic and passionate person
   B. he is open-minded and studious
   C. he is critical and wise
   D. he is scholastic and academic

II. Judgments and Implications:

Do the following statements agree with the information given in the passage?
True   if the statement is true according to the passage
False if the statement contradicts the passage

1. Bruner and other pioneers of cognitive development no longer get the recognition they deserve because their theory is out of time.
2. Even though Bruner was sidelined, he never wanted to change his view on the studies.
3. Bruner agreed with his teacher McDougall that interaction is the key to a person's understanding and development.
4. Bruner went to work in Oxford because people in Harvard could not agree with his academic thoughts.
5. According to Bruner, the context in communication is important because no matter what words we use, the way we interact defines how we understand something.

III. Chart Filling:

Read the last section of the text concerning Bruner's life and fill in the information to complete the chart below with no more than three words.

Childhood life	Adulthood life
He grew up on the south shore of Long Island and looked after by his mother.	He tried to sign up for the Republicans and attempted to _____.
Playtime spent with _____	Served in the Office for Strategic Studies with a useful lesson learning.
His father died at his age of 12, his sister married young, and he learned to be _____ and _____.	While Bruner's academic life proceeded more smoothly, he explained his personal life with "nothing random going on at all." Because of _____.
His respects to his father is high, even if he advocates _____.	He admitted critics, but addressed _____ always needs to be researched thoroughly.

IV. Critical Questions:

What does Bruner emphasize in his interview? What positive elements can we learn from his remarks?

Text C

Brainstorming

Constructivism: A perspective in education, is based on experimental learning through real life experience to construct and conditionalize knowledge. It is problem based adaptive learning that challenges faulty schema, integrates new knowledge with existing knowledge, and allows for creation of original work or innovative procedures. The types of learners are self-directed, creative, innovative, drawing upon visual/spatial, musical/rhythmic, bodily kinesthetic, verbal/linguistic, logical/mathematical, interpersonal, intrapersonal, and naturalistic intelligences. The purpose in education is to become creative and innovative through analysis, conceptualizations, and synthesis of prior experience to create new knowledge.

Questions before reading:
In what ways can constructivism be applied in the process of teaching?

Curriculum Development from a Constructivist Perspective[1]
Martin Brooks

Children at all grade levels can learn more effectively if we teach them to build relationships and connect new information with concepts they already know.

Constructivism as a Philosophical Base

Piaget has been the major figure in promulgating the constructivist perspective. However, Piaget viewed constructivism not as a theory of learning, but as a theory of development, stating that human beings develop through predictable stages, each of which is typified by the emergence of new cognitive structures that increase the complexity of our thinking. Piaget's research did not focus on learning because he viewed learning as externally provoked, development as internally spontaneous. He concluded that learning cannot account for development, but development accounts for learning: Teaching children concepts that they have not attained in their spontaneous development...is completely hopeless. Therefore, it is often developmentally appropriate for children to be "wrong", to be cognitively unable to construct an adult understanding of specific concepts.

---

[1] Excerpt from "Curriculum Development from a Constructivist Perspective", *Journal of Education Leadership*, January 1987, pp. 63—67.

Constructivism can be defined as a psychologically based notion of development: we come to know our world by interacting with it and using our operative cognitive structives to "explain" what we have perceived. Constructivism is also a model of learning. Since construction of knowledge is often accompanied by the emergence of new cognitive structures. Eventually our second graders will recognize that the pie is the whole and each slice cannot also be the whole, at this point they will have gained a different, more complex, understanding of part /whole relationships.

Curriculum from a Constructivist Perspective

The following two examples describe curriculum development from a constructivist perspective, one at the elementary level and one at the middle school level, one resulting in a new written curriculum, and one as an example of how curriculum development occurs through instruction.

Symmetry. Disenchanted with the isolation of different curriculums at the primary level (grades K-3), a group of teachers decided to develop an integrated arts curriculum. They based their decision on the constructivist notion that children learn when they are able to build relationships and make connections among common concepts.

One such concept is "symmetry" and the symmetrical design "A-B-A". In the new curriculum, the art teacher helps his first-grade children visually recognize shapes and patterns having an A-B-A symmetrical design, such as certain trees and buildings with center halls and identical wings to the left and right. The music teacher helps her students compose or perform pieces of music having an A-B-A symmetrical design, such as verse-refrain-verse songs and high-low-high sounds on instruments. The physical education teacher helps children move their bodies in A-B-A shapes, such as arm-trunk-arm. And the regular classroom teacher helps children use blocks, chain links, unfix cubes, and other materials to create A-B-A designs and teaches them to recognize symmetry in disciplines such as math: 1+2=2+1.

Photosynthesis. The New York State Education Department requires students to learn about life sciences in the seventh grade. One topic in the life science sequence is photosynthesis. The text used in our district describes photosynthesis in this way:

Photosynthesis is the chemical change that produces food. In photosynthesis, carbon dioxide gas and water are combined to produce sugar and oxygen. The sugar may be changed to starch. Sunlight is necessary for photosynthesis. It supplies the energy for the chemical change. This energy becomes locked in the sugar and starch molecules that are produced.

$$6CO_2 \text{(carbon dioxide)} + 6H_2O \text{(water)} \xrightarrow{\text{energy}} C_6 6_{12}O_6 \text{(chlorophyll glucose oxygen)} + O_2$$

Note in the equation above that oxygen is produced in photosynthesis.

Unit 6 Educators Philosophies and Teaching Theories

The reading level of this passage is appropriate for seventh graders, and the description of photosynthesis is technically correct and logical from an adult perspective. However, although they are able to memorize this information for a test, most seventh graders understand neither the explanation nor the symbols in the equation. From the students' perspective, the curriculum is not appropriately matched to their cognitive abilities.

"Unlike competency-based teaching models, in which teacher reflection is often subordinate to written curriculums, the success of constructivist approaches to curriculum development and delivery is contingent on the thoughtful mediation of the teacher."

One of our seven-grade science teachers who has a constructivist perspective adapted this curriculum unit to match the instructional demands imposed by the cognitive abilities of her pupils. She recognized that to understand the textbook explanation requires abstract mental structures not yet developed in most 12 and 13-year-old children, structures such as the ability to coordinate multiple frames of reference (the interdependence of oxygen, carbon dioxide, sugar, etc.), and correlational reasoning (sunlight affects the plant's production of oxygen).

To help her student understand the process of photosynthesis, she decided to guide them in constructing it for themselves. She asked the students to think about how to bake a cake. They knew they would need eggs, milk, butter, and flour. She then asked if a cake would form it if these products were placed on a table. The students responded that the products must be mix together. She asked if mixing them together would make the cake. The students added that the mixed products must be placed in an oven and baked. She asked if there is a way to tell, before the cake comes out of the oven, that it is baking in the oven. After thinking a bit, the students agreed that the aroma of the baking cake is a way to tell. She asked if we bake cakes for their aroma. The students agreed that we bake cakes to eat them, not smell them. She identified the aroma as a by-product, then drew an analogy to photosynthesis plants, using energy from sunlight and having a special ingredient in their leaves(chlorophyll), produce food for their own growth and survival while giving off oxygen as a by-product. Armed with that analogy, the students were then asked to draw a flowchart of another process, similar to photosynthesis, in which a product and a by-product are created in the presence of some sort of energy. An example of the work she received is in figure 1.

Fig. 1 Milk Shake

This teacher analyzed a highly abstract part of the curriculum and employed an analogy to help her students use their large concrete cognitive structures to construct selected features of it for themselves. She asked them to seriate and use one-to-one correspondence in moving through the analogy and from the analogy to photosynthesis. Next, she asked students to classify certain outcomes as either product or by-product. Finally, she had them concretely illustrate the process in a drawing.

The Role of the Teacher

Curriculum development and delivery from a constructivist perspective is a highly complex, idiosyncratic endeavor. Unlike competency-based teaching models, in which teacher reflection is often subordinate to written curriculums, the success of constructivist approaches to curriculum development and delivery is contingent on the thoughtful mediation of the teacher. Although written curriculums are valued as general guides denoting what students often force teachers to shift direction. This requires teachers to think on their feet and reflect on their practice. Competency based models view teachers largely as implementers of curriculum developed elsewhere in the local, state, or national hierarchy. Constructivist models view teachers as developers and deliverers of curriculum. If students are not constructing knowledge as anticipated by the teacher, the teacher must quickly analyze the reasons and alter the curriculum or develop a new curriculum.

This is not a revolutionary notion. Good teachers have always been able to read the class, shift gears, and adapt constructivism gives teachers another lens through which to read the class, an important one that has been largely ignored in our endless search for simple answers to complex problems. Models that attempt to be teacher proof miss an essential point we are all constructors, students and teachers alike. Effective teachers are constantly constructing knowledge about the abilities of their students. They resist being tied to fixed. Static curriculum sequences and seeks opportunities to develop curriculum consistent with their expanding knowledge or students.

Unit 6 Educators Philosophies and Teaching Theories

Nevertheless, teachers in Shoreham Wading River report that approaching curriculum development from a constructivist perspective is difficult. In an elementary classroom reading lesson, for example, it is much easier to use prepackaged kits with all students than to assess which students comprehend the written word literally and which inferentially and then to develop appropriate curriculums for each group. However, our teachers also report that it is precisely this complexity that makes the constructivist perspective to curriculum development meaningful for them and their students.

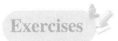

I. Reading Comprehension:

There are four suggested answers marked A, B, C and D. Choose the best answer for each question.

1. Which one of the following about constructivism is NOT true according to the text?
   A. Constructivism is a psychologically based notion of development.
   B. Constructivism is a model of studying and learning.
   C. The construction of knowledge is often accompanied by the emergence of new cognitive structures.
   D. People come to know our world by interacting with it and using our operative cognitive structures to "explain" what we have perceived.
2. Which one of the following about the second example is true?
   A. The reading level of this passage is too difficult for seventh graders.
   B. The description of photosynthesis is technically correct and logical for seventh graders.
   C. The seventh graders are not able to memorize this information for a test.
   D. Most seventh graders understand neither the explanation nor the symbols in the equation.
3. In the example of "photosynthesis", the seven-grade students couldn't understand the description of photosynthesis in the textbook because _____.
   A. the textbook explanation is too complex to understand and memorize
   B. the textbook explanation requires abstract mental structures not yet developed in most 12 and 13-year-old children
   C. seventh graders lack the cognitive ability to forming logic reasoning
   D. seventh graders think textbook knowledge is dull and out-dated
4. Which one of the following choices could not draw the features of constructivist teaching model?
   A. Complex, idiosyncratic.
   B. Flexible, adaptive.
   C. Static, abstract.
   D. Difficult, demanding.

5. This article is mainly about _____.
   A. definition and structure of constructivism
   B. Piaget's understanding and explanation of constructivism
   C. differences of curriculum development between constructivist perspective and competency-based perspective
   D. how to develop curriculum from a constructivist perspective

II. Judgments and Implications:
   Do the following statements agree with the information given in the passage?
   True   if the statement is true according to the passage
   False   if the statement contradicts the passage
   1. Piaget viewed connstructivism as human beings' development through predictable stages, each of which is typified by the emergence of new cognitive structures.
   2. Based on the connections among common concepts, children learn symmetry when they are able to build relationships between learning and constructivist notion.
   3. The teacher analogized photosynthesis to making cakes because they are similar.
   4. The success of constructivist approaches to curriculum development and delivery lies in well-prepared written curriculums.
   5. If students are not constructing knowledge as anticipated by the teacher, the teacher must quickly analyze the reasons and help student to adjust to the curriculum.

III. Critical Questions:
   Chinese classroom teaching has always been criticized for less interactive activities, and can you make a constructive lesson plan in Chinese context?

Learning Skills

Note-taking Skills

Effective note-taking from lectures and readings is an essential skill for university study. Good note-taking allows a permanent record for revision and a register of relevant points that you can integrate with your own writing and speaking. Good note-taking reduces the risk of plagiarism. It also helps you distinguish where your ideas came from and how you think about those ideas.

Effective note-taking requires:
- recognising the main ideas
- identifying what information is relevant to your task
- having a system of note-taking that works for you

Unit 6　Educators Philosophies and Teaching Theories

- reducing the information to note and diagram format
- where possible, putting the information in your own words
- recording the source of the information

Reading Note-taking Strategies

1. Be selective and systematic

As you take notes from a written source, keep in mind that not all of a text may be relevant to your needs. Think about your purpose for reading.

- Are you reading for a general understanding of a topic or concept?
- Are you reading for some specific information that may relate to the topic of an assignment?

Before you start to take notes, skim the text. Then highlight or mark the main points and any relevant information you may need to take notes from. Finally—keeping in mind your purpose for reading—read the relevant sections of the text carefully and take separate notes as you read.

A few tips about format:

Set out your notebooks so that you have a similar format each time you take notes.

- Columns that distinguish the source information and your thoughts can be helpful.
- Headings that include bibliographic reference details of the sources of information are also important.
- The use of colour to highlight major sections, main points and diagrams makes notes easy to access.

2. Identify the purpose and function of a text

Whether you need to make notes on a whole text or just part of it, identifying the main purpose and function of a text is invaluable for clarifying your note-taking purposes and saving time.

- Read the title and the abstract or preface (if there is one)
- Read the introduction or first paragraph
- Skim the text to read topic headings and notice how the text is organised
- Read graphic material and predict its purpose in the text

Your aim is to identify potentially useful information by getting an initial overview of the text (chapter, article, pages...) that you have selected to read. Ask yourself: will this text give me the information I require and where might it be located in the text?

3. Identify how information is organised

Most texts use a range of organizing principles to develop ideas. While most good writing will have a logical order, not all writers will use an organising principle. Organising principles tend to sequence information into a logical hierarchy, some of which are:

- Past ideas to present ideas
- The steps or stages of a process or event
- Most important point to least important point
- Well known ideas to least known ideas
- Simple ideas to complex ideas
- General ideas to specific ideas
- The largest parts to the smallest parts of something
- Problems and solutions
- Causes and results

4. Include your thoughts

When taking notes for an assignment it is also helpful to record your thoughts at the time. Record your thoughts in a separate column or margin and in a different colour to the notes you took from the text.

- What ideas did you have about your assignment when you read that information.
- How do you think you could use this information in your assignment.

Many of the strategies for reading note-taking also apply to listening note-taking. However, unlike reading, you can't stop a lecture and review as you listen (unless you listen to a taped lecture). Therefore preparation prior to listening can greatly improve comprehension.

- Have a clear purpose
- Recognise main ideas
- Select what is relevant, you do not need to write down everything that is said
- Have a system for recording information that works

Lecture Survival Tips

Strategies to increase comprehension and improve note-taking:

Before the lecture:

- Revise the previous lecture or tutorial
- Pre-read about the topic
- Check the pronunciation of any new words or discipline-specific language in the pre-readings.
- Rule up pages according to your note-taking system. This saves time in the lecture.

During the lecture:

- Be on time and sit near the front
- Distinguish between main points, elaboration, examples, repetition, "waffle", restatements and new points by:
- Listen for structural cues (signpost/ transition words, introduction, body and summary stages)
- Look for non verbal cues (facial expression, hand and body signals)

- Look for visual cues (copy the content of any visual aids used [*e.g.* OHTs], note references to names and sources)
- Listen for phonological cues (voice change in volume, speed, emotion). Generally with more important information the speaker will speak slower, louder and they will direct their attention to the audience

After the lecture
- Revise lecture notes within 24 hours
- Tidy up your handwriting and fill in any missing bits. Reviewing makes remembering lectures much easier.
- Write a short summary of the lecture (1 paragraph) in your own words
- Attach any handouts to your lecture notes

1. Use symbols and abbreviations

The use of symbols and abbreviations is useful for lectures, when speed is essential. You also need to be familiar with symbols frequently used in your courses.
- Develop a system of symbols and abbreviations; some personal, some from your courses
- Be consistent when using symbols and abbreviations

Some examples of commonly used symbols and abbreviations are presented in the following tables.

Symbols for note-taking are as follows:

$=$	equals/is equal to/is the same as
$\neq$	is not equal to/is not the same as
$\equiv$	is equivalent to
$\therefore$	therefore, thus, so
$\because$	because
$+$	and, more, plus
$>$	more than, greater than
$<$	less than
$-$	less, minus
$\rightarrow$	gives, causes, leads to, results in, is given by, is produced by, results from
$\nearrow$	rises, increases by
$\searrow$	falls, decreases by
α	proportional to
$\alpha/$	not proportional to

Abbreviations:

These can be classified into three categories

a. Common Abbreviations

Many are derived from Latin.

c.f. (confer) = compare

i.e. (id est) = that is

e.g (exempla grate) = for example

NB (nota benne) =note well

no. (numero) = number

etc. (et cetera)= and so on

b. Discipline—Specific Abbreviations

In chemistry:

Au for gold

GM for magnesium

In the case of quantities and concepts, these are represented by Greek letters in many fields.

A or a (alpha) B or b (beta)

c. Personal Abbreviations

Here you can shorten any word that is commonly used in your lectures.

diff =different

Gov = government

NEC = necessary

Some abbreviations are so well known and widely used that they have become an acronym—an abbreviation pronounced as a word.

For example, the word "laser" was originally an abbreviation for "Light Amplification by Stimulation Emission of Radiation". It now is a noun in its own right!

2. Use concept maps and diagrams

You can set down information in a concept map or diagram. This presents the information in a visual form and is unlike the traditional linear form of note-taking. Information can be added to the concept map in any sequence.

Concept maps can easily become cluttered, so we recommend you use both facing pages of an open A4 note book. This will give you an A3 size page to set out your concept map and allow plenty of space for adding ideas and symbols.

- Begin in the middle of the page and add ideas on branches that radiate from the central idea or from previous branches.
- Arrows and words can be used to show links between parts of the concept map.
- Colour and symbols are important parts of concept maps, helping illustrate ideas and triggering your own thoughts.

Concept map

Concept maps, also called target maps, should be used when you are exploring a topic that is not complex. To make one, draw a circle and add spokes radiating from it. Put your central idea or problem in the middle, and add possible solutions around it in any order. As you can see from the example that follows, a concept map visually arranges a simple decision and the factors that may be used in making that decision.

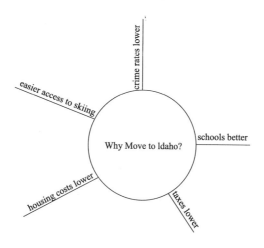

Practice

Imagine that you are considering purchasing a new car. Come up with at least five reasons why you should make the purchase. Use a concept map to organize your answer.

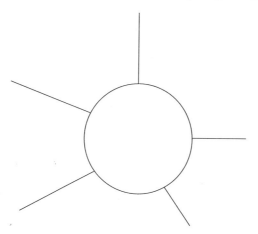

Webbing

Webs are visual organizers that are more structured and complex than concept maps. They are most useful when you are exploring possible solutions to a problem that has a number of symptoms or causes. To develop a web, write your problem in a circle. Next, write the symptoms or possible causes of the problem in smaller, or secondary, circles, each connected to the center by a line. From each of the secondary bubbles, draw smaller bubbles in which you brainstorm possible solutions. Each possible solution is connected to the corresponding secondary bubble by a line.

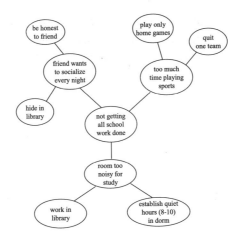

Practice

Create a web for the following problem: you want to deposit $50 per month of disposable income in an investment account, but never seem to have the money. Causes of this problem are eating out at restaurants four times per week, not returning videos on time and paying late fees, and buying too many clothes. Brainstorm possible solutions using a web.

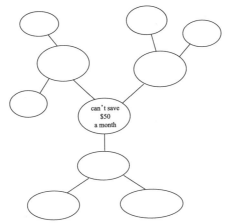

Chart

Consider brainstorming with a chart if you have two or more elements that you want to compare and contrast. Charts let you clearly see how each item is similar to the others, and how it differs. In order to make an effective chart, you need to define the elements you wish to compare, and then come up with two or more areas in which to compare them. Then, you may need to conduct some research to accurately fill out your chart. The chart will keep you focused on your purpose, and on relevant information as you conduct your research.

Practice

You are trying to decide whether to take a job offer in another state or stay where you are. The considerations are salary, housing, schools, and standard of living. While you already have the salary information, you will need to go to the library or Internet to find out the other facts you need to make your comparison. To guide you in your search, you create a chart that looks like this:

Decision	Salary	Housing	Schools	Standard of Living
Move to Chicago				
Stay in Atlanta				

 Group Work Activities

Work in groups to complete the following two tasks:

Task 1: Listening episode practice

Search for an online listening episode or IELTS listening episode to practice note-taking skills.

Requirements:
- Listening episode should be kept in academic genres.
- The complexity of the episode can be adjusted in consideration of students' competence.
- The exercises need to focus on the training of note-taking skills.

Task 2: Reading materials practice

Search for an academic reading material in any subjects or educational topics in preference to practice note-taking skills.

Requirements:
- Reading materials should be kept in academic genres.
- The complexity of the materials can be adjusted in consideration of students' competence.
- The exercises need to focus on the training of note-taking skills.

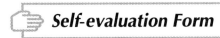

Self-evaluation Form

What are the main objectives in this unit?
_____
_____
_____

What useful vocabularies or expressions have you learned from this unit?
_____
_____
_____

What key terms and educational knowledge have you learned?
_____
_____
_____

Have you used the learning skills before? Why do you think they are useful or not useful?
_____
_____
_____

If possible, what would you like to add to make learning more interesting and relevant?
_____
_____
_____

Unit 7

My Perspectives on Education from Pedagogies to Globalization

Introduction

Education and Globalization: Some Hypotheses[1]
Corlos Alberto Torres

Let me propose the following hypothesis: there are multiple processes of globalization interacting simultaneously in a fairly convoluted fashion. Yet, all of them are deeply affected by the dynamics of international relations from the past few years, and by implication, they affect the role education and educational reform may play in the improvement of people's lives and societies. The idea of multiple globalizations deserves to be discussed in detail before we embark in a discussion about their educational impacts.

There is one layer of globalization, which I have called "globalization from above", in which an ideology of neoliberalism has called for the opening of borders, the creation of multiple regional markets, the viability of faster economic and financial exchanges, and even the presence of forms of state other than the nation-state, shrinking state services, and its overall presence in civil society. Selective deregulation is the motto of this globalization process.

There is a second layer of globalization representing the antithesis of the first, known as the "anti-globalizers", or what could be named "globalization from below". These are individuals, institutions, and social movements that have actively opposed what is perceived as the neoliberal globalization. For these social sectors, groups, individuals, and communities, no globalization without representation is their motto.

There is a third layer of globalization that pertains not so much to markets, but to rights: the globalization of human rights. With the growing ideology of human rights taking hold on the international system and international law, a number of traditional practices (from religious practices to esoteric practices) that have always been considered inherent to the fabric of a particular society or culture are now being called into question, challenged, forbidden, or even outlawed. Advancement of cosmopolitan democracies and

---

[1] Excerpt from *Education and Neoliberal Globalization*, Routledge, 2009.

plural citizenship is the motto of this globalization process.

There is also a fourth layer of globalization that goes beyond markets, and to some extent against human rights, that pertains to the globalization of the international war against terrorism. This new globalization has been prompted in full scale by the events of September 11th—which were interpreted as the globalization of the terrorist threat—and the reaction of the United States. The anti-terrorist response has been military in nature, with two coalition wars led by the United States against Muslim regimes in Afghanistan and Iraq. Yet, the overall feeling of this process was not only its military flavor, but also its emphasis on security and control of borders, people, capital, and commodities—that is, the reverse of open markets and fast commodity exchanges. Security, as a precondition of freedom, is the motto of this anti-terrorist globalization. Not surprisingly, its nemesis—terrorism based on religious fundamentalism—will endorse the motto that only chaos will bring about freedom.

Hence, globalization is a multiple and contradictory phenomenon, with deep-rooted historical causes, and, if one thinks of the tenets of human rights, for instance, a historical process that is difficult to reverse or even confront. Let us now explore in some detail these four possible layers of globalization vis a vis its educational implications.

The Educational Impact of the Multiple Layers of Globalization

There has been a wave of educational reforms influenced by the globalization process under neoliberal inspiration. Martin Carnoy has classified these recent reforms in three types. The first type is reforms that respond to the evolution of the demand for better-qualified labor in the national and international labor markets; these reforms are based on new ideas of how to reorganize schools and improve the professional competence for a successful performance. Carnoy has classified these as "competition-based reforms". There is a second type of reform that responds to the restriction of budgets in the private and public sectors. These reforms are termed by Carnoy as "reforms based on financial imperatives". Finally, there is a group of reforms that try to improve the political role of education as a source of mobility and social equality. Carnoy has classified these reforms as "equity oriented reforms".

The first type, or competition-based reforms, are characterized by four conventional strategies, including: a drive toward decentralization of educational governance and administration of schools (e.g., a drive toward municipalization), new educational norms and standards that usually are measured through extensive testing (the new standards and accountability movement), introduction of new teaching and learning methods leading to the expectation of better performance at low cost (e.g., universalization of textbooks), and improvements in the selection and training of teachers.

The second type of reform, based on financial imperatives, is usually advocated by the IMF and the World Bank as a pre-condition to educational lending to the countries. These reforms also include a series of strategies. Among these are, first and foremost, the transference of educational financing from higher education to lower levels of education—under the premise that to subsidize higher education is to subsidize the rich, since the majority of the students enrolled in higher education are mostly from middle class and/or affluent families. Discussing access to higher education in Argentina, a university professor argued that:

If you take 100 students at first grade what you will find is that the number of people who finally make it to a university and graduate is less than four. So, there is very little access, because there is dramatic attrition at the very initial levels of the primary system. So the university is essentially an elitist university. Although not all of the people who are there are members of the elite. At best, it is a middle-class phenomenon. The poor do not make it to the university. The poor dessert the system and we can never recover them.

The third major type of reform, equity-based reforms, seems to be simply a smokescreen, an add-on to the first two as their main legitimation. As Carnoy explains, the argument to transfer funds from higher education to lower levels of education is justified on the premise of investing for equity purposes. Similarly, equity policies attempt to serve and provide educational opportunities to women, girls, indigenous people, and rural populations—all of who are at a disadvantage in absolute and comparative terms with their counterparts, namely men, boys, and non-indigenous and urban populations. For instance, bilingual and multicultural programs destined to address the needs of linguistic minorities, special education programs, or out of school programs for disadvantaged and "at-risk" children, are all examples of equity focus reforms seeking quality of education for those sectors.

Questions after reading:
Can you define the term "Globalization" and describe the impacts of Globalization? How do you interpret the correlated relations between globalization and education? Can you take examples to illustrate them?

Group work:
Topic: Globalization as an irresistible wave affects educational policy making in around the world, so that China has reformed its primary and secondary education to keep up the pace with the world. Can you provide information to demonstrate China's Educational Reforms since the open-door policy from 1978?
Directions: Work as a group and share your ideas with others.

Text A

Brainstorming

Quality Education:
- Learners who are healthy, well-nourished and ready to participate and learn, and supported in learning by their families and communities;
- Environments that are healthy, safe, protective and gender-sensitive, and provide adequate resources and facilities;
- Content that is reflected in relevant curricula and materials for the acquisition of basic skills, especially in the areas of literacy, numeracy and skills for life, and knowledge in such areas as gender, health, nutrition, HIV/AIDS prevention and peace;
- Processes through which trained teachers use child-centred teaching approaches in well-managed classrooms and schools and skilful assessment to facilitate learning and reduce disparities;
- Outcomes that encompass knowledge, skills and attitudes, and are linked to national goals for education and positive participation in society.

Questions before reading:

Do you agree the tiger mother's way of parenting?
What is the major difference of family education between the West and East?

Tiger Moms: Is Tough Parenting Really the Answer?[①]

Annie Murphy Paul

This is a story about a mother, two daughters, and two dogs. It's also about Mozart and Mendelssohn, the piano and the violin, and how we made it to Carnegie Hall. This was supposed to be a story of how Chinese parents are better at raising kids than Western ones. But instead, it's about a bitter clash of cultures, a fleeting taste of glory, and how I was humbled by a thirteen-year-old.

A lot of people wonder how Chinese parents raise such stereo-typically successful kids. They wonder what these parents do to produce so many math whizzes and music prodigies, what it's like inside the family, and whether they could do it too. Well, I can

---

① Excerpt from "Tiger Moms: Is Tough Parenting Really the Answer?" *Time*, Thursday, Jan. 20, 2011.

tell them, because I've done it. Here are some things my daughters, Sophia and Louisa, were never allowed to do:
- attend a sleepover
- have a playdate
- be in a school play
- complain about not being in a school play
- watch TV or play computer games
- choose their own extracurricular activities
- get any grade less than an A
- not be the #1 student in every subject except gym and drama
- play any instrument other than the piano or violin
- not play the piano or violin.

It was the "Little White Donkey" incident that pushed many readers over the edge. That's the name of the piano tune that Amy Chua, Yale law professor and self-described "tiger mother", forced her 7-year-old daughter Lulu to practice for hours on end—"right through dinner into the night", with no breaks for water or even the bathroom, until at last Lulu learned to play the piece.

For other readers, it was Chua calling her older daughter Sophia "garbage" after the girl behaved disrespectfully—the same thing Chua had been called as a child by her strict Chinese father. And, oh, yes, for some readers it was the card that young Lulu made for her mother's birthday. "I don't want this," Chua announced, adding that she expected to receive a drawing that Lulu had "put some thought and effort into". Throwing the card back at her daughter, she told her, "I deserve better than this. So I reject this."

Even before *Battle Hymn of the Tiger Mother*, Chua's proudly politically incorrect account of raising her children "the Chinese way", arrived in bookstores Jan. 11, her parenting methods were the incredulous, indignant talk of every playground, supermarket and coffee shop. A prepublication excerpt in the *Wall Street Journal* (titled "Why Chinese Mothers Are Superior") started the ferocious buzz; the online version has been read more than 1 million times and attracted more than 7,000 comments so far. When Chua appeared Jan. 11 on the *Today* show, the usually sunny host Meredith Vieira could hardly contain her contempt as she read aloud a sample of viewer comments: "She's a monster"; "The way she raised her kids is outrageous";

"Where is the love, the acceptance?"

Chua, a petite 48-year-old who carries off a short-skirted wardrobe that could easily be worn by her daughters (now 15 and 18), gave as good as she got. "To be perfectly honest, I know that a lot of Asian parents are secretly shocked and horrified by many aspects of Western parenting," including "how much time Westerners allow their kids to waste — hours on Facebook and computer games — and in some ways, how poorly they prepare them for the future," she told Vieira with a toss of her long hair. "It's a tough world out there."

Chua's reports from the trenches of authoritarian parenthood are indeed disconcerting, even shocking, in their candid admission of maternal ruthlessness. Her book is a *Mommie Dearest* for the age of the memoir, when we tell tales on ourselves instead of our relatives. But there's something else behind the intense reaction to *Tiger Mother*, which has shot to the top of best-seller lists even as it's been denounced on the airwaves and the Internet. Though Chua was born and raised in the U.S., her invocation of what she describes as traditional "Chinese parenting" has hit hard at a national sore spot: our fears about losing ground to China and other rising powers and about adequately preparing our children to survive in the global economy. Her stories of never accepting a grade lower than an A, of insisting on hours of math and spelling drills and piano and violin practice each day (weekends and vacations included), of not allowing playdates or sleepovers or television or computer games or even school plays, for goodness' sake, have left many readers outraged but also defensive. The tiger mother's cubs are being raised to rule the world, the book clearly implies, while the offspring of "weak-willed", "indulgent" Westerners are growing up ill equipped to compete in a fierce global marketplace.

One of those permissive American parents is Chua's husband, Jed Rubenfeld (also a professor at Yale Law School). He makes the occasional cameo appearance in *Tiger Mother*, cast as the tender-hearted foil to Chua's merciless taskmaster. When Rubenfeld protested Chua's harangues over "The Little White Donkey", for instance, Chua informed him that his older daughter Sophia could play the piece when she was Lulu's age. Sophia and Lulu are different people, Rubenfeld remonstrated reasonably. "Oh, no, not this," Chua shot back, adopting a mocking tone: "Everyone is special in their special own way. Even losers are special in their own special way."

With a stroke of her razor-sharp pen, Chua has set a whole nation of parents to wondering: Are we the losers she's talking about? Americans have ample reason to wonder these days, starting with our distinctly loserish economy. Though experts have declared that the recent recession is now over, economic growth in the third quarter of 2010 was an anemic 2.6%, and many economists say unemployment will continue to hover above 9%. Part of the reason? Jobs outsourced to countries like Brazil, India and China. Our housing values have declined, our retirement and college funds have taken a beating, and we're too concerned with paying our monthly bills to save much, even if we had the will to change our ingrained consumerist ways. Meanwhile, in China, the economy is steaming along at more than 10% annual growth, and the country is running a $252.4 billion trade surplus with the U.S. China's government is pumping its new wealth right back into the country, building high-speed rail lines and opening new factories.

If our economy suffers by comparison with China's, so does our system of primary and secondary education. That became clear in December, when the latest test results from the Program for International Student Assessment (PISA) were released. American students were mired in the middle: 17th in reading, 23rd in science and 31st in math—17th overall. For the first time since PISA began its rankings in 2000, students in Shanghai took the test—and they blew everyone else away, achieving a decisive first place in all three categories. When asked to account for the results, education experts produced a starkly simple explanation: Chinese students work harder, with more focus, for longer hours than American students do. It's true that students in boomtown Shanghai aren't representative of those in all of China, but when it comes to metrics like test scores, symbolism matters. Speaking on education in December, a sober President Obama noted that the U.S. has arrived at a "Sputnik moment": the humbling realization that another country is pulling ahead in a contest we'd become used to winning.

Such anxious ruminations seem to haunt much of our national commentary these days, even in the unlikeliest of contexts. When the National Football League postponed a Philadelphia Eagles game in advance of the late-December blizzard on the East Coast, outgoing Pennsylvania governor Ed Rendell was left fuming: "We've become a nation of wusses," he declared on a radio program. "The Chinese are kicking our butt in everything. If this was in China, do you think the Chinese would have called off the game? People would have been marching down to the stadium. They would have walked, and they would have been doing calculus on the way down."

These national identity crises are nothing new. During the mid-20th century, we kept a jealous eye on the Soviets, obsessively monitoring their stores of missiles, their ranks of cosmonauts and even their teams of gymnasts, using these as an index of our own success (not to mention the prospects for our survival). In the 1980s, we fretted that Japan was besting us with its technological wizardry and clever product design—the iPod of the '80s was the Sony Walkman—and its investors' acquisitions of American name-brand companies and prime parcels of real estate.

Now the Soviet Union has dissolved into problem-plagued Russia, and our rivalry with the Japanese has faded as another one has taken its place: last year, China surpassed Japan as the world's second largest economy. The U.S. is still No. 1—but for how long? We're rapidly reaching the limit on how much money the federal government can borrow—and our single biggest creditor is China. How long, for that matter, can the beleaguered U.S. education system keep pace with a rapidly evolving and increasingly demanding global marketplace? Chinese students already have a longer school year than American pupils—and U.S. kids spend more time sitting in front of the TV than in the classroom.

Exercises

I. Reading Comprehension:

There are four suggested answers marked A, B, C and D. Choose the best answer for each question.

1. The phrase "pushed many readers over the edge" at the beginning of the article indicates_____.
   A. the readers realized how malicious Amy Chua was
   B. the readers could hardly understand Amy Chua's good intention even if she is the mother of two daughters
   C. the readers could not understand Amy Chua, but also they feel sorrowful and unacceptable for her parenting
   D. the readers somewhat considered that the tiger mother's parenting was reasonable

2. "Chua's proudly politically incorrect account of raising her children 'the Chinese way'" implies that_____.
   A. Chua's way of education is different from the Chinese way
   B. Chua's method is incorrect and radical
   C. Chua's exemplified way is to distinguish the Western way of parenting with her uniqueness
   D. Chua's way of education is the same with the Chinese pedagogy

3. The "national sore spot" refers to_____.
   A. the declining quality of education in America
   B. the economic threatens from China
   C. the challenges American confronted from China in all round ways
   D. the downfall of America's national strength and its fears about losing the leading position

4. The anecdote of The National Football League implies that_____.
   A. Pennsylvanian governor Ed Rendell laughed at Americans' timidity
   B. it is widely accepted that Chinese are much more progressive than contemporary Americans
   C. it is a public concern that the uneven race of development between China and America would erode USA
   D. a pervading propaganda of China's threatening has over spread

5. The author's attitude in writing this article is_____.
   A. hypercritical
   B. hysteric
   C. pessimistic
   D. critical

Unit 7　My Perspectives on Education from Pedagogies to Globalization

II. Judgments and Implications:
Do the following statements agree with the information given in the passage?
True　if the statement is true according to the passage
False　if the statement contradicts the passage
1. It has been indicated that most Americans disapprove of the Chua's way of parenting.
2. Rubenfeld claims that each individual owns their specialty.
3. Americans attributed the decline of educational qualities to economic slow down.
4. In the 1980s, Japanese beat Americans on economy and technology, because businesses had been merged by Japanese enterprises.
5. China has become the new rivalry of America who claims to be a leading power replacing it.

III. Summary:
Read the following paragraph and complete the summary with the words in the table. Write with only one word.

| proclaim | impoverished | reveal | conflict | superior | perform | behave |
| poverty | controversy | outperform | excel | acknowledge | debunk | |

　　"Tiger mother" Amy Chua, who sparked _____ three years ago with her attack on Western parenting, returns next month with a claim that certain "cultural groups" in America—including Jews, the Chinese and Mormons—"starkly outperform" others.

　　Chua and her husband posit that eight "cultural groups" in America—Jews, Mormons, Chinese, Cuban exiles, Nigerians, Indians, Lebanese-Americans and Iranians, as outlined by the Post-"starkly _____ others". Why, they ask, do Jews win so many Nobel and Pulitzer prizes, why are Mormons running the business and finance sectors, and "why do the children of even _____ and poorly educated Chinese immigrants _____ so remarkably at school?"

　　"That certain groups do much better in America than others—as measured by income, occupational status, test scores, and so on—is difficult to talk about", they _____. In large part this is because the topic feels racially charged. The irony is that the facts actually _____ racial stereotypes.

IV. Critical Questions:
　　How does globalization impact cultural values? How does Tiger Mother's case reflect the process of globalization?

Text B

> **Brainstorming**
>
> *Seminar:* A seminar is, generally, a form of academic instruction, either at an academic institution or offered by a commercial or professional organization. It has the function of bringing together small groups for recurring meetings, focusing each time on some particular subject, in which everyone present is requested to actively participate.
>
> *Workshop:* A workshop is an intensive, short-term learning activity that is designed to provide an opportunity to acquire specific knowledge and skills. In a workshop, participants are expected to learn something that they can later apply in the classroom and to get hands-on experience with the topic, such as developing procedures for classroom observation or conducting action research.

Questions before reading:

What approaches of teaching have you experienced in China's universities? How are they different?

The Tutorial System: The Jewel in the Crown[①]
Ted Tapper & David Palfreyman

What an Oxford tutor does is to get a little group of students together and smoke at them. Men who have been systematically smoked at for four years turn into ripe scholars... A well-smoked man speaks and writes English with a grace that can be acquired in no other way.

The Rise of Tutorial Teaching

Although the Oxbridge colleges shared teaching responsibilities with their respective Universities, it was not until the nineteenth century that Oxbridge's distinctive contribution to pedagogy, the college tutorial, emerged in its present form (tutorials at Oxford, supervisions at Cambridge). While it is unwise to make too sweeping an assertion, it is evident that as the eighteenth century progressed that both Universities, along with most of their colleges, shamefully neglected their responsibilities towards teaching and learning. Oxbridge fell into disrepute, stimulating its ardent critics to call for parliamentary intervention. While most historians concur with the judgment that the rebirth of the ancient universities owed much to parliamentary action, they also point to

---

① Excerpt from *Oxford, the Collegiate University: Conflict, Consensus and Continuity,* Springer, 2012.

the impact of internally driven reforms. The most far-reaching changes centred on the examination system: examinations became more rigorous, written examinations were introduced and class lists were published. In essence, the examination process was partially rationalised, made highly competitive and became more amenable to public scrutiny. University-wide reforms were complemented by changes in some of the more progressive colleges, invariably nudged into action by far-sighted heads acting in concert with a cadre of reform-minded fellows. For example, in spite of bitter internal conflict in the first part of the nineteenth century, Oriel College eased existing restrictions upon the election of fellows, moving towards selection by merit. And at about the same time a group of New College and Balliol tutors started to regenerate the commitment of the colleges to teaching.

If examination reform was the pebble that stimulated change, then innovations in the teaching and learning process were the ripple effect. While the social status of most of the gentlemen commoners was assured and even if they felt the need for a degree then a mere pass would suffice, many of the scholars were not so favoured. They required a good degree, or even the opportunities afforded by a college fellowship, to make their way in the wider world. Thus competition was both intensified and made more precarious by the reformed examination process. Where was the ambitious scholar to look for help? Few of the unreformed colleges would have inspired confidence. The inevitable consequence was the emergence of the private coach who, although often despised in official college circles, fulfilled — and often admirably fulfilled—a glaring need.

What could the ambitious scholar acquire from his private coach that he would be most unlikely to obtain from his college tutor? Although Curthoys, in his research into the "unreformed" colleges, makes the point that there is disputed evidence as to precisely how many Oxford undergraduates used private coaches, and indeed whether they were really needed at all, he concludes: "But for 'reading' men private tutors offered two facilities which could not be generally obtained from their college tutors: specialised tuition and individual attention." And the same was true of Cambridge where the coaches not only offered academic competence and rigorous training but also the student "could expect from the coach the warm and personal interest which college officers failed to provide". While such a claim may be too sweeping, the provision of private tuition was a competitive marketplace in which the competence of the tutors was measured by the examination success of their students. Either the coach delivered results or his fees were in jeopardy for there were others waiting in the wings to take his place. The publication of the class lists was therefore as much a trial for the private coaches as for their students.

Whilst there may have been no inevitability about the eventual demise of the private coach, it is difficult to imagine that this state of affairs could continue indefinitely. The very futures of the two collegiate universities were at stake, either they reformed or they stagnated. With the wisdom of hindsight the reinstatement of the colleges as the major focus of teaching and learning under the guidance of the college tutors seemed the most logical outcome to the reform of the ancient English universities. Not only were the tutors a large organised interest (the Tutors Association was convened in 1852 at Oriel College in direct response to the creation of the first nineteenth century Royal Commission) but also their preeminence was assured by the emergence of new social forces. Like the public schools in the latter half of the nineteenth century, both Oxford and Cambridge were responding to the needs of an expanding bourgeoisie that was intent on using education to sustain its newly won social status. The clerical party represented a declining past while "the endowment of research" party constituted an interest whose time had yet to arrive. In the meantime, it was the day of the college tutor.

The consequence was that the college tutors secured for themselves a respected career built upon teaching and the pursuit of scholarship while the colleges were reinvigorated as centres of national learning. Although the collegial ties to the established church were steadily eroded, there remained—at least for the time being—a favoured place for the gentleman commoner. What the colleges offered the bourgeoisie was not simply an academic education but the possibility of acquiring a highly valued form of cultural capital, the possession of which almost guaranteed rich returns in the job market. The colleges were integral to the process through which the student acquired the correct cultural capital, and intrinsic to college life was a teaching and learning experience built around the tutorial system. When Rose and Ziman trumpet Oxbridge's fame as teaching universities they are recognizing the powerful allure of the college tutorial. It is the tutorial that has been given the credit for stimulating "intellects to sparkle", of filling "heads with knowledge" and imparting "great wisdom". It is critical to remember that the college tutorial was not merely a pedagogical method, the best means of giving untutored undergraduates a higher education. Tutorials also provided the context for moral instruction; although the moral flavour could be either religious (Newman) or secular (Jowett), the purpose was to impart social values as well as learning. The dons, like the public school masters, were acquiring in the latter half of the nineteenth century the role of in loco parentis. So, for many well-heeled Victorian parents the purchase of an Oxbridge education represented not only a sound economic investment but also a vital stage in the rite de passage of their male offspring, the best means of making them both economically secure and worthy citizens.

The Long Love Affair

Throughout the past century in which the tutorial system has taken root in Oxbridge, the belief that it remains a highly effective pedagogical method has persisted. For example, in 1909 Oxford's Chancellor, Lord Curzon, was moved to observe: "...if there is any product of which Oxford has special reason to be proud, which has stamped its mark on the lives and characters of generations of men, and has excited the outspoken envy of other nations, it is that wonderful growth of personal tuition which has sprung up in our midst almost unawares..." Some 60 years later, the Franks Inquiry gave its own powerful endorsement:

Unit 7 My Perspectives on Education from Pedagogies to Globalization

At its heart is a theory of teaching young men and women to think for themselves. The undergraduate is sent off to forage for himself....and to produce a coherent exposition of his ideas on the subject set. The essay or prepared work is then read by its author and criticized by the tutor.

In this discussion the undergraduate should benefit by struggling to defend the positions he has taken up, by realizing the implications of the argument, and by glimpsing the context in which a more experienced scholar sees his problem.

In a very similar vein, we read in the North Report that the tutorial system "encourages the student to take an active rather than passive role in learning and develops skills in self-directed study and working independently, as well as analytical and critical skills", and, moreover, it provides the undergraduate with "the opportunity to discuss particular topics in considerable detail with the tutor, who may well be a leading expert in the subject or a young active researcher at the forefront of the discipline..." And vice-chancellors, especially in Oration speeches, have felt no need to be coy: "A properly organized tutorial is the *best method ever devised* for training minds and exposing fallacies. Generations of Oxford graduates owe their subsequent success in life to their tutors", and, while there may be shortcomings, "None of this detracts from *the special excellence* of the tutorial or the esteem in which it deserves to be held." In his incoming address the current vice chancellor referred to Oxford's "commitment to excellence" and concluded the list of virtues with, "And excellence in those twin Oxford jewels, the collegiate structure and the tutorial system." And to complete the story, one of the authors of this book has edited *The Oxford Tutorial* (New College's homage to tutorial teaching), which significantly has the sub-title, *"Thanks, you taught me how to think"*, and is due to appear—illustrating the international fascination with the topic—in a Chinese edition.

How is this protracted love affair to be explained? There are two key elements. First, as the quotations we have presented demonstrate, there is a very powerful sentiment within Oxbridge that tutorials are an immensely effective pedagogical tool. Second, like the idea of collegiality itself, as this chapter will show, the tutorial as proven to be an exceedingly flexible concept. This is in spite of the fact that there is considerable consistency in the debate about both their supposed virtues and how they should function—teaching undergraduates how to think critically through the constructive intellectual interaction of tutor and undergraduate(s). Therefore, as with the idea of collegiality, we have to reflect on how far the tutorial as a pedagogical tool can be stretched before it fails to achieve its central purpose.

In the classical model the student is advised by a tutorial fellow or (at Cambridge) by the Director of Studies who arranges his or her programme of tuition. Ideally the tutor is a teaching fellow of the student's own college and they meet weekly, one—to one, to analyse a piece of work prepared by the student. Even if this ideal model exists, there is far less certainty as to the precise conduct of a tutorial, although there is a measure of consensus as to how they should *not* proceed. There is widespread agreement that tutorials should not be used either to cover the full syllabus or to convey only factual information, and certainly tutors should *not* impose their own interpretations upon their tutees. On the contrary, the tutorial is perceived as a forum in which an exchange of views occurs; the tutor is a participant rather than an authority figure. Furthermore, as tutorial discussion is centred around the student's reading aloud a prepared essay, he or she has a significant say in determining the pace and direction of the analysis.

What are the qualities that this process instills? Franks argued that undergraduates were taught "to think for their themselves": that in the process of preparing their weekly essays they learnt how "to forage" independently and "to produce a coherent exposition" of their own ideas; however, in the course of the tutorial hour itself they acquired the ability "to defend" the positions they had adopted in face of the tutor's critique. All this was reiterated by the North Commission, which also added, in genuflection to the emerging concern with "transferable skills": "to gain experience in debating" and "to develop effective oral communications skills".

For the tutor the teaching situation itself may bring its own rewards (especially at Oxbridge where the students are likely to be both talented and motivated) and, should the examination results of your tutees be especially good, it is not unreasonable to suspect that this is direct consequence of your skilled teaching. Inevitably, the occasional tutor is bound to allude to the deep insights that have been revealed during the course of an undergraduate tutorial, but one suspects that for every time this occurs there have been literally thousands of tutorials in which the hour follows well-trodden paths. Does the occasional flash of insight compensate for this large expenditure of teaching energy? If the teaching experience itself is considered by the tutor to be rewarding presumably the reply is positive; otherwise one suspects that the answers would be more circumspect.

Undoubtedly, central to the longevity of the tutorial system has been its flexibility as a pedagogical method. Whereas the Franks Inquiry maintained that tutorial teaching could succeed only when "the tutor takes undergraduates singly, or in pairs", it is clear that tutorial teaching has become in some cases little more than small-group teaching. For example, while the North Commission found that only a very small proportion of tutorials "had four or more students attending", it was still prepared to describe these as tutorials. Furthermore, the proportions are not as small as the North Report implies because its own evidence shows that some 17.3% of Oxford undergraduates were taking tutorials with four or more students and only 25.0% were in single-student tutorials.

While the development of inter-collegiate lecturing was a nineteenth century innovation, the trend towards undergraduates taking tutorials at Oxford with either a fellow of another college or a non-fellow (mainly a graduate student) is a more recent growth. The Franks Inquiry revealed that in Michelmas Term 1964, 67% of undergraduates received tutorial supervision from a fellow and/or lecturer of their own college, whereas the North Commission shows that in the Hilary Term of 1996 the same figure ranged from 64.8% for the wealthier colleges to 55.4% for the poorer colleges.

Unit 7 My Perspectives on Education from Pedagogies to Globalization

The evidence suggests that while most students may continue to receive the majority of their tutorials in their own colleges, it is sometimes a close-run thing. Moreover, although the North Commission may feel that the graduate student can justifiably be described as "a young active researcher at the forefront of the discipline", she or he may in reality be little more than a conveniently located and relatively cheap source of untrained and untested academic labour. However, it is more than possible that energy and enthusiasm may compensate for experience and potential *ennui*.

In "An Open Letter to the Chairman of the North Commission", a group of college fellows argued, "....our combined experience suggests that to use a Cambridge expression, the 'director of studies' element of what we do is the cornerstone of the tutorial system. With a model of this kind, it is possible to regard the senior academic as at the centre of tutorial teaching, whilst also paying heed to the value of a reasonable proportion of that teaching being undertaken by junior academics, including graduate students." However, if the key, and indeed only variable explicitly defined, is who is in control of the system then it is possible to imagine that the model of tutorial teaching could be stretched indefinitely. And it is not surprising to find that the "Open Letter" offers a very liberal interpretation of what constitutes tutorial teaching:

There is certainly no intention on our part of supporting the idea that this must necessarily involve the one-to-one tutorial with an essay read by the undergraduate to the tutor and commented upon by the latter....we believe that our system encourages tutors to use and develop their own teaching methods and styles.

Exercises

I. Reading Comprehension:

There are four suggested answers marked A, B, C and D. Choose the best answer for each question.

1. What measures cause of the emergence of the tutorial system?
   A. Parliamentary intervention.
   B. Internally driven reforms.
   C. Reform on examinational system.
   D. Malperformance and irresponsibility of most colleges.

2. The reforms of examination system in 19th century included all of the following except _____.
   A. examinations became more rigorous
   B. written examination was introduced
   C. test results were published
   D. selection by merit was introduced

3. The boom of the private coach was inevitable because _____.
   A. private coach delivered individual attention
   B. private coach was more competent than college tutor

C. private coach offered more vigorous training
   D. private coach met the demands of social progress
4. The tutorial system helped students to develop all of the following skills except_____.
   A. independent learning skills
   B. analytical and critical skills
   C. communication skills
   D. social skills

II. Judgments and Implications:

Do the following statements agree with the information given in the passage?
True   if the statement is true according to the passage
False   if the statement contradicts the passage

1. The examination system reformation in 19th century was quite successful and met the social demands.
2. Curthoys doubted the necessity of private coach and held no favorable points toward them.
3. Only few undergraduates in Oxford and Cambridge used private coaching.
4. College tutorial not only aimed to provide cultural values but also emphasized on imparting moral instruction and social values.
5. In the ideal tutorial system, the tutor only taught one student and his major task was to impart knowledge and information.

III. Critical Questions:

What are the advantages of tutorial teaching? What kind of teaching activities do you like? Why and Why not?

Text C

Brainstorming

Nation State: The nation state is a state that self-identifies as deriving its political legitimacy from serving as a sovereign entity for a nation as a sovereign territorial unit. The state is a political and geopolitical entity; the nation is a cultural and/or ethnic entity. The term "nation state" implies that the two geographically coincide.

The concept and actuality of the nation state can be compared and contrasted with that of the multinational state, city state, empire, confederation, and other state forms with which it may overlap.

Unit 7　My Perspectives on Education from Pedagogies to Globalization

Questions before reading:
　What is your view of national identity?
　Do you think learning English would weaken the national identity of a country? Why?

Education, the Nation-State, and Global Movement[1]

Joseph I. Zajda

　We begin this section with a short personal reflection. Recently, one of us (Nadine) returned from South Africa. On the flight back from South Africa, she sat next to a woman, Riannon, from Cape Town, and her daughter, Tamara. During the flight, Nadine discovered that Riannon had only just returned from a 6-week holiday to the USA a few days before, on Wednesday. It was now Sunday, and Riannon and Tamara were back on the plane again—a 30 plus hour journey—as Riannon's father was having emergency heart surgery in the USA. Riannon was born in South Africa, but has lived most of her life in Canada and the USA. However, it was Tamara, her 10-year-old daughter, whose story—whose identity—was the most fascinating. Of Indian descent, Tamara was born in Canada of South African and Canadian parents, and has lived her life between South Africa and the USA. Her parents recently divorced, and her mother remarried—to a Zimbabwean of British descent. It occurred to Nadine that, in the complexity of her situation, national belonging may present a formidable and daunting dilemma. Tamara might very well feel more comfortable—more at "home"—on a plane, for the ground presents a dizzying array of conflicting affiliations: Canada, South Africa, the USA, India, Zimbabwe, and Britain. To whom, to what, does Tamara owe allegiance? Her mother expressed dismay that Tamara's expensive private school in Cape Town required her to learn two local languages—Afrikaans and Xhosa; neither appears useful in her decidedly global future. French, Spanish, even Chinese, Riannon observed, would be more useful to Tamara than languages spoken only on a speck of the earth.

　Tamara's reality, and her (possibly large) stack of passports and permanent residence visas, highlights some of the challenges of applying a bounded paradigm of "nation" to the decidedly less bounded inhabitants of the globe at the turn of the twenty-first century. While certainly Tamara is among the global elites in her multiple affiliations and constant jet travel the cracks in the edifice of nation extend well beyond those who are economically privileged and physically mobile.

　National identities are grounded in sustaining mythologies, which assume that lines are easily drawn between one "people" and another. Nations, of course, have been heavily invested in this inventing and policing of lines: the borders that separate nations

---

[1] Excerpt from "Global Pedagogies: Schooling for the Future", *Springer Science & Business Media*, 2010.

can be porous (as between the USA and Canada, particularly before September11), extremely rigid and tension-filled (as between North and South Korea), or a combination of the two. For example, the border between the USA and Mexico is both fluid and rigid. While American companies, such as Tyson Foods, are accused of actively recruiting and facilitating illegal migration to fill low-paying, hazardous processing jobs (such as in slaughterhouses), US border patrol agents simultaneously capture dozens of Mexicans every night, as they unsuccessfully attempt to cross the "no-man's land" between Mexico and Texas. Thus, states often face contradictory impulses: to maintain national borders and national identities, and simultaneously to erode these same borders when it suits their economic and political purposes.

At the same time, there are forces that are increasingly beyond the control of states. As Saskia Sassen observes, the "global cities" of New York, London, and Tokyo are situated in, but are not of, their corresponding nation-states of the USA, Britain, and Japan. Thus, "New York" is not necessarily the quintessential "American" city, but is, in fact, the exact opposite. Less economically advantaged states are also forced to respond to global forces, and rework their ideas of national identity. Peggy Levitt's research on the Dominican Republic exemplifies the way in which states reshape their notions of citizenship to accommodate new global realities. Dominican communities are increasingly transnational and diasporic, and the economic health of the Dominican Republic depends on the movement of its citizens residing abroad. In response, the state is rethinking its idea of "citizenship" and parliamentary representation, to ensure the continuation of close national ties between the state, the nation, and Dominican nationals living abroad. Many other nation-states, including Mexico, Brazil, Ecuador, Portugal, and India are similarly revamping and broadening the way the "nation" is imagined, to embrace those beyond the physical borders of the nation. Aiwha Ong's writing similarly documents the way that Chinese nationals deploy "flexible citizenship" to develop new spaces of attachment that defy traditional national borders. Flexible citizenship is also evident in multiple other venues: Mexican President (then presidential candidate) Vicente Fox campaigning in the USA for Mexican votes, and calls in South African newspapers reminding Greek citizens to vote in upcoming Greek elections. Instead of rejecting their diasporic citizens, many states are embracing, and in some cases, even encouraging, the extension of the national imaginary well beyond geographic, political lines. As Appadurai observes, there are increasing patterns of "sovereignty without territoriality", where the assumed connection between a geographical locale and a "people" is fractured.

In the following section, we turn to a discussion of two qualitative studies that suggest that youth's identities are increasingly being formed in this "postnational space", the interstice that runs between, above, and below nations, and seriously disrupts homogeneous national identities promoted by educational systems.

Unit 7 My Perspectives on Education from Pedagogies to Globalization

The United States: Destabilizing Center Identities

The data discussed in this section are drawn from a comparative study of 46 American and Australian undergraduates who studied abroad for 5—12 months during the period 2001—2002. For comparative purposes, the study was limited to American students studying abroad in Australia, and Australian students studying abroad in the USA. All students were interviewed before their study abroad experience, and when they returned. Students were also e-mailed a series of questions approximately 2 months after the beginning of their study abroad experience.

While data were collected from both American and Australian students, for purposes of this essay, we will discuss only data from the American students, who were enrolled at a large, public research university in the Midwest.

Before studying abroad, American undergraduates had a strong, though undeveloped, sense of their national identity, and little to no understanding of how they would be positioned as "Americans" outside of the USA. Thus, they are surprised at their predeparture orientation when an invited Australian student comments "Australians hate Americans". While the study abroad advisor, and other professional members of the staff, attempted to tone down and smooth over her observations, the impact of her statement was significant, as outgoing students were surprised, puzzled, and alarmed by this (largely) new information. For example, during the predeparture interview, Danielle commented, "Because I live in America, I don't really understand how Americans are mean".

For the American students in Australia, the most meaningful challenge to their sense of a national self emerges as they begin to realize that they are not the sole "authors" of their American identity, and how "America" as symbol is deployed in the world. For example, Karen comments,

I saw how much information that the rest of the world, or Australia specifically, gets about us. Because they actually get a lot of information about what is going on here, and I felt almost disappointed that I didn't know, it seemed like I didn't know as much stuff as some people knew about the United States.

While some students retreat into what Calhoun would label a "thick" or exclusionary identity, others actively attempt to disrupt this closed sense of nation, and to broaden their sense of the possibilities of a national identity that is not invested solely in itself and its superiority. Linda reflects,

I had no idea that people had this view of Americans, that we thought that we were just so great and we just dominate and are in charge. We're very snotty and rude and get our way. And that was kind of a shock to me. So the whole time I was there, I tried not to portray that image as much as I could because I think that's sort of terrible.

In this instance, Linda's encounter with Australians and the resultant encounter with her own American identity leads to a practice and rewriting that does not sway between "thick" and "thin" identities. Students like Linda do not reject their national identity, but attempt to rewrite it outside of the mythology of American domination that they have been surrounded by since birth. Thus, they explore a decidedly postnational aspect of their American selves. While retaining an "American" trace, they simultaneously explore the connections and possibilities that exist in understanding the perspectives of others, and of formulating an identity that is grounded in the multiple, local attachments.

Malaysia: Diasporic and National Selves

Malaysia is a particularly rich arena for examining the interplay between national and global imperatives, because the Malaysian government simultaneously insists on binding the nation together through the promulgation of Malay culture and language, while embracing global capitalism, and the importance of international education for its youth. Thus, Malaysian youth confront a national identity that is much less exclusionary, much more open to and of the world, than their American counterparts, though it still insists on a strictly bounded sense of culture and identity.

Malaysian students in Australia are aware of the contradictory nature of "national" identity in Malaysia. As Ahmad reflects, "English is the global language and even in Malaysia you cannot go very far unless you are a confident speaker of English. That is why the Malaysian government now realizes it can't be anti-English like it was." Here, we see one of the contradictory moments in the emergent paradigms of nation: for Malaysia to succeed as a nation, to maintain its sovereignty, and to grow economically, it is forced to embrace English, a language that is not of its nation. To refuse to do so, as Ahmad suggests, would be to undercut the growth of the Malaysian nation. For Chinese Malaysians, whose opportunities are limited in Malaysia by government affirmative action policies that favor the Bumiputras (Muslim and indigenous Malays), studying in Australia expands their employment possibilities. For many Malaysian Chinese students, their ability to speak English and Chinese gives them a global competitive advantage unavailable to Bumiputras: what is a disadvantage within the bounds of their nation (their Chinese heritage) becomes an advantage within a broader, global landscape. These Chinese Malaysian students do not solely reject their Malaysian national identity, but embrace a diasporic Chinese one—a specific node of identity (or what Appadurai might refer to as a "new patriotism") that is available to them through their experience in Australia.

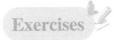

I. Reading Comprehension:

There are four suggested answers marked A, B, C and D. Choose the best answer for each question.

1. The author used the example of American companies to show _____.
   A. the relationship between the two countries on their board could be loose
   B. the relationship between the two countries on their board could be tight
   C. the relationship between the two countries on their board could be random

Unit 7 My Perspectives on Education from Pedagogies to Globalization

   D. both A and B
2. Dominican communities are increasingly _____.
   A. tolerant
   B. unbounded
   C. exclusive
   D. unrest
3. A lot of countries now broaden the way in which the nation is imagined, because _____.
   A. the boards between countries would not exist any more
   B. each country wants to broaden their territory
   C. they want to include those beyond the physical borders of the nation
   D. people could not anticipate what would happen to every nation
4. Karen realized that American could not interpret American identity, but should consider _____.
   A. how the world develop the idea of America as a symbol
   B. how the expert explains
   C. how the constitution regulates
   D. how their competitors understand
5. As Linda reflects, she thinks that _____.
   A. Americans are so great and dominant in the whole world
   B. there is nothing to fear about people's idea about Americans
   C. people's opinion could only be served as references
   D. Americans are arrogant and vulgar

II. Judgments and Implications:

Do the following statements agree with the information given in the passage?
True   if the statement is true according to the passage
False if the statement contradicts the passage

1. Malaysian government devotes a lot of efforts on promoting its culture and language by refusing other languages to endanger its own.
2. The national identity of Malaysian youth is rather exclusionary, while their American counterpart confronts a national identify which is much less exclusionary.
3. Malaysian students in Austria have been aware of the contradictory nature of "national" identity in Malaysia.
4. In order to be successful as a nation, to protect its sovereignty and develop its economy, Malaysian government has realized the importance of learning English.
5. If Malaysian people do not study English, it would not influence their development, for they could purely rely on themselves.

III. Summary:

Complete the summary below. Choose ONLY ONE WORD from the text for each answer.

In the United States: Destabilizing Center Identities section, the author adopted a _____ study between _____ and _____ undergraduates who studied abroad for 5—12 months during the period 2001—2002. In order to compare, it would be confined to study American students studying abroad in Australia and Australian students studying in America and _____ all the students before they left and after they left their home country. Also the students needed to accomplish a series of _____. Although the author collected both data, this essay only focused on the data from American students. In fact, the American students had little sense of their national identity, so they could not understand how they could be positioned as "Americans" outside _____. Therefore, they were quite _____ when Australian students said _____. The author also provided us with two cases by Karen and Linda, who explore a decidedly _____ aspect of American selves. While retaining an "American" trace, they simultaneously explore the connections and possibilities that exist in understanding the perspectives of others, and formulate an identity that is grounded in the multiple, local attachments.

IV. Critical Questions:

How do people respond to identity change and face the challenges of globalization in education?

Learning Skills

Critical Reading Skills I

One key aspect of reading smarter is taking active control of the reading process. Analytical reading techniques help students mentally organize information, make decisions about their reading, and engage critically with what they read. Students integrate speed reading, previewing, and reporting skills into an active, flexible approach that takes into account both their reader's purpose and the material at hand.

1. Building an Organizational Map

One important analytical reading skill is keeping track of a book or article's organization. Building an organizational map helps readers mentally organize information and follow the author's development of ideas, an important reader's purpose for nonfiction.

In any nonfiction book or article, the author presents an idea (or ideas), develops that idea, and finally resolves it. Each author does this differently. In order to build an organizational map, students consider what the author is trying to accomplish in each part of the book. Doing this helps them get a solid grasp of the author's purpose and how the material is organized to achieve that purpose.

2. Making Decisions Throughout the Reading Process

Another key aspect of analytical reading is making active decisions about which skills to use and when to use them. When making decisions about their reading, students consider both their reader's purpose (why they are reading the material) and features of the material, like length and difficulty level. Students learn to experiment and figure out which tools are most appropriate for their reading tasks.

The first decision students make with any reading is how to preview: what to look at in order to ensure maximum comprehension, concentration, and recall. Previewing also sets students up to make good decisions as they read, including determining what to read and what to skip, as well as what speed and which speed reading skills are appropriate for particular material.

Once students begin reading, they need to decide how to approach the material.

Top-down and **bottom-up** are strategies of information processing and knowledge ordering, mostly involving software, but also other humanistic and scientific theories (see systemics). In practice, they can be seen as a style of thinking and teaching. In many cases top-down is used as a synonym of analysis or decomposition, and bottom-up of synthesis.

Top-Down	Bottom-Up
Holistic reading	Reading word by word
Paragraph comprehension	Sentence understanding
Sentence understanding	Paragraph comprehension
Reading word by word	Holistic reading

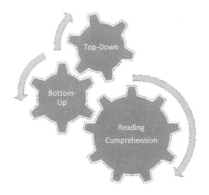

3. Basic Skills in Reading English Articles

Predicting (preview): Using the first paragraph to make predictions

The first paragraphs of a passage can help you make predictions about the context of a passage.

The first paragraph often contains:
- The topic sentence (a summary of the main idea of the passage)
- A definition of the topic
- The author's opinion
- Clues to the organization of the passage

Guessing: As we read English textbook for college courses, we may find many words that are unfamiliar words to us. Don't expect we will know all words in our texts. By guessing word meanings we will be able to figure out the meanings of words without consulting a dictionary.

Work out the meaning of a word in the context, three steps need to be followed:
- Identify the part of speech
- Guess the meaning with knowledge of vocabulary (prefix, root, suffix)
- Detect the meaning of a word in the context

Skimming: Speed is often important when we are reading. We may have a lot to read but not much time. For this kind of reading we usually do not want to know and remember everything. We only want to find out something about the book or article. We can do this by skimming.

We may want to skim:
- Newspaper or magazine articles
- Book covers in a bookstore
- Library books
- Mystery, detective, or other novels

Scanning: Scanning is very fast reading. When the learners scan, they skip over many words. They have to look for some information as precise as they can. Scanning is especially important for improving the learners' accuracy. Many of learners try to read every word. If they learn to scan, they can learn to read information they need understand faster.

The purposes to use scanning are:
- Understanding descriptions
- Understanding details
- Understand specific information

4. Reading Critically

When students read critically, they bring their own thoughts and opinions to what they read. Reading is like engaging in a mental conversation with the author—the reader isn't merely absorbing what the author has to say, but contributing his or her own thoughts and ideas.

Here are some things students learn to ask themselves as they read:
- What are the author's main ideas?
- Do I agree with this author's ideas? What questions do I have?
- What are some additional examples that support or disprove what this author is saying? Have I read other materials in the past that support or contradict this author's ideas?
- Where might the author go next with these ideas?
- How does this material connect to my own experiences?

Brainstorming

Use brainstorming activities in diverse subject areas. Brainstorming encourages students to think open-endedly and creatively. For instance, if presenting a science lesson on the seasons of the year, challenge students to brainstorm differences between winter and summer. If presenting a lesson on animal species, challenge students to brainstorm characteristics about a certain animal or species. No matter the subject area, brainstorming reinforces critical thinking skills and encourages mental development.

Reading reflections

Take advantage of group reading to develop analytical thinking skills. After reading a chapter or short story aloud to students, ask the students an open-ended question that cannot be answered affirmatively or negatively. For instance, ask the children to evaluate a character or to predict the action or outcome of the next chapter. Facilitate a discussion between students, encouraging them to contribute new ideas and to respond to classmates' ideas.

Making connections

An essential component of analytical thinking is the ability to make connections between personal experience or knowledge to new material or concepts. To practice this, challenge students to think critically about instances or scenarios that they have experienced that are similar to scenarios in narratives or stories. Use this activity in a social studies lesson, such as a lesson about historical treatment of minorities. Ask each student to think about a time when he felt unjustly persecuted by others or excluded from a group. Invite students to share their experiences aloud with the class and have a discussion about the implications of discrimination.

5. Discourse Analysis

In analytical reading, analyzing the functions of sentences and organizational structures enables readers to understand the text deeply.

General-particular

In more recent years the curriculum widened beyond the basic skills and exercise in general knowledge to encompass a wider range of subject areas and contents. The methods of teaching these new subjects also became more sophisticated, although retaining the elements of telling, writing, rehearsal and recall. Three models have been elaborated to describe, post hoc, some of the changes which have taken place in teaching methods...

Problem-solving

While it is unwise to make too sweeping an assertion, it is evident that as the eighteenth century progressed that both universities, along with most of their colleges, shamefully neglected their responsibilities towards teaching and learning. Oxbridge fell into disrepute, stimulating its ardent critics to call for parliamentary intervention. While most historians concur with the judgment that the rebirth of the ancient universities owed much to parliamentary action, they also point to the impact of internally driven reforms. The most far-reaching changes centred on the examination system: examinations became more rigorous, written examinations were introduced and class lists were published.

Cause-effect

The child has his own instincts and tendencies, but we do not know what these mean until we can translate them into their social equivalents. We must be able to carry them back into a social past and see them as the inheritance of previous race activities. We must also be able to project them into the future to see what their outcome and end will be. In the illustration just used, it is the ability to see in the child's babblings the promise and potency of a future social intercourse and conversation which enables one to deal in the proper way with that instinct.

6. Cohesion and Coherence

Read these sentences again and find out why they are important.

The methods of teaching these new subjects also became more sophisticated, although retaining the elements of telling, writing, rehearsal and recall.

While it is unwise to make too sweeping an assertion, it is evident that as the eighteenth century progressed that both universities, along with most of their colleges, shamefully neglected their responsibilities towards teaching and learning.

While most historians concur with the judgment that the rebirth of the ancient universities owed much to parliamentary action, they also point to the impact of

Unit 7 My Perspectives on Education from Pedagogies to Globalization

internally driven reforms.
The child has his own instincts and tendencies, <u>but we do not know what these mean until we can translate them into their social equivalents.</u>

Notice the following underlined words in the sentences and use another appropriate word to replace them without changing its meaning in the context.
While it is unwise to make too sweeping an <u>assertion</u>, it is <u>evident</u> that...
Three models have been <u>elaborated to describe...</u>
They also <u>point to</u> the impact of...
<u>In the illustration just used,</u> it is the ability to see in...

Group Work Activities

Analytical reading practice
Directions: Analytical reading as a means of study skills enables readers to further understanding from superficial level to the deep insights of the literature. Therefore, teachers need to provide sample texts from extensive reading materials or IELTS reading exercise to let students practice.

Students need to work in groups to complete the following tasks:
1. Share your own reading experience with your members to discuss the key points of analytical reading.
2. Search for reading materials to practice analytical reading skills.

Requirements:
- Reading materials need to be selected in academic standards. (No stories)
- The length of reading materials need to be kept in at least 1,000 words.
- The completion of the reading task should be kept in a time limit.

Self-evaluation Form

What are the main objectives in this unit?
_____
_____
_____

What useful vocabularies or expressions have you learned from this unit?
_____
_____
_____

What key terms and educational knowledge have you learned?
_____
_____
_____

Have you used the learning skills before? Why do you think they are useful or not useful?
_____
_____
_____

If possible, what would you like to add to make learning more interesting and relevant?
_____
_____
_____

Unit 8

Education and Teachers' Development

Introduction

Defining Teaching and Teacher Education[1]
James Calderhead & Susan B. Shorrock

"What makes a good teacher?" is a question that has intrigued and challenged philosophers, researchers, policy-makers and teachers for many centuries. It is also a question that has generated diverse answers, varying in their nature and degree of specificity in different countries and across different periods in history. Educational thinkers and writers have variously emphasized different aspects of the teaching role— the teacher as expert in their subject; the teacher as facilitator of learning; the teacher as a motivator and source of inspiration; the teacher as upholder of moral standards. Recent educational policy documents in the UK, and in many other countries, have tended to become more prescriptive in the views of teaching which they support— often construing teachers as the deliverers of a prescribed curriculum, necessitating the acquisition of particular skills and competences. At the same time, media reports would suggest that public expectations of schools and teachers have become more extensive: schools are not only institutions in which children acquire knowledge and skills, they are also places where children learn to socialize and cooperate with others, learn about the world of work and prepare for responsible citizenship.

Views about the role of the teacher are culturally embedded. Substantial variations in how school teachers think about their roles and responsibilities have been found across France, Spain and the UK, for example. Spanish teachers, working within a democratic management system, in which head-teachers are elected from amongst teachers within the school, have been found to be more likely to think of teaching as a collaborative activity and to have a stronger sense of responsibility to the local community. French school teachers, on the other hand, tend to think of their role as relating much more to expertise in their subject specialisms and do not regard their responsibilities as encompassing the pastoral care that their English counterparts value more highly.

---

[1] Excerpt from *Understanding Teacher Education*. London: The Falmer Press, 1997.

How we conceptualize the work of teachers inevitably influences how we think about their professional preparation, and ultimately shapes suggestions for the further improvement of teacher education. Zeichner and Feiman-Nemser provide interesting classifications of ideologies, or conceptual orientations, in teacher education which they suggest have characterized reform movements within the United States over the past century. These orientations refer to a body of values and beliefs about teaching and teacher education that at different points in history have been particularly influential in shaping the nature of initial teacher education courses. The academic orientation, for example, emphasizes teachers' subject expertise and sees the quality of the teacher's own education as his/her professional strength; in this view, a sound liberal arts education is seen as the crucial ingredient of teacher preparation. The practical orientation, on the other hand, emphasizes the artistry and classroom technique of the teacher, viewing the teacher as a craftsperson; it therefore attaches importance to classroom experience and apprenticeship models of learning to teach. The technical orientation derives from a behaviourist model of teaching and learning, emphasizes the knowledge and behavioural skills that teachers require and has been associated with microteaching and competency-based approaches to teacher education. The personal orientation emphasizes the importance of interpersonal relationships in the classroom, often derives support from humanistic psychology, and views learning to teach as a process of "becoming" or personal development; in this view, teacher education takes the form of offering a safe environment which encourages experimentation and discovery of personal strengths. The critical inquiry orientation views schooling as a process of social reform and emphasizes the role of schools in promoting democratic values and reducing social inequities; an important aspect of teacher education is therefore seen as enabling prospective teachers to become aware of the social context of schools and of the social consequences of their own actions as teachers; within this orientation, teacher education functions to help teachers become critical, reflective change-agents.

These ideologies or value positions are clearly identifiable across national boundaries. In many countries one can distinguish similar, competing ideologies or orientations in how teaching and teacher education are viewed. Arguably all of these orientations offer a perspective on teachers' professional preparation and all simultaneously have implications for the design of teacher education courses, although frequently they appear to vie with each other for precedence in the prevailing language with which teacher education is publicly discussed, rather than being thought of as complementary or mutually relevant and informative. Inevitably, learning to teach involves the acquisition of certain knowledge and skills, but teaching is also a matter of individuality and personal expression; it is also often subject focused, but teachers' actions are embedded within a particular institutional context to which they need to adapt and which may well require them to analyse critically its nature and structure and its contribution to the overall goals of education. Teacher education, in effect, is too complex to be characterized by any one of these orientations alone, and inevitably encapsulates aspects of them all.

Questions after reading:

What teaching ideology is of most concern? Can you explain and illustrate with examples?

Group work:

Topic: What qualities have to be equipped with to become a good teacher? Can you provide a list of good qualities?

Directions: Work as a group and share your ideas with others.

Brainstorming

Pre/In-service education: The education and training provided to student teachers before they have undertaken any teaching. /The education and training provided to teachers after they have undertaken any teaching.

Novice/Master teacher: A novice teacher is any teacher having less than one school year of public school, or accredited private school, classroom teaching experience. / A leader who has mastered the management of their classrooms and found a way to accelerate learning for all their students. These educators are exceptional communicators who have a strong connection with their students.

Questions before reading:

What would be the biggest problem for the first lesson of a novice teacher?

What would frustrate a novice teacher so desperate that he or she may abandon teaching profession?

The Novice Teacher: Armed and Dangerous
—A Cautionary Tale[①]

As professors whose primary experience at the college level has been in teacher education programs, we have had the opportunity to teach and learn with hundreds of prospective teachers. Many leave their training with an almost palpable zeal for change. Unfortunately, enthusiasm, strong teaching skills, and even a love for students and learning are not enough. Making change, any change, is slow, sometimes painful, and

---

① Excerpt from *Creating and Sustaining the Constructivist Classroom*. California: Corwin Press, 2005.

exponentially more difficult as the number of people one wants to include in the change process increases—which is why we begin this book with a cautionary tale about the peril of banking on achieving too much too soon.

Susan Jackson

One of our best students, a young woman we'll call Susan Jackson, was as excited about teaching as anyone we can remember. Susan was crackerjack student. She was dynamic, engaging, and highly inquisitive. She was interested not only in how things worked in educational settings but also in why the pieces fit together the way they did. Her curiosity was contagious. In fact, of all the students we have known, Susan stood out in terms of both her intellectual curiosity and her enthusiasm—enviable traits for a teacher charged with actively engaging students in learning. Susan also was among the very strongest students we had in terms of her ability to grasp theoretical issues, articulate her arguments, and integrate theory with practice. Finally, she had excellent writing and verbal communication skills, and by the time she graduated, Susan had accumulated a solid repertoire of very creative ideas about how to help students develop these important skills. In short, Susan represented the best our system has to offer, and in many ways she seemed like a perfect candidate for becoming a strong change agent as well.

Susan's story is a common one. Armed, ready, and excited for constructivist teaching, she found herself surrounded by teachers who simply did not see things her way and students unprepared to play along—but we're getting ahead of ourselves. Let's start at the beginning with Susan's culminating college experience of working in a ninth-grade English classroom. Here is what Susan had to say about what her "dream school" would look like shortly before her culminating project began.

Susan's Ideal World

In my ideal world, I will graduate and get a well-paying, teaching job at a progressive school where the students and teachers are self-motivated—where teachers, administrators, and students work together to create exciting, fascinating, fun learning experiences. The best part of working in my dream school, though, is that it is filled with problem solving yes-sayers rather than griping nay-sayers. When an exciting or unusual opportunity for teaming presents itself, the numbers of my school community will get together and say, "We really must find a way to make this happen," rather than, "Oh, we couldn't possibly do that because..." In addition, I want to be in a school just to be in a school. I want to sit at a lunch table with good teachers who care about their students and just listen to what they have to say. I want to be in a place where I can ask more than one teacher, "This is what happened to me today. What would you do in this situation?" I want to see for myself what it is like to have 5 special-needs students in a class of 20. I want to hear the kinds of things that teachers gripe about in low voices during free periods in the day.

Unit 8　Education and Teachers' Development

Susan's Experience at the High School

As Susan would later discover, high school freshmen, classrooms, and schools are often significantly shy of her dream. Nevertheless, Susan had the good fortune of working with a teacher who was open to new ideas, ready for some experimentation, and willing to follow her lead for at least one major project. The excerpt below comes from Susan's self-evaluation of her culminating experience.

One of the first questions I asked Marcia (the cooperation teacher) was, "How much freedom do we have in terms of what the students can explore, how they go about doing it, and how they show us what they have learned?" She explained that the school had already decided that all 9th grade students would do a unit on Greek mythology. She said that this had been the case for several years. She explained the ways in which she had taught the topic in the past but said that she was willing to try a new approach. From what I gathered, her approach in the past was fairly "traditional". As I understood it, she had the class begin with the Greek story of the creation of the earth, which the whole class read and discussed together. She then had them move on to several of the other well-known myths. She said that in the past she gave weekly quizzes on vocabulary and content and ended the unit with a comprehensive exam. In other words, Marcia's approach in the past had been to try to expose each student to several (and all the same) of the Greek myths and to discuss some of the broad themes like the role of the hero in Greek mythology.

The approach I advocated was a bit different. The model I used was basically the model used in many of my college classes. I suggested that each student either alone or with a partner, pick a myth, a mythological character, or some other aspect of Greek culture and create an original exhibition to present to the class. Using this approach, each student would have the opportunity to become an expert on some aspect of Greek culture or mythology and, because they had to present to the entire class, all of the students would be exposed to every topic. Marcia said that she liked the idea of projects, although she also said that she had never given the students total freedom in choosing the topics, and she was interested to see how well they would handle it.

For my first lesson, I introduced myself, told them a bit about my philosophy of learning, and explained to the class that I needed their help. I needed to know what they thought were the qualities of a good teacher. We spent the rest of the period generating this list. For their homework assignment, Marcia asked the students to pick the two or three qualities they thought were most important and to explain why these qualities were at the top of their personal lists. In addition, I asked the students to write me a short letter that began, "Dear Miss Jackson, one thing I liked about today's class was that... and one thing I did not like or did not understand about today's class was that.." The letters were a wonderful way to begin to get to know the students. I could also begin to identify which students were willing to take some time to think about the question and which students just wrote something down to get it over with.

The next step in this process was to try to determine what the students already knew about the Greeks and Greek mythology. In addition, I wanted the students to begin thinking about ways they could demonstrate their understanding of a topic other than by taking a test or writing an essay. We spent the last half of the class talking about what authentic assessment means. We generated another list, similar to the good teacher list, and I gave each student a copy. Following these discussions I struggled with the following questions:

How do I get them to understand what a great project looks like?

What would be a good way to have students tell me what they are thinking of exploring for their exhibitions?

How will I know if my expectations are clear?

How can I make sure that the students are actually doing something productive and moving forward, and not just goofing off in the library?

I came up with the idea of an update sheet. I asked the students to fill out an update sheet during the last few minutes of each class period. I intended to look over the sheets at the end of each day to try to assess process and to help me pinpoint students who might need my help finding resources. Approximately two weeks into the project, I asked the students to fill out a final where each student was in the contract telling me exactly what they had planned to do for their exhibitions. I also gave the students a document that explained the criteria (which they helped develop) on which they would be evaluated. Attached to the evaluation sheet was a calendar which showed the students which days they were scheduled to present.

Overall, the presentations went well. Many of the students' exhibitions were exceptional. Some of the students made video—and audiotapes. Others wrote and performed original monologues in costume. One student made an incredibly lifelike clay sculpture of Hercules slaying the Hydra. After the students' presentation, the principal asked if he could display the statue in the center of the front hall. Two students even researched the eating habits of the ancient Greeks and cooked an ancient Greek feast for the entire class. While we ate, our chefs used a map they had created to explain the ancient Greeks' trade routes and the origins of the products they bartered.

Preparing for the Real World

Susan's experience was, in many ways, both transformative and validating. She had learned about constructivist approaches in her college classes and had a positive and successful experience trying them out. As she prepared for her first full-time teaching job in the Northeast, where she was hired as a member of a middle school team specifically to nudge some of the older teachers toward more progressive practice, the following questions that she created as part of her culminating college experience guided her:

• How can I facilitate students' learning in such a way that I provide opportunities for them to discover, create, and apply knowledge for themselves while working within a public school setting?

- How can I get students to push themselves beyond what they dreamed they were capable of?
- How can I get them to want to truly understand what they learn and to demonstrate that understanding in a meaningful and creative way, rather than just memorizing information and spitting it back out on a test?
- How do I get students to understand that learning for learning's sake is cool and fun, and hard, and much more worthwhile than memorizing information for a grade and then forgetting it?

The Reality and the Poem

These are tough questions, but Susan, buoyed by her successful culminating experience, a long summer break, and the confidence of a much more experienced teacher, felt ready to tackle them head-on. What she found when she arrived was anything but what she expected.

By October of her first year of teaching, six short weeks into the semester, Susan sent us the following poem.

I Hate—A Poem by a First-Year Teacher

I hate preparing lessons.
I hate that feeling of panic of "what am I going to do tomorrow?"
I hate vomiting in the morning.
I hate kids who try to slime out of doing things like Steve and Billy do.
I hate getting up at five o'clock (or four-forty-five, or four-thirty).
I hate it when Pamela reminds me of Stacy Jefferson, the girl who made my life hell in seventh grade.
I hate it when Elizabeth Milios yells at a kid who is crying because he is having problems with his ex-girlfriend.
I hate it when Cindy Tuppan looks at me with that bitchy smirk and I know she would secretly love to see me fail.
I hate territorial teachers.
I hate feeling incompetent.
I hate crying when I feel like this.
I hate not having any friends here.
I hate feeling lost.
I hate it when a 14-year-old can make me feel exactly the way I felt when I was 14 years old.
I hate it when kids talk when I am trying to tell them something.
I hate it more when kids who while talking ask me, "Now what are we supposed to do?"
I hate Fridays because that means Monday is only three days away.
I hate Sundays because that means Monday is tomorrow.

What happened? Could this be the same Susan Jackson who left our program so confident, determined, and excited about teaching? By November things had not improved. Another letter, this one more urgent, followed:

Last Monday was definitely the lowest point in my life. We had a great in-service. We had to sit at tables with our teammates and the workshop leader told us all about the kinds of things that he has done with interdisciplinary units, and he showed us how to start with a topic that middle school kids are interested in and then make a web of related topics, etc. Things were going well, overall. After lunch, we met with him as grade-level teachers for about an hour and he asked us to voice concerns that we had with our particular students. It was then that I realized how little faith the teachers at this school have in the students at our school. They truly don't believe that the kids have any desire to learn. They really believe that the kids have to be bribed to do anything.

So after we met with the workshop leader, we were supposed to go upstairs as a team and brainstorm ideas about ways we might be able to do an interdisciplinary unit ourselves. So... I got upstairs and John (the social studies teacher who only lectures and teaches straight out of the social studies textbook) was sitting at his desk, and I said, "So do you want to meet in here?" At the same moment, Cindy Tuppan (a science teacher) walked in and John said, "Yeah—whatever. Do we even need to meet? What is the point? I'll tell you what we could do. We could just sit here and pretend to be meeting in case Mr. Schwartz (the principal) walks by—or we could just leave." I had no idea what to say.

Then Cindy said, "Well, I can't do this. I can't teach like this. I'm a science teacher. I can't teach a unit on freedom (the topic we had been webbing in the in-service as an example)." "There is absolutely no place for science in anything we were talking about down there. I can't teach like that."

And I lost it.

I felt all the frustration come up from the pit of my stomach, and I said something like, "Well Cindy I know how you feel... (and the tears started flowing). I feel so frustrated everyday because that was the way I learned to teach. I wasn't trained to teach from a textbook. Everyday I feel so frustrated..." (I'm not sure if that was where I said), but I said it "because I feel like I was hired to teach here because I do know how to teach like that, but nobody else in this place, or at least on this team, teaches like that or even wants to teach like that and I hate it!"

At some point during this outburst, Elizabeth Milios walked in and said, "Well then, maybe you're in the wrong place! But you don't start blaming the team. It is not the team's fault. There are plenty of people in this school who would love to be on this team." Then Cindy pipes in with this: "Your insecurities and your inabilities are not my problem. You are not my problem. I don't care about your problems. I don't care about you!"

Ahh, yes, teaming at its finest.

At some point I told Elizabeth not to yell at me like I was one of her students, I did stop crying, but I literally felt like someone had dropped a barbell on my stomach. The rest of the day is a fog. We had to go down to the library to wrap things up. Everything in my whole being wanted to run away from that place. At the end of the in-service, one of the other new teachers, Reggie, looked at me and said, "Are you all right?" I looked at him and shook my head no, but I couldn't speak.

He said, "Come to my room." I followed him out of the library and the tears just started pouring out of my eyes. We got to his room and I started sobbing and I kept saying, "I can't do this. I can't do this. I thought I could but I can't. I have to resign. This is killing me. I can't do this."

Reggie just sat there on his knees and listened to me and he kept saying. "Don't quit. Don't quit. I'll help you. We'll do it together, whatever it takes. I swear I'll help you. You are meant to be a teacher."

Exercises

I. Reading Comprehension:

There are four suggested answers marked A, B, C and D. Choose the best answer for each question.

1. What does the author most likely to convey in this article?
    A. Susan's experience was a single case due to her defects in personality.
    B. Susan's teaching was not contextualized.
    C. Susan's experience was rather typical for novice teachers.
    D. Susan's teaching was not conventional and constructive.
2. Susan's failure of teaching may be explained in the following reasons except that _____.
    A. her teaching education at the college
    B. her poor performance at the workplace
    C. her abilities to apply theory to practice
    D. her individual teaching beliefs can be hardly carried out in the school
3. Why Susan's internship at the high school was successful?
    A. Because Susan taught what she had learned at university.
    B. Because Susan taught students who were highly motivated.
    C. Because Susan was well prepared with teaching expertise.
    D. Because Susan's coordinator supported her experiment.
4. Which one of the following choices has not shown the features of Susan's constructivist teaching?
    A. Discovering, experiencing, and applying knowledge.
    B. Understanding in a meaningful way.
    C. Learning for the sake of fun.
    D. Fostering abilities to exert potentials.
5. What can we infer from reading the poem of Susan?
    A. Susan's approach is not suitable for teaching children.
    B. Susan is not able to get along with children.

C. Susan has changed her minds to be a teacher.
D. Susan meets troubles in teaching practices.

II. Judgments and Implications:

Do the following statements agree with the information given in the passage?
True   if the statement is true according to the passage
False   if the statement contradicts the passage

1. The article indicates that students and teachers are filled with enthusiasm and professional training to meet the prospective challenge in their career development.
2. Susan Jackson exemplified the best ideal of student teacher, because she had been armed with all the potentials and qualities that a good teacher needed.
3. For her first lesson, Susan introduced her teaching philosophy to learn students' feedbacks.
4. Susan changed to hate teaching, because she was not able to get along with other colleagues at that school.
5. Susan's case indicates the failure of pre-service teacher education in her college.

III. Critical Questions:

Three months after beginning what promised to be a stellar teaching career, Susan Jackson found herself crying on the floor of an eighth-grade public classroom, at a crossroads. Should she forge ahead or quit? Was the enthusiasm and energy, her love for teaching, knocked out of her so early in the game? What went wrong?

We share this story not to discourage current or future teachers but to generate thinking and to raise questions by all involved in the teaching profession. Was Susan's teacher preparation program inadequate? Were her goals too lofty? Were the teachers in Susan's school woefully uninformed or inflexible? Was Susan expecting too much? How typical is Susan's experience?

Text B

Brainstorming

Professional Development refers to skills and knowledge attained for both personal development and career advancement. Professional development encompasses all types of facilitated learning opportunities, ranging from college degrees to formal coursework, conferences and informal learning opportunities situated in practice. It has been described as intensive and collaborative, ideally incorporating an evaluative stage.

Unit 8　Education and Teachers' Development

Questions before reading:
What elements should be included in teachers' development? Do you think teachers' professional development may influence students' achievements? Why?

Teaching Teachers: Professional Development to Improve Student Achievement[1]

Good teachers form the foundation of good schools, and improving teachers' skills and knowledge is one of the most important investments of time and money that local, state, and national leaders make in education. Yet with the wide variety of professional development options available, which methods have the most impact on student learning?

Research on professional development is scattered throughout subject areas, with its focus ranging from classroom processes and structures to teachers' personal traits. We have limited our review to learning opportunities for teachers that are explicitly aimed at increasing student achievement.

What Are Teachers' Learning?

Focus on teaching skills

Research on the links between teacher learning and student achievement is divided into two waves. The first wave, beginning in the 1960s, focused primarily on "generic" teaching skills, such as allocating class time, providing clear classroom demonstrations, assessing student comprehension during lectures, maintaining attention, and grouping students. These studies showed small to moderate positive effects on students' basic skills, such as phonetic decoding and arithmetic operations; in a few cases, reasoning skills also improved. For example, in an experimental study of fourth-grade mathematics in urban schools serving primarily low-income families, student achievement was greater when teachers emphasized active whole-class instruction—giving information, questioning students, and providing feedback—and more frequent reviews, among other measures. Student achievement also was enhanced when teachers learned to follow the presentation of new material with "guided practice"—asking questions and supervising exercises.

Focus on subject matter and student learning

In the 1990s, a second wave of research delved deeper into student learning, focusing on students' reasoning and problem solving potentials rather than only on basic skills. It suggested that professional development can influence teachers' classroom practices significantly and lead to improved student achievement when it focuses on (1)

---

[1] Excerpt from *Teaching Teachers: Professional Development to Improve Student Achievement*, AERA Research Points. Volume 3, Issue 1, Summer 2005.

how students learn particular subject matter; (2) instructional practices that are specifically related to the subject matter and how students understand it; and (3) strengthening teachers' knowledge of specific subject-matter content. Close alignment of professional development with actual classroom conditions also is a key. In one study, Thomas Carpenter and colleagues randomly placed first-grade teachers either in a month long workshop that familiarized them with research on how students understand addition and subtraction word problems or in professional development that focused on mathematical problem-solving strategies but not on how students learn. Teachers who participated in the student learning workshop more often posed complex problems to students, listened to the processes students used to solve those problems, and encouraged them to seek different methods of finding answers. By contrast, teachers who were not in the workshop emphasized basic fact recall, getting answers quickly, and working alone rather than in groups. Student achievement was consistently higher and growth in students' basic and advanced reasoning and problem-solving skills was greatest when their teachers' professional development focused on how students learn and how to gauge that learning effectively. This suggests that professional development that is rooted in subject matter and focuses on student learning can have a significant impact on student achievement. In another study, Paul Cobb and colleagues provided opportunities for teachers to examine new curriculum materials, solve mathematics problems that they would teach to students, and then study student learning. At the end of the school year, these teachers' students did better on conceptual understanding and maintained their basic (computational) skills. Although research in teacher professional development is dominated by mathematics studies, good examples of such research also exist in other subjects including science, literacy, and basic reading skills. In reading, Deborah McCutchen and colleagues studied two groups of kindergarten and first-grade teachers. One group received professional development that improved their knowledge of word sounds and structure, whereas the other group had no additional training. Students' reading performance then was tracked over the course of a year. Teachers who got the extra training spent more time explicitly teaching the building blocks of words and language, and their students did better on tests of word reading, spelling, and in first grade, comprehension.

Linking professional learning to teachers' real work

To be effective, professional development must provide teachers with a way to directly apply what they learn to their teaching. Research shows that professional development leads to better instruction and improves student learning when it connects to the curriculum materials that teachers use, the district and state academic standards that guide their work, and the assessment and accountability measures that evaluate their success. Two recent studies that support focusing professional development on curriculum have implications for states striving to connect education policy to instruction. David Cohen and Heather Hill found that teachers whose learning focused directly on the curriculum they would be teaching were the ones who adopted the

Unit 8 Education and Teachers' Development

practices taught in their professional development. These teachers embraced new curriculum materials when they were supported by training and, in some cases, workshops about the new state-required student assessment. The study also showed that students of teachers who participated in this kind of curriculum-focused professional development did well on assessments. Unfortunately, most teachers received less effective forms of training. In another study, Michael Garet and colleagues surveyed a nationally representative sample of teachers who, in the late 1990s, participated in the Eisenhower Professional Development Program, which emphasized mathematics and science. The study found that teachers were more likely to change their instructional practices and gain greater subject knowledge and improved teaching skills when their professional development linked directly to their daily experiences and aligned with standards and assessments. How Much Professional Development Is Enough, and How Well Is It Working? Studies suggest that the more time teachers spend on professional development, the more significantly they change their practices and that participating in professional learning communities optimizes the time spent on professional development. Therefore, it is striking that one national survey found that in nine of 10 content areas, most teachers said that they spent one day or less on professional development during the previous year. While adequate time for professional development is essential, studies also show that by itself, more time does not guarantee success. If the sessions do not focus on the subject-matter content that research has shown to be effective, then the duration will do little to change teachers' practices and improve student learning. Most states and school districts do not know how much money they are spending on professional development for teachers or what benefit they are actually getting from their outlays because they do not systematically evaluate how well the additional training works. An effective evaluation includes an examination of actual classroom practices, the training's impact on teacher behavior, and its effect on student learning. Evaluation should be an ongoing process that starts in the earliest stages of program planning and continues beyond the end of the program.

In a study of a federal program supporting professional development, teachers reported that a focus on content knowledge was one of two elements that had the greatest effect on their knowledge and skills and led to changes in instructional practice. The other element was coherence, which included building on what teachers already have learned, aligning professional development with state and district standards and assessment, and encouraging communication among teachers who were striving to reform their instruction in similar ways. Other things that mattered but had less impact were time span (how long the training lasted over time) and contact hours (the number of hours spent in professional development). Therefore, professional development is likely to be more effective if it is sustained over time and involves a significant number of hours.

Collective participation, which involves professional development designed for groups of teachers from the same school, department, or grade level, tended to create more active learning (e.g., observing and being observed while teaching; planning for classroom use of what was learned in professional development; reviewing student work; and giving presentations, leading discussions, and producing written work), and this had some effect on teacher knowledge and skills.

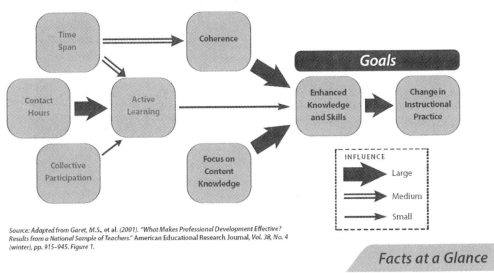

Aspects of Teacher Professional Development and Their Relationship to Better Instruction

Source: Adapted from Garet, M.S., et al. (2001). "What Makes Professional Development Effective? Results from a National Sample of Teachers." American Educational Research Journal, Vol. 38, No. 4 (winter), pp. 915-945. Figure 1.

Conclusion

Our changing goals for learning, coupled with shifts in curriculum emphasis and a deeper understanding of teacher learning and student thinking, have led to new findings about the impact of teacher professional development and how best to sharpen teachers' skills and knowledge. What matters most is what teachers learn. Professional development should improve teachers' knowledge of the subject matter that they are teaching, and it should enhance their understanding of student thinking in that subject matter. Aligning substantive training with the curriculum and teachers' actual work experiences also is vital. The time teachers spend in professional development makes a difference as well, but only when the activities focus on high-quality subject-matter content. Extended opportunities to better understand student learning, curriculum materials and instruction, and subject-matter content can boost the performance of both teachers and students.

Unit 8 Education and Teachers' Development

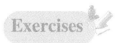

I. Reading Comprehension: analytical reading practice

Organizational Structure

While reading a long article, it seems to be a contradiction to maintain a high reading speed with a good comprehension. Sometimes, fluency and accuracy could reach a balance when we apply analytical reading. Read the following exercises and complete each task.

Example:

"Focus on teaching skills"

① Research on the links between teacher learning and student achievement is divided into two waves. (Transitional sentence)

② The first wave, beginning in the 1960s, focused primarily on "generic" teaching skills, such as allocating class time, providing clear classroom demonstrations, assessing student comprehension during lectures, maintaining attention, and grouping students. (Topic Sentence)

③ These studies showed small to moderate positive effects on students' basic skills, such as phonetic decoding and arithmetic operations; in a few cases, reasoning skills also improved. (Argumentation)

④ For example, in an experimental study of fourth-grade mathematics in urban schools serving primarily low-income families, student achievement was greater when teachers emphasized active whole-class instruction—giving information, questioning students, and providing feedback—and more frequent reviews, among other measures. Student achievement also was enhanced when teachers learned to follow the presentation of new material with "guided practice"—asking questions and supervising exercises. (Supporting details)

The main idea of the paragraph:
The function of skills training in teachers' professional development is not completely invisible.

Read the paragraph of "Focus on subject matter and student learning" and complete the following exercises.

In the 1990s, a second wave of research delved deeper into student learning, focusing on students' reasoning and problem solving potentials rather than only on basic skills. (Topic Sentence)

教育文论选读

Main coverage:

```
            ┌─────────────────────────┐
            │  Focused Professional   │
            │      Development        │
            └───────────┬─────────────┘
        ┌───────────────┼───────────────┐
┌───────────────┐ ┌───────────┐ ┌───────────┐
│Students' learning│ │           │ │           │
│ of a particular │ │           │ │           │
│  subject matter │ │           │ │           │
└───────────────┘ └───────────┘ └───────────┘
```

Empirical study on focused professional development:

In one study	Objects	Specific skills
Experimental group	Teachers participated in workshop	On mathematical problem-solving strategies
Control group		
Study results		

Judgment:
This suggests that professional development that is rooted in subject matter and focused on student learning can have a significant impact on student achievement.

Transitional sentence:
Although research in teacher professional development is dominated by mathematics studies, good examples of such research also exist in other subjects including science, literacy, and basic reading skills.

Another study of kindergarten and first-grade teachers:_____
Study result: _____

II. Judgments and Implications:

Do the following statements agree with the information given in the passage?
True   if the statement is true according to the passage

Unit 8 Education and Teachers' Development

False if the statement contradicts the passage

1. Professional development could both affect teachers' classroom practices and student achievement.
2. Professional development is a practical way to link teachers' learning and teaching together.
3. Sufficient time would promise the teacher more successful professional development.
4. Only a small number of states or school districts know exactly how much money they spent on professional development for teachers.
5. A focus on content and coherence are the two factors which have great impact on knowledge and skills and result in changes in instructional practice.
6. The time and money matter most on the teachers' professional development.

III. Summary:

Read the paragraph of "Linking professional learning to teachers' real work" and complete the summary below, Choose ONLY ONE WORD from the text for each answer.

Teachers' professional developments result in positive effects on students' learning if "professional developments" contextualize materials, individualize academic study guides, and _____ . Two recent studies that support focusing professional development on curriculum have promising implications for connecting education policy to instruction and teachers evaluation. The more time teachers professional development, the more significantly they change their practices. However, _____ doesn't guarantee success, only when the sessions centre on the subject-matter of curriculum can ensure effectiveness. Finally, the evaluation is an _____ process which is carried out from the beginning to the end.

IV. Critical Questions:

What has been the most effective way to improve teachers' learning? Besides what have been mentioned to in the text, what other ways can be employed to improve teachers' professional development?

Text C

Brainstorming

The No Child Left Behind Act of 2001 (NCLB) is a United States Act of Congress that is a reauthorization of the Elementary and Secondary Education Act, which included Title I, the government's flagship aid program for disadvantaged students. NCLB supports standards-based education reform based on the premise that setting high standards and establishing measurable goals can improve individual outcomes in education.

The Act requires states to develop assessments in basic skills. To receive federal school funding, states must give these assessments to all students at select grade levels. The Act does not assert a national achievement standard. Each individual state develops its own standards. NCLB expanded the federal role in public education through annual testing, annual academic progress, report cards, teacher qualifications, and funding changes.

Questions before reading:

What would you comment on NCLB?

Regardless of countries varied economic status, cultural beliefs and teacher evaluations, what should be the priority of teacher education?

An Education President for the 21st Century[①]
Hilda Borko, Jennie Whitcomb, Dan Liston

As this editorial goes to press, Super Tuesday[②] is still spinning in the news cycle. The dramatic primary and caucus season are in full swing, as no candidate has yet clinched his or her party's nomination. Whether a political junkie or a more casual follower of national politics, a record number of individuals have been swept up in the drama of the presidential campaign. Who will be the next president rivets the nation.

Whoever he or she is, the 44th president will inherit a troubled educational system, one ready for transformation despite persistent reform efforts since the 1980s. Whatever one's position on the reauthorization of No Child Left Behind, a legacy of this federal policy has been to make salient the two profoundly unequal public education systems in the United States. All candidates recognize the moral and cultural imperative to ensure that all children receive an education on par with our most advantaged. The next

---

① Excerpt From *Journal of TeacherEducation*, Vol. 59, 3, May/June 2008, pp. 207—211.
② Super Tuesday: 总统竞选(初选)日

president will also find a general public and policy community that grasp how much teachers matter. It is now conventional wisdom among researchers and policy makers to assert that teachers are the single most important school-based intervention to foster student learning. But the next president faces daunting challenges to ensure that all children are in the company of quality teachers. With regard to education, the concerns are vexing.

As editors, we invited individuals whose work centers on teaching and teacher education to pen letters to the 44th president of the United States offering their advice to ensure quality teaching and teacher education. Our aim was to engage individuals from a range of perspectives and to provoke conversation and lively deliberation about our nation's educational future. Their letters make up this theme issue and were also the focus of the JTE/AACTE (American Association of Colleges for Teacher Education) major forum at the annual meeting in New Orleans earlier this spring. Collectively, the invited letter writers challenge the next president to be bold and clear in his or her vision to value children and teaching. They urge that individual to use the mechanisms available to the office—the bully pulpit①, selection of a secretary of education, and budget development and federal funding for our public education system—to realize that vision. We highlight here two themes that cut across the eight letters published in this issue, improving the conditions of children's lives and lending dignity to the teaching profession. In doing so, we necessarily leave out details and subtleties of each author's message. Thus, we encourage you to read the letters in their entirety.

Lending Dignity to the Teaching Profession

Points made in the previous section highlight powerful, sometimes overpowering, factors outside of school that influence what happens inside school. In school buildings, the most important factor in any child's learning and development is the quality of teachers encountered. Bush's signature legislation, No Child Left Behind, attempts to improve teacher quality through its requirement that all teachers be "highly qualified" in the subject areas they teach, where *highly qualified* is defined almost exclusively in terms of content knowledge. States' varied compliance approaches to this requirement for quality resulted in little progress. The federal approach taken over the past 8 years seems to us to have diminished the dignity of the profession in several critical ways. For example, it has focused on narrow criteria to define teacher quality that underplay the importance of professional knowledge and teachers' ongoing learning. It has also not attended to the conditions in which teachers work and how those conditions affect their willingness to stay. And, it has tolerated, even encouraged, sweeping critiques of teacher education.

The next president has an opportunity to reframe the teacher quality movement in

---

① bully pulpit: 白宫

ways that both expand components of teacher quality and affirm teachers' professional and vocational commitments. From a policy perspective, one critical challenge the next president must attend to is recruiting, preparing, and retaining high quality teachers who both choose and stay in schools serving our poorest communities. All contributors to this theme issue take up the topic of this challenge by bidding the next president to use the office to lend dignity to the profession of teaching. Their recommendations cover broad terrain, and each requires the next president to exercise a combination of the power of the bully pulpit, the power of sound policies, and the power of the purse and support, the power of teaching and the work teachers do in service to our nation.

First, all letters argue for valuing teacher preparation and ongoing teacher learning. Christine Sleeter outlines the characteristics that diverse students' need of their teachers:

Students need teachers who hold high expectations for their learning, who can engage them academically by building on what they know and what interests them, who can relate to their families and communities and read them as well as their families in culturally accurate ways, and who can envision them as constructive participants in a multicultural democracy.

These characteristics are developed through well-structured teacher learning experiences. Yet, not all teacher education pathways offer such learning opportunities. For this reason, several appeal to the next president to promote the importance of teacher preparation that attends to the needs of diverse learners (see especially Christine Sleeter).

Julia Freeland, Julie Mikuta, and Andrew Rotherman argue that "Washington can encourage more pluralism in teacher preparation and training organizations". They point to charter management organizations (e.g., teacher residency models, Teacher for America) as promising models to encourage highly motivated and academically accomplished individuals to choose teaching. Seeking to bridge the now familiar professionalization versus market-based pitches at reform in teacher preparation, Freeland and her colleagues argue for a "third way approach". For them, drawing from the best aspects of each approach will yield policies that "open the teaching profession to a wider pool of higher quality candidates, enable the development of more and better preparation programs, and encourage more innovation while still maintaining an important credentialing function and role for the public sector". Freeland, Mikuta, and Rotherman challenge the received wisdom in current teacher education circles, and the challenge needs to be heeded.

Along with improving initial teacher preparation, several letters tackle ways that the president can improve teachers' opportunities to continue learning throughout their careers. Most professional development is disconnected from teachers' immediate questions and challenges. In addition, Freeland and her colleagues argue that it is often not cost-effective, in particular because professional development dollars are not spent on approaches aligned with improving student learning or meeting teachers' professional goals. To guide the next president, Ann Lieberman and Desiree Pointer-Mace synthesize what we know about teacher learning communities (TLCs) and highlight reform networks and TLCs as an exemplary approach to improve teachers' practice. In their analysis, key features of TLCs include the following:

They focus on instruction; are sustained and continuous, rather than short term and episodic; provide opportunities for teachers to learn from one another both inside and outside school; make it possible for teachers to influence how and what they learn; and engage teachers in thinking about what they need to know.

Lieberman and Pointer-Mace urge the president to promote opportunities for teachers to "open the doors" to their practice, both literally and virtually.

A second way that the president can encourage quality and lend dignity to the profession is to support the provision of external markers that value particular features of the profession. Berliner asserts, "Our nation needs the pay scales and social rituals to honor all its teachers and to recruit and retain highly qualified teachers for our classrooms." The authors offer a number of specific strategies. Freeland and her colleagues, for example, look to Britain's successful and "aggressive $50 million media campaign [that] managed to attract a wider audience to the teaching profession, elevating teaching from the 92nd most desirable next job for 25—35 year olds to the most desirable". Arthur Levine argues for "creating the equivalent of a Rhodes Scholarship for teachers". His proposal, now being implemented in several states as Woodrow Wilson Scholarships, provides substantial fellowships (on the order of $50,000) to "America's best" who attend a 1-year graduate program in teacher education and agree to teach in urban or rural schools for 3 years. In a culture that lives by the expression "show me the money", creating financial incentives to teach is intuitively appealing. On one hand, Levine's model holds promise as an incubator of innovative and excellent teacher preparation; on the other hand, it is also a harbinger for growth of teacher preparation programs financed by philanthropies and administered through school districts. Such programs are not, in principle, weak, but they do have the potential to become apprentice-based job training that diminishes the value and values added by grounding teacher preparation in the liberal arts and social sciences.

As a third strategy to dignify the profession, the authors encourage the next president to nurture creativity and innovation in teacher preparation, professional development, and research in teaching. Given that states and districts bear the central responsibility for teacher quality, the federal government can promote innovation. Clift asks the president to learn from and expand "unique initiatives" that foster coordination and collaboration across the varied institutions (universities and colleges, districts, and other agencies) who support teachers across their developmental continuum. Freeland and her colleagues encourage "innovations based on demand rather than supply", that is, giving teachers more choice in their selection of professional development programs while holding those programs accountable for results in student achievement. To improve research, Berliner suggests funding more teacher research and implementation studies. Sleeter requests funding for research on teacher education practices that "have promise [to prepare] teachers for diverse and historically underserved learners". Freeland and colleagues call for funding quality data collection systems that allow states to track "teachers' student gains back to their training institutions".

A final approach to lend dignity to the profession comes from Lee Shulman, who asks the next president to serve as a paragon of an educated person. Speaking directly to the next president, he writes,

I want you to support the work of teachers at all levels by serving as a persistent, relentless, and selfconscious model of an educated person. I further implore you to define the president's role as the principal teacher of our nation, the model educator, whose responsibility is to exemplify the habits of mind, habits of practical judgment and action, and habits of heart that we associate with our ideal for all well educated citizens in our democracy. Even more important, I implore you to define your roles as the principal learner taking every opportunity to make your own intellectual and moral development visible and transparent to your fellow citizens.

Shulman's message reminds us that the next president's leadership, more than policies or purse strings, may be the most essential factor in reframing the tenor and substance of reform talk about teaching and learning. Such a shift may yield fertile ground for the many excellent suggestions made in the letters written to our next president.

In closing, it is too early to tell whether this will be a national security election, an economy election, a change election. It is unlikely that it will be an education election. The primary season has been marked by record turnouts in nearly every primary election or caucus. Yet, as Arthur Levine reminds us, education was largely ignored in speeches, meetings with voters, and televised debates. Similarly, the 44th president may or may not be an "education president". There will be many issues competing for that president's time. For us, one key moral and pragmatic imperative of the 21st century is to redesign our education system to serve those who have been historically underserved and marginalized. Thus, the 44th president must be an education president for the 21st century; he or she must commit vigorously to improve factors outside educators' control that dramatically shape what children and teachers are able to do in school. Read our lips: It's about the poverty. The next president must also reframe the teacher quality movement. A quality teacher is one prepared to work in schools serving our nation's English language learners and new arrivals, low-income families and communities, and students of color. We look forward to the race ahead in the fall and hope that the bloggers, campaign staffers, and speech writers will attend to the thoughtful advice offered by our eight contributors.

Unit 8　Education and Teachers' Development

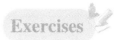

Exercises

I. Reading Comprehension:
There are four suggested answers marked A, B, C and D. Choose the best answer for each question.

1. What is the author's purpose to write this letter?
   A. The letter aims at highlighting the issue of education and calls for efforts from U.S. government.
   B. The letter targets on issues of children and teaching.
   C. The letter mainly focuses on the issue of teachers' dignity.
   D. The letter draws on the educational problems that the next president of America confronts with.
2. A highly qualified teacher means_____.
   A. a fully competent knowledge in subject matters
   B. a fully competent knowledge in subject and pedagogic matters
   C. components of qualified teaching
   D. qualified teaching, career development and commitments
3. Which one of the followings has not been mentioned in teacher education?
   A. Well-structured teacher education.
   B. Pluralism in teacher preparation and training organizations.
   C. Recruiting teachers familiar with multi-culture.
   D. Bridging professionalization with market-based reform.
4. What is the most likely reason to explain teaching as the most desirable job in Britain?
   A. Teaching profession has attracted public attentions.
   B. Teaching profession has been combined with market forces.
   C. Teaching profession has provided a one-year graduate study and scholarship.
   D. Teaching profession has lent dignity to the youth.
5. In the last paragraph, what is the author's attitude toward the next president?
   A. The author criticized the election and felt disillusion to the president.
   B. The author was looking forward to the next president and felt optimistic to the educational development.
   C. The author was pessimistic to the new election and felt little hope to the education president.
   D. The author kept a sober mind to the election and felt somewhat pressure to improve education.

II. Judgments and Implications:

Do the following statements agree with the information given in the passage?
True   if the statement is true according to the passage
False   if the statement contradicts the passage

1. Lending dignity to the profession of teaching may include reinforced teacher education, external incentives, and the president's leadership.
2. Teachers' professional development at current stage has focused on improving student learning or meeting teachers' professional goals.
3. Woodrow Wilson Scholarships serves as a mentoring model that teachers' training has been elevated in values from subject matters.
4. The nature of innovation in professional development is to reinforce demand and evaluation for both teachers and students.
5. Lee Shulman defines the role of the next president as a perfect model and an educator who exemplifies the habits of behavior, habits of mind, and habits of spirit.

III. Matching:

Read the definitions of fact and opinion carefully, and fill in F (Fact) or O (Opinion) if the sentence is a fact or if the sentence is an opinion.

Fact: *A fact is something that has really occurred or is actually the case.*
Opinion: *In general, an opinion is a subjective belief, and is the result of emotion or interpretation of facts.*

1. Whoever he or she is, the 44th president will inherit a troubled educational system, one ready for transformation despite persistent reform efforts since the 1980s.
2. Along with improving initial teacher preparation, several letters tackle ways that the president can improve teachers' opportunities to continue learning throughout their careers.
3. For us, one key moral and pragmatic imperative of the 21st century is to redesign our education system to serve those who have been historically underserved and marginalized.
4. The next president must also reframe the teacher quality movement.
5. Lieberman and Pointer-Mace urge the president to promote opportunities for teachers to "open the doors" to their practice, both literally and virtually.

IV. Critical Questions:

In the initial part, the author has indicated that several writers of the original letters highlighted the importance between children and teaching. What would they argue for the perspective of children and what are the correlations between children and teaching?

Unit 8 Education and Teachers' Development

Learning Skills

Critical Reading Skills II

Critical reading requires you to focus your attention much more closely on certain parts of a written text, holding other information in mind. As it involves analysis, reflection, evaluation and making judgments, it usually involves slower reading than that used for recreational reading or for gaining general background information. As you develop critical reading skills, these reading skills will become faster and more accurate.

A. Preparing for critical reading

It is not usually easy to make sense of any information taken out of context. When reading new material, some basic preparation can help you to:
- see how the main argument fits together;
- better remember the overall argument;
- better comprehend specific pieces of information;
- recognize how reasons and evidence contribute to the main argument.

Find the argument

Once you have worked quickly to locate where the information is in general terms, apply the critical thinking methods to identify the arguments:
- Identify the author's position: what does the text want you to do, think, accept or believe?
- Look for sets of reasons that are used to support conclusions.

Key terms

Position: A point of view.
Agreement: To concur with someone else's point of view.
Disagreement: To hold a different point of view from someone else.
Argument: Using reasons to support a point of view, so that known or unknown audiences may be persuaded to agree. An argument may include disagreement, but is more than simply disagreement if it is based on reasons.

Once you have located the argument, you are likely to need to read more slowly and carefully, applying further critical thinking strategies.

B. Identifying the theoretical perspective

What is a theory?

In professional research and academic thinking, a theory is usually an elaborated system, or "school", of ideas, based on critical analyses of previous theories and research. Much research sets out to test or further refine existing theories so that they are more useful in providing explanations, and for creating models for future action.

Example:
The flight still hasn't been announced. My theory is that a storm is brewing so they think they can't take.

Everyday use of the word tends to be an expression of opinion, but it shares the characteristics of academic theory in being:
- an attempt to provide an explanation, or a prediction of likely outcomes;
- an idea, or set of abstract ideas, that haven't been fully proved;
- based on the facts as far as they are known at the time, and acknowledging there is still more to find out.

Task: *What are the main schools of thought for your own areas of interest?*

Theoretical-based argument: A theory may be used as the basis of an argument.
Example:
Marx's theory of economics argues that wealth will become concentrated into a few hands. This research project is based on an interpretation of Marx's theory, and argues that although the denationalisation of public services in Britain led to more companies being set up in the short term, over a few decades, mergers and buy-outs have resulted in many smaller companies closing. As a result, the wealth of those industries is now in the possession of a small number of "super-companies". The research hypothesis is that after three decades, 75 per cent of the wealth of former British nationalised industries will, in each case, be in the hands of three or fewer super-companies.

C. Identifying argument from academic reading

Usually, arguments are not provided separately from other material. They may be surrounded by:

> introductions
> descriptions
> explanations
> background information
> summaries
> other extraneous materials

Example:
Satellite imaging has been used to match water temperature swirls drawn on a map of ocean currents made as long ago as 1539. The map was produced by a Swedish

cartographer, Olaus Magnus. It had been thought that the rounded swirls, located between pictures of serpents and sea monsters, were there for purely artistic reasons. However, the size, shape and location of the swirls match, change in water temperature too closely for this to be a coincidence. The map is likely to be an accurate representation of the ocean eddy current found to the south and east of Iceland. It is believed that the map-maker collected his information from German mariners of the Hanseatic League.

Analysis of the example:

The overall argument in the example above is that an old sea map is likely to be an accurate chart of part of the ocean.

Description: The passage opens with a description of the method used to test the map: Satellite imaging has been used to match water temperature swirls drawn on a map of ocean currents...

Background information: ...a map of ocean currents... made as long ago as 1539. The map was produced by a Swedish cartographer; Olaus Magnus. It had been thought that the rounded swirls, located between pictures of serpents and sea monsters, were there for purely artistic reasons.

Task: *Complete the following details based on the above paragraph.*
  Reason to support:
  Explanatory detail:
  Conclusion:

D. Identifying reasoning from academic reading

Deductive reasoning

What is deduction?

Deduction is the process of reasoning from two general premises, or things that are known, to a specific conclusion. These three parts are:
  a. major premise
  b. minor premise
  c. conclusion

For instance, we know, A, that dogs have four legs, and we know, B, that Fido is a dog. Therefore, since A and B are true, we can conclude with certainty that, C, Fido has four legs.

From this example, you may see that a deductive argument is sound when the premises are true, and the conclusion logically follows from the premises.

Task: *Which one is an example of a deductive argument?*
  1. There are 25 CDs on the top shelf of my bookcase and 14 on the lower shelf. There are no other CDs in my bookcase. Therefore, there are 39 CDs in my bookcase.
  2. Topeka is either in Kansas or Honduras. If Topeka is in Kansas, then Topeka is in

North America. If Topeka is in Honduras, then Topeka is in Central America. Therefore, Topeka is in Kansas.

3. No one got an A on yesterday's test. Jimmy wasn't in school yesterday. Jimmy will make up the test today, and get an A.

4. All human beings are in favor of world peace. Terrorists don't care about world peace. Terrorists bring about destruction.

Inductive reasoning

What is induction?

Induction is the process of reasoning from the specific (particular facts or instances) to the general (principles, theories, rules). It uses two premises that support the probable truth of the conclusion.

Thus, an inductive argument looks like this: If A is true and B is true, then C is probably true.

How can you determine or measure what is probable or improbable?

By using two things:

a. past experience

b. common sense

Past experience tells you what you might be able to expect. For instance, "for the past three weeks, my colleague has showed up a half hour late for work. Today, she will probably be late, too." Common sense allows you to draw an inference, or a "smart guess," based on the premises, such as, "They need five people on the team. I'm one of the strongest of the seven players at the tryouts. It's likely that I will be picked for the team."

Because you must make a leap from the premises to the truth of the conclusion, inductive reasoning is more likely to fail and produce fallacies. Even so, most reasoning is inductive. One of the basic theories of modern biology, cell theory, is a product of inductive reasoning. It states that because every organism that has been observed is made up of cells, it is most likely that all living things are made up of cells. There are two forms of inductive arguments. Those that compare one thing, event, or idea to another to see if they are similar are called **comparative arguments**. Those that try to determine cause from effect are **causal arguments**.

Tasks:

1. Use possible past experience and common sense to choose the best conclusion for the inductive argument that begins: The other thirteen people who work on my team

    a. liked the design of the new product, so I should too.

    b. got positive evaluations from our boss, so I should too.

    c. got sick after eating the tuna salad, so I will too.

    d. who met the new employee liked him, so I will too.

2. Which one is NOT an example of comparative argument?
a. This month I paid my bills on time and I didn't get charged any late fees. Next month I'm going to pay them on time too so I can avoid the fees.
b. I got so tired at work yesterday afternoon after I had a bagel for lunch. Tomorrow, I think I'll order a roast beef sandwich.
c. Tom works out every morning and so does Bill. They are both in great shape and have lots of energy. If I work out every morning, I could get in shape and have more energy.
d. The chunky peanut butter was 50 cents cheaper at the supermarket every week for the past month. This week, it will probably be 50 cents cheaper, too.

3. Look for causation in the following scenario:
Yesterday, I pulled out of a diagonal parking spot, and was starting to turn my wheel and move forward, when another car backed out of a spot behind me. She drove right into me, smashing my left rear door with the corner of her bumper. The other driver told the police officer that I hit her. But he agreed with me that it was her fault, and wrote down why on the police report.

4. What did the police officer write? Circle all that could apply.
a. Drivers must wait their turn if another car is already pulling out of a parking space behind them. It is clear that the first car was already out of her space when she was hit on her door.
b. It is impossible to hit the corner of someone's bumper with your rear door when backing out of a parking spot. It is possible to hit the rear door of someone's car with the corner of your bumper.
c. Speeding in parking lots is prohibited by law.
d. The other driver must not have been looking in her rearview mirror, or she would not have backed into the other car.

E. Making notes to support critical reading
Important questions to ask:
- Do the reasons support the argument? Is there any supporting evidence?
- Does this match what I know about the subject already?
- Does it fit what other people say about the subject?
- Is this relevant and useful to my current purpose?
- How does this add to previous research on the subject?

Critical reading checklist
Identify the main argument (topic sentence)
Identify the introduction/background

Identify descriptions and transitions
Identify evidence to support reasons/argument
Identify facts and opinions
Identify counter arguments put forward by the author
Identify intermediate conclusion
Identify summative conclusion

 Group Work Activities

Task 1:
Read the following topic and list as many reasons as possible to argue about.
Global warming is one of the most serious issues that world is facing today. What are the causes of global warming and what measures can governments and individuals take to tackle the issue.

Task 2:
Read an academic article to identify the structure and writing elements mentioned in the checklist above.

Global Warming Requires a Global Solution

The increase in greenhouse gas emissions over the past 50 years is viewed as a major factor in global warming. Research by the leading world authorities on global warming, the Intergovernmental Panel on Climate Change (1PCC) suggests that even if all carbon dioxide emissions ceased today, there would be climate changes for a number of years to come, leading to water shortages for 5 billion people and increased flooding across Northern Europe by 2025. However, scientists have proposed a range of solutions from increasing efficient use of fossil fuels to incentives for using cleaner forms of energy, which they believe are sufficient to make a real impact on climate change.

The Kyoto Protocol was proposed in 1997 as a means of working towards a reduction in greenhouse gas emissions and the halting of long-term climate change. It focuses on developed countries, the world's greatest polluters, and seeks to establish an overall reduction in greenhouse gas emissions of 5 per cent on 1990 levels over the period of 2008—2012. Many key developed industrial nations have ratified the Protocol but a number of others have been resistant towards signing it, as they feel it is unfair that developing countries are exempt from the Protocol. Although a global solution to global warming is required, developed countries need to take the lead.

Politicians, scientists and businesses in developed countries have given a number of reasons for not signing up to the Protocol. These include doubt about the real link between carbon dioxide emissions and global warming, concerns about the effect on their own economies and a rejection of the need for imposed, rather than voluntary, reductions in emissions. A number of leaders of state have cited the lack of emission reduction targets for developing countries as the key reason behind their rejection of the protocol. On the surface, this appears a fair argument--global warming is a problem for everyone, not just those in developed countries, and requires every nation to participate. William K. Stevens (1997) makes the point that, if left unchecked, emissions from developing countries will surpass those from developed countries in 20—30 years.

Self-evaluation Form

What are the main objectives in this unit?
___
___
___

What useful vocabularies or expressions have you learned from this unit?
___
___
___

What key terms and educational knowledge have you learned?
___
___
___

Have you used the learning skills before? Why do you think they are useful or not useful?
___
___
___

If possible, what would you like to add to make learning more interesting and relevant?
___
___
___

Unit 9

English Language and Teaching

Introduction

Approaches to Language Learning and Teaching[1]

The Environmentalist Approach to Language Learning

Up to the end of the 1960s, the field of language learning was dominated by environmentalist ideas. The theory underlying these ideas was rooted in two parallel schools of thought in linguistics and psychology. In linguistics, the structural school of linguistics was strongly influential in the 1940s and 1950s. The approach arose from the attempts to analyze Indian languages, many of which had no written system and therefore the only data available was the oral form of the language. Based on the evidence that many languages did not have a written form and that people learnt to speak before they learnt to read or write, structural linguists assumed that language was primarily an oral phenomenon. Furthermore, written language was a secondary representation of speech. To the structuralists, language was viewed as consisting of different elements related to each other in a linear way by means of a series of structures or rules, these elements being phonemes, morphemes, words, and sentence types. The target of language learning was to master all the elements of the system and to learn the rules by which these elements were combined, from phoneme to morpheme to word to phrase to sentence. This specific theory of the nature of language learning, which was attracting language teachers' attention at that time, was the general learning theory then dominant in mainstream psychology, behaviorism.

In psychology, the behaviorist school dominated thinking in the field during the same time period, that is, in the 1940s and 1950s. This approach stemmed from early learning theorists who attempted to describe the learning process in terms of conditioning. To the behaviorists, behavior happened in associative stimulus-response chains, and all learning was seen as associative learning or habit-formation which became stronger with reinforcement. Therefore, the occurrence of behavior was

---

[1] Excerpt from *Current Trends in the Development and Teaching of the Four Language Skills*, Ed. by Usó-Juan, Esther and Martínez-Flor, Alicia. Walter de Die Deutsche Bibliotbek, 2008.

dependent upon three crucial elements in learning: a *stimulus*, which elicited the behavior; a *response*, which was triggered by the stimulus; and *reinforcement*, which marked the response as being appropriate or inappropriate and encouraged repetition or suppression of the response. Behaviorist theory placed emphasis on the role of the environment and denied the existence of internal mental processes, which were regarded as "inaccessible to proper scientific investigation".

The main proponent of this approach to the study of (learning) behavior was generally considered to be Skinner, who constructed a system of principles to account for human behavior from the observation of animal responses to stimuli in laboratory experiments. In his view, language learning, like any other kind of learning, was simply seen as a stimulus—response—reinforcement chain which led to the establishment of the appropriate habits of the language being learnt through automatic conditioning processes. Children received linguistic input from language users in their environment and positive reinforcement for their (grammatically) correct repetitions. As a result, and encouraged by the environment, they continued to practice until habits were formed. Imitation and practice, according to Skinner, were strong contributing factors in the language learning process.

Structural linguistics, in conjunction with behaviorist psychology led to the environmentalist approach to language learning. The American structuralist Bloomfield made the marriage between these two schools of thought clear in his book *Language*, which provides an excellent description of how language is acquired from a behaviorist point of view. The implications of this theoretical approach for language teaching were, thus, twofold. First, it was believed that learning took place by imitating and practicing the same structures time after time. Second, teachers should make it explicitly clear what was to be taught and focus mainly on the structures that were presumably more difficult.

The Innatist Approach to Language Learning

By the 1960s, the fields of linguistics and psychology witnessed major changes. Linguistics saw a paradigm shift from structural linguistics, which was based on the mere description of surface forms of utterances, to generative linguistics, which was concerned with both surface forms of utterances as well as the abstract structures underlying sentences, thus emphasizing the creative nature of human language. This paradigm shift was initiated by the publication of Chomsky's revolutionary book *Syntactic Structures*, in which he explained Transformational-Generative Grammar. This linguistics theory contends that language has a deep structure, which consists of the essential meanings, and a surface structure, which is made up of the particular way in which ideas are stated. Thus, there is one type of rules, phrase structure rules, which generate deep structures, and a second type, called transformational rules, which are responsible for converting deep structure into surface structure. Chomsky was interested not only in describing language, but also in explaining language behavior by studying the rules by which speakers and writers transformed their meanings (deep structure) into the particular sentences they say or write (surface structure) and the rules by which listeners and readers answered to these sentences by discovering their meanings. Following Saussure's dichotomy of langue (the language system) and parole (actual speech), Chomsky made the theoretical distinction between competence and performance and it was this competence or langue that generative theory was trying to explain.

Two years later Chomsky reviewed Skinner's *Verbal Behaviour* and made a critique of behaviorism by arguing consistently that a theory that only considers the observable responses in linguistic interaction could not hope to account for language behavior. He proved that statement to be true with two kinds of evidence. First, children can create and understand new sentences that they have never learnt before. He contended that this creativity implies that children have internalized an underlying system of rules (what he calls language *competence*) rather than strings of words. Second, all children successfully learn their native language at an early age in life despite the complexity and abstractness of linguistic rules. Furthermore, they accomplish this complex task of language learning without being systematically corrected on language points. Chomsky claimed that children were innately predisposed to acquire the language of the community into which they were born because they were born with some kind of Language Acquisition Device (LAD) to tackle the language learning task. In later work, Chomsky and his followers replaced the term LAD by the idea of *universal grammar*. This was a theory of innate principles and rules of inferences that enable the child to learn any grammar, or what Cook defined as "the black box responsible for language acquisition".

Around the same period of time, the field of psychology also underwent a major change as a result of the emergence of the hybrid field of psycholinguistics, which in its initial years of existence, aimed to test Chomsky's innatist theory of language acquisition. In direct contrast to the antimentalistic and mechanic view of human learning advocated by the behaviorist approach, this new approach was mentalistic and dynamic. The learner was seen as possessing an innate ability to process language and as actively participating in the learning process, using various mental strategies in order to sort out the language system to be learnt. Psycholinguistics studies showed conclusively that children were *active* rather than *passive* participants in the language learning process, since they inferred rules to test how language worked. This insight enabled researchers to explain why sentences such as "I drinked the juice" or "I have two foots" are produced in early childhood. In the first construction children are inferring that the past tense is made by adding -ed, whereas in the second construction they infer that the plural is formed by adding -s. In addition, this research also found that children's language development was incremental and could be characterized as going through similar stages. Longitudinal studies and cross-sectional studies also found that there was a consistent order of acquisition in a number of grammatical morphemes. All these findings, therefore, seemed to support Chomsky's assumptions that children are born with a predisposition to language acquisition. The implications of this theoretical approach for language teaching were, thus, twofold. First, it was believed that language learning was a rule-governed internal behavior (not the automatic formation of new habits). Second, teachers should develop learners' mental.

The Interactionist Approach to Language Learning

By the 1970s additional developments could be seen in the fields of linguistics and psychology. In the linguistics field, researchers began to turn their attention to discourse or language beyond the sentence. The development of discourse analysis supposed a shift within the field of linguistics away from the study of isolated sentences and toward understanding how sentences were connected. This new orientation advocated the study of both structure and function in order to understand what language was. The functional analysis of language was mainly represented by Halliday's systemic grammar, which attempted to explain how the function of language determines the form of language. Towards acquiring communicative competence through the four skills, Halliday postulated a total of seven communicative functions characterizing the child's early communicative development, all of which were related to aspects of social life. These functions were: *instrumental*, which involves the use of language to get things; *regulatory*, which involves the use of language to regulate people's behavior; *interactional*, which involves the use of language to interact with other people; *personal*, which involves the use of language to express one's feelings; *heuristic*, which involves the use of language to explore the outside world; *imaginative*, which involves the use of language to create an environment, and *representational*, which involves the use of language to communicate information. He theorized that children learned to talk because it served a function for them. Halliday's theory underscored the crucial importance of context of situation in the description of language systems and language was viewed as *meaning potential*. Therefore, the descontextualized analysis of formal structures followed by structural and generative linguistics was losing ground in favor of a contextualized perspective followed by systemic functional linguistics.

Questions after reading:

How do different theorists explain language learning? How do they affect the development of language teaching?

Group work:

Topic: Work in groups and provide a list of different English teaching approaches and methods. Can you build the correlated relations between the approaches and learning theories above?

Directions: Work as a group and share your ideas with others.

Text A

Brainstorming

Teachers' belief: A belief is a proposition that maybe consciously or unconsciously held, is evaluative in that it is accepted as true by the individual, and is therefore imbued with emotive commitment, further it serves as a guide to thought and behavior.

Teachers' belief, a term usually refers to teacher's pedagogic beliefs, or those beliefs of relevance to an individual's teaching. The areas most commonly explored are teachers' beliefs about teaching, learning, learners, subject matter, teacher identity and the role of teacher.

Questions before reading:

What is the function of language? What happens in the process of language learning? Is English a subject? Can language learning be taught by teachers? Why?

Illiteracy at Oxford and Harvard: Reflections on the Inability to Write[①]

Peter Elbow

In college, my experience of writing was the experience of being knocked down, but then stubbornly picking myself up, dusting myself off, and finally succeeding. On my third essay for freshman English, my teacher wrote, "Mr. Elbow, you continue your far from headlong rise upward" and the grade was D. The teachers I met in 1953 at Williams College were sophisticated and I was naive. But I was eager to do well and I worked hard at it—and by the end of my first year had begun to do so. Indeed, I gradually found myself wanting to enter their world and be like them a college professor, not just a teacher. I wanted to be a learned, ironic, tweedy, pipe-smoking, professor of literature.

As for writing, I took no particular pleasure in it. I wrote when assigned. I no longer experienced any imaginative element in the writing I did; it was all critical. I found it difficult, but I sometimes got excited working out a train of thought of my own. Toward the end of my four years, however, I began to notice out of the corner of my consciousness, an increase in the "ordeal" dimension of writing papers: more all-nighters; more of them the night after the paper was due; more

---

① Excerpt from *Reflective Stories: Becoming Teachers of College English and English Education,* National Council of Teachers of English, USA, 1998.

not-quite-acknowledged fear. But still I got those As.

Tutorials were conducted in the tutor's rooms. Once a week, I'd knock on the oak door and come in and read my essay to him, and be instructed, and then at the end he'd say something like, "Why don't you go off and read Dryden and write me something interesting?" My first essay was on Chaucer and he was pretty condescendingly devastating. ("What are we going to do with these Americans they send us?" Interesting again that Chaucer was my Ph.D. topic.) During one tutorial, he cleaned his rifle as I read my essay to him. On another occasion I quoted Marvell. As I pronounced the title of the poem in my broad-vowelled American accent, "On a Drohp of Doo," he broke in with his clipped Oxford accent, "On a Drup of Djyew," and remarked, "Maybe that's why you don't understand poetry, Elbow. You don't know what it sounds like." Before the end of the fall term, I was coming in every week saying, "I don't have an essay for you. I tried as hard as I could, but I couldn't write it." And I really had tried hard, spending the whole week writing initial sentences, paragraphs, and pages and throwing them all away.

Eventually, I changed tutors and limped through my second year. I took a lot of Valium as exams approached. For in fact, it turned out that the Oxford degree didn't depend at all on any of these essays written for tutors over two years. They were nothing but practice for the nine three-hour exams you took during your last four-and-a-half days. I was terrified, but it turns out that the exams didn't throw me as much as the essays had done: in each exam there were only three hours for at least three essays and there wasn't time to agonize even to revise. I survived with acceptable results (an "undistinguished second") and very grateful too. "Pretty much what we expected," was Jonathan's comment on the card on which he mailed me my results.

My sense of failure was total. It wouldn't have been so bad if I had been less invested or hadn't tried so hard. But I'd long announced my career commitment to my family and relatives, my friends, and my teachers and I'd tried my damndest. I'd defined and staked my identity on this business of getting a Ph.D. to become a college professor. And I'd also defined myself to others and to myself as "successful", particularly at school. So when I quit, I felt ruined. I felt I never wanted to have anything to do with the world of books and teaching again.

First Reflection: On the Experience of Failure

I realize now that much of the texture of my academic career has been based in an oddly positive way on this experience of complete shame and failure. In the end, failing led me to have the following powerful but tacit feeling: "There's nothing else they can do to me. They can't make me feel any worse than they've already done. I tried as hard as I could to be the way they wanted me to be, and I couldn't do it. I really wanted to be good, and I was bad." These feelings created an oddly solid grounding for my future conduct in the academic world. They made it easier for me to take my own path and say whatever I wanted.

In subsequent years, I've noticed that lots of people's behavior in schools and colleges is driven by the opposite feelings sometimes unconscious: "Uh-oh. They could really hurt me. I must do this or I'll fail. I couldn't say that or they'd kick me out. To fail or be kicked out is unthinkable." When you live with these feelings as I had certainly done through all the years before I failed you sometimes notice a faint impulse to say or do something unacceptable (for example, to skip an assignment, or to do it in a way that the teacher would find unacceptable, or to stand up to the teacher with some kind of basic disagreement or refusal). But you scarcely notice this impulse because acting on it would be unimaginable; insupportable. I realize now that the most unsuccessful students are often the most adventuresome or brave or mentally creative. They operate from the feeling of, "They can't hurt me any worse. What the hell!" That feeling can be empowering. In truth, the most successful students are often the most timid and fearful. They have the most at stake in getting approval. They do the most cheating in school; they have the most suicides.

Second Reflection: Language to Convey, Language to Disguise

There emerges here a curious and pregnant fact: that language can be used not only to convey meaning, but to disguise it. We characteristically articulate our meaning in words so people will understand us; but sometimes we do it so that they won't or at least some of them won't. This may seem perverse. And perverse is what I was being "contrary" with my teachers. And I get mad when I feel others using language this way such as when professionals and academics write not just to communicate their meaning, but to exclude the unwashed.

Yet this "game" of using language to convey-but-also-to-disguise was explicitly celebrated in medieval theology and criticism as a model for poetry. According to this theory, the poem consists of a tough husk that hides and protects, and a sweet and tender kernel inside. The function of a good poem is to convey the kernel of wisdom or sweetness but only to those worthy of it; and to hide it from the unworthy.

This wasn't just a theory spun by intellectuals and theoreticians. Christ proclaimed it openly in his parable talking about his very use of parables, and from the Gospels, it became common currency. Here is Matthew's version:

Then the disciples went up to him and asked, "Why do you talk to them in parables?" "Because," he replied, "the mysteries of the kingdom of heaven are revealed to you but they are not revealed to them. For anyone who has will be given more, and he will have more than enough; but from anyone who has not, even what he has will be taken away. The reason I talk to them in parables is that they look without seeing and listen without hearing or understanding."

Helen Fox points out that many traditional, non-Western cultures value this indirect, and often metaphorical, way of conveying meaning and scorn the modern Western value of being direct and literal. Here is an account by Deborah Fredo of the difference between traditional and modern ways of conveying knowledge in Senegal:

The [traditional] kind of knowledge that is sought after is that kind which can come from *"minds that bleed best" [the wisest minds]....[I]n direct thought... is more valued than direct thought because what can be attained through direct thought is said to be the kind of knowledge you don't have to work for, the kind that is given to you. Riddles are used as a kind of intelligence test to see if the mind is open enough to "bleed".*

Being modern, on the other hand, is associated with being direct, a decidedly inferior attribute of the mind. Being true to traditional form means being able to speak in ways which require a listener to decode what you are saying and analyze your meaning. Making meaning, in such a process, always involves some inquiry and analysis but it is the qualities of the person seeking to understand meaning or knowledge that guarantee its acquisition.

So even though I resent this use of language (which I now think I engaged in with my college teachers) and dislike this parable about parables, I must recognize that language-to-convey-and-to-disguise is not only a venerable tradition but a perennial human impulse. It lies behind much spontaneous and unsophisticated word play. And isn't much, or even most, poetry an attempt, in a way, to slow down comprehension? (The poet Richard Hugo famously remarked, "If I wanted to communicate, I'd pick up the telephone.") Almost every-one loves riddles, which are a central art form in most oral cultures. In short, humans naturally use language to make their meaning more clear and striking; but they also like to use language to make their meaning less clear to use language as a kind of filter or puzzle or game to distinguish among receivers.

Third Reflection: Writing as Giving in

My story seems to be about the movement from compliance to resistance. As a good student, I had been expert at compliance, at doing what my teachers wanted me to do, but too much compliance got me in trouble. I was so unable to notice or experience any resistance or refusal or anger so mistaken about my feelings, so unable to find a path for these feelings that they found their own underground path to short circuit my entire ability to write or even be a student. My story seems to be about the need to learn fruitful or healthy ways to resist rather than ways that undermine oneself.

This is a familiar theme in studies of the learning process. These commentators emphasize not only how learning leads inevitably to resistance, but also that we can't learn well without resistance. It seems clear that an important goal for teachers is to help students find fruitful or healthy ways to resist. This became my theme too in most of my subsequent writing about writing: I have been a celebrator of writing without teachers, writing that is free, writing that ignores audience.

But at this stage in my autobiographical reflections, I'm noticing something different in the story. Yes, it's about ineffective resistance, but now I'm struck with how it's also about ineffective compliance. When I couldn't write my papers at all, I may not have been resisting very effectively, but I certainly was resisting. What I wasn't doing at all was complying. During the earlier stages of writing this paper, I was noticing my gift for compliance; now I'm noticing my problem with compliance. Something tugs at me now to learn more about this side of the authority relationship of a student to a teacher.

Once I open this door, I'm struck at how many ways writing involves complying or giving in. The need for compliance is most obvious in the case of writing in school and college. There is always a teacher and an assignment and criteria to be met. Someone other than the writer is in charge. The writing has to conform to the teacher's criteria or it's not acceptable (Cleary gives us good pictures of this in her interviews with students). But even when scholars write for learned journals, there is often a strong sense of the need to conform to some-one else's criteria. The constraints can be even stronger with a supervisor or employer sometimes, in fact, the obligation to say exactly what the person in charge wants you to say. Thus in many, or even most, writing situations, there is a subtle, or not so subtle, pressure to give in. When we send writing to journals, publishers, and teachers, what is the verb we use? We "submit".

Exercises

I. Reading Comprehension:

There are four suggested answers marked A, B, C and D. Choose the best answer for each question.

1. What are the author's attitudes towards good writing?
   A. Simple, clear, straightforward.
   B. Direct, literal.
   C. Muddy, unclear, sophisticated.
   D. Ambitious, thoughtful, ironic.

2. What can be inferred from the author's experiences in school?
   A. If you work hard in school, you will succeed.
   B. The most successful students are often lack of creativity and having psychological problems.
   C. If your writings are indirect and unclear, you will probably be praised by teachers in college.
   D. Writing is actually a word game between teachers and students in college.

3. Which one of the following statements is incorrect about language to convey and to disguise?
   A. It has a long and valuable tradition.
   B. It has based on spontaneous human activity.
   C. It has only used among intellectuals and professionals.
   D. It has used as a kind of filter to distinguish receivers.

4. Scholars agree that learning inevitably leads to resistance because_____.
   A. writing is free and writing ignores audience
   B. we can't learn well without resistance
   C. accepting conventions means losing integrity and creativity
   D. complying to the conventions and traditions will meet condemnations

5. What is the genre of this passage?
   A. Argumentation.
   B. Narration.
   C. Description.
   D. Exposition.

II. Judgments and Implications:

Do the following statements agree with the information given in the passage?
True   if the statement is true according to the passage
False   if the statement contradicts the passage

1. The author had pleasant and fruitful writing experiences and he got all As in college.
2. The author's learning experiences in Oxford were terrible, so he quited school.
3. The practice of using language to convey-but-also-to-disguise was celebrated in medieval theology and poetry but condemned by modern writing.
4. For intellectuals and theoreticians, the major use of language is to conceal, not just to reveal.
5. Most professionals believe that good writing always means clear writing.
6. When scholars write for learned journals, they are writing to comply to someone else's criteria.

III. Critical Questions:

The novelist Helen Oyeyemi said in an interview that she forced herself to write with a word-gobbling application (app), sparking a conversation about other aids for procrastinating writers. Helen Oyeyemi offered the following rather startling writing tip:

Download the Write or Die computer application. When you activate kamikaze mode, the screen lets you pause typing for about 45 seconds before it begins deleting words you've already written. Because, sometimes, fear is the only motivator.

What are your tips? Let us know if you have any other tips for new-era aids to the writing life.

Text B

Brainstorming

English as a lingual franca: In recent years, the term "English as a lingua franca" (ELF) has emerged as a way of referring to communication in English between speakers with different first languages. Since roughly only one out of every four users of English in the world is a native speaker of the language, most

ELF interactions take place among "non-native" speakers of English.

Although this does not preclude the participation of English native speakers in ELF interaction, what is distinctive about ELF is that, in most cases, it is "a 'contact language' between persons who share neither a common native tongue nor a common (national) culture, and for whom English is the chosen foreign language of communication".

Questions before reading:

What problems do Chinese schools have in English language teaching?
If possible, what would you suggest to make progress?

TESOL in China: Current Challenges[①]
Bonny Norton & Yian Wu

English Language Teaching in China: Trends and Challenges

Learning English in a Chinese language environment is a rather daunting task. Millions of ELF learners (There are more than 200 million primary and high school pupils in China. In September 2000, 2 million school leavers were enrolled in universities.) task regular English courses, 4 class hours a week, 18 weeks a term, for 12 terms in high school and 48 terms at university. For those not majoring in English, the goal is to function adequately in English at work, but not many have developed the necessary competence. In fact, although English language teaching (ELT) is a huge profession in the process of reform and renovation, it seems to fall far short of meeting the needs generated from the country's rapid developments in the economy, science, and technology, and from increasing contact with the outside world. As a consequence, the importance of English at all levels of education cannot be overemphasized.

Although English education may not be able to keep up with the need for it, over the years Chinese universities have provided tens of thousands of competent English users, a great majority of these having been English majors educated in over 300 intensive English programmes. However, this number is actually rather small relative to China's needs and compared with the huge number of young adults trying to master English in addition to their other areas of study. Programmes designed for majors face a different challenge. A recent large-scale investigation, initiated by the Higher Education Division of the Ministry of Education, reveals that in general the country's need for foreign language workers equipped with target language skills alone has dropped to zero. All foreign language majors are expected to develop knowledge of other areas in addition to competence in a foreign language. The Ministry of Education responded quickly to the

---

① From *TESOL Quarterly*, Volume 35, Issue 1, Spring 2001, pp.191—194.

need for English for students across disciplines by organizing major curriculum reviews for schools and for major and non-major English programmes at universities nationwide. Long-distance ELT and English on-line programmes are joining forces with formal ELT programmes in attempting to upgrade English proficiency levels across the nation. The ELT profession has felt the impact throughout the country, where many people are demanding reform.

In what follows, the outline of what I see as the dominant trends of reform. I also discuss the accompanying challenges, with a view to appealing for support and efforts to promote ELT in China and for research in formal English language learning in a non-target language environment.

English Language Planning

In recent years, English has been introduced into the primary school curriculum in an increasing number of cities across China. Efforts are being made to plan a two-stage learning process consisting of the primary/junior high/senior high stage and the university stage, which cover a total span of 14—16 years. Ideally, the learning process should be a cumulative one with varying sub-goals and approaches for different stages, necessarily constrained by the developmental characteristics of the learner's cognitive growth and their learning environment. In reality, the reformers are still far from knowing a sound basis on which to plan the sequence of learning. Nor do curriculum reformers have a system of evaluating the planning yet. An added complication is that in a huge country like China, any planning has to accommodate the very uneven development in English proficiency levels among the learners. Research is needed to address these curriculum and evaluation issues.

Teacher Education

Administrators and teachers themselves are increasingly aware that it is teachers who hold the key to the outcome of reform and therefore of ELT. Teacher education has received increasing attention, especially for university EFL teachers, who in general have not been trained for the profession. The Ministry of Education, teachers' universities, leading linguistics and applied linguistics programmes, and ELT publishers have all been involved in organizing training programmes, and teachers are eager to take advantage of the opportunities.

But questions remain about how to develop teacher education programmes most effectively. What are suitable models of teacher development in China, where there is an acute shortage of ELT teachers and the need for development is often threefold—in (a) English proficiency levels; (b)knowledge about language in general, English in particular, and language learning; and (c) language teaching philosophies and methodology. What are we as TESOL professionals in China to draw from our own traditional ELT and from contemporary theories, research findings, and trends of practice in the profession? How can we best organize research with a view to meeting the challenges we face? These seem urgent questions to take up before teacher education can significantly affect ELT in China.

Materials

Textbooks are essential in formal ELT in China. They provide input, suggest approacher and methodology, and guide or impose the course of learning. Materials also offer education of a sort. The major curriculum reviews and the subsequent launching of new curricula call for high-quality materials that frame and support systematic, efficient, and effective English language learning. ELT publishers and teachers have attempted to respond to the need.

Challenges to material writing include (a) a shortage of source materials, (b) a lack of full understanding of Chinese learners' learning process in the formal school environment, and (c) the need to combine traditional and multimedia materials effectively. To meet the first challenge, in recent years Chinese publishers and publishers in native-English-speaking countries have tended to form collaborative relationships. More crucially, though, material writers need to be critically informed in relevant theories and research findings concerning language teaching and learning, in task design, and in principles and methods that work in the traditional language teaching paradigm.

Assessment

As a form of assessment, language testing is especially influential in education in China. Indeed, large-scale exams whose design is based on structuralism and whose format is predominantly multiple choice have been found to constrain language teaching in a rather negative way. Teachers and administrators demand improvements in test design.

While existing test designs are being improved, organized effort have been directed to alternative, more task-based test designs guided by contemporary language testing theories. Unlike the earlier tests, these new tests give due attention to speaking and writing. They are designed with a view to promoting learning. Formative assessment has been a means of teaching for many experienced language teachers over the years, but little research has been conducted on formative assessment in China and abroad. There seems a need for such research to complement language testing.

Research

All the trends outlined above, however immature or robust, must depend upon systematic research and information practice to sustain and bloom. To upgrade ELT in China and to contribute to the TESOL field, China will need to organize nationwide research teams in each of the subareas of study and to draw on international expertise. Initial efforts are being made toward this end.

Unit 9 English Language and Teaching

Exercises

I. Reading Comprehension:

There are four suggested answers marked A, B, C and D. Choose the best answer for each question.

1. Which one of the following options is NOT one of the challenges of TESOL in China?
   A. Chinese universities have cultivated tens of thousands of English users but the number is rather small compared with its needs.
   B. All foreign languages majors are expected to develop knowledge of other areas.
   C. The country's need for foreign language workers equipped with target language skills has dropped to zero.
   D. English education is not able to keep up with the need.
2. "Efforts are being made to plan a two-stage learning process", it means that _____.
   A. it is made up of the primary, junior high, senior high stage and the university stage, and with the total span of 14—16 years
   B. it should be a cumulative one with constant sub-goals and approaches for different stages
   C. it is a process consisting of two stages—the primary stage and the university stage, which cover a total span of 14—16 years
   D. it is a cumulative process with one major target and approach for different stages
3. Which one of the following questions has NOT been included on how to develop teacher's education programmes?
   A. What are suitable models for teachers' development in China?
   B. What can we as TESOL professionals in China draw from our own traditional ELT and from contemporary theories?
   C. Where is an acute shortage of Teacher Education?
   D. How can we best organize research with a view to meeting the challenges we face?
4. Challenges to material writing include all of the followings, except for _____.
   A. a shortage of source materials
   B. the need to form collaborative relationships
   C. a lack of full understanding of Chinese learners' learning process in the formal school environment
   D. the need to unite traditional and multimedia materials effectively
5. Which one of the following statements is TRUE?
   A. University English teachers have been trained for the profession and they are eager to take advantage of the opportunities.

B. Material writers need to be critically informed in irrelevant theories and research findings concerning language teaching and learning.
C. The multiple choice questions in large-scale exams have been found appropriate for language teaching.
D. To upgrade ELT in China and to contribute to the TESOL field, China needs to form nationwide research teams in every aspect.

II. Judgments and Implications:

Do the following statements agree with the information given in the passage?
True   if the statement is true according to the passage
False   if the statement contradicts the passage

1. For students who are not majoring in English, their English learning goal is to function adequately in English at work, but not many have developed the necessary competence.
2. Long-distance ELT and English on-line programmes are joining forces with formal ELT programmes trying to promote English proficiency levels in China.
3. As a huge country, China has plenty of English learning plans, but all of these plans have to accommodate the very equilibrium development in English proficiency levels among the learners.
4. In order to combine traditional and multimedia materials effectively, Chinese publishers have tended to form collaborative relationship.
5. Different from the earlier tests, the new tests give due attention to speaking and writing. They are designed with a view to promoting the assessment of learning.

III. Read the following two paragraphs and decide which one is an academic text, and why?

In recent years, English has been introduced into the primary school curriculum in an increasing number of cities across China. Efforts are being made to plan a two-stage learning process consisting of the primary/junior high/senior high stage and the university stage, which cover a total span of 14—16 years. Ideally, the learning process should be a cumulative one with varying sub-goals and approaches for different stages, necessarily constrained by the developmental characteristics of the learner's cognitive growth and their learning environment. In reality, the reformers are still far from knowing a sound basis on which to plan the sequence of learning. Nor do curriculum reformers have a system of evaluating the planning yet. An added complication is that in a huge country like China, any planning has to accommodate the very uneven development in English proficiency levels among the learners. Research is needed to address these curriculum and evaluation issues.

In recent years, we have introduced English into primary school curriculum to many cities over China. Our main efforts have been dedicated to developing English proficiency at both primary, secondary and university levels. The full coverage of English language teaching has been expanded to learners whose ages are from 14—16 years old. We naturally hope the well-designed goals of curriculum could be reached in light of the cognitive and learning development, but the order of learning process and evaluation of planning as fundamental elements have been overlooked. What have been more complicated are the apparent flaws on the analysis of uneven proficiency in China, which shows the invalid unprofessional values of those who used to be proclaimed professionals.

Read each sentence above again and list the features of academic text from the aspects of structure, pronoun, voice and lexis.

pronoun	
voice	
lexis	
structure	

IV. Critical Questions:

To tackle the problems mentioned in the article, measures need to be taken through policy making and implementation. In English language teaching, what policy has to be issued and how to evaluate its effects?

Text C

Brainstorming

Evidence-based education: It is an approach to all aspects of education—from policy-making to classroom practice—where the methods used are based on significant and reliable evidence derived from experiments. It shares with evidence-based medicine the aim: to apply the best available evidence, gained from the scientific method to educational decision making.

Questions before reading:
Do you think that language skills should be taught separately or integrally? Why and Why not? How can you illustrate your assumptions in a scientific way?

From Reading to Writing, from Elementary to Graduate Students

Sandra Stotsky

My intellectual curiosity about the nature of reading as a language process and about the most successful methods for reading instruction remained after I stopped teaching full time to raise a family. I avidly followed the controversies about reading instruction as they were reported in the popular press. Rudolph Flesch's *Why Johnny Can't Read and What You Can Do about It* had appeared in 1955, beginning an unnecessarily polarized battle between those advocating a sight word approach and those arguing for systematic phonics instruction that has continued uninterrupted to this day (although with somewhat different labels for the antagonists over the years). In 1967 appeared the most famous book of all about the controversy over approaches to reading instruction Jeanne Chall's *Learning to Read: The Great Debate*. I read it eagerly and experienced a minor epiphany. It was the first account of the issues in reading instruction that made sense to me in light of my own teaching experience. And it wasn't filled with opinions, dogma, or cant; it was a careful, clear, and systematic presentation of research evidence by someone who seemed to know what children and classrooms were like. This was somebody I wanted to study with. I applied and was admitted to the Harvard Graduate School of Education (HGSE), with the intention now of examining the pieces of the reading puzzle from a research perspective.

My entry into graduate school in 1970 brought me immediately in touch with all the major currents of academic thinking about the teaching of reading. The tenets of transformational grammar dominated reading research, and a "psycholinguistic" approach to reading (the term for the sight word approach at that point in time) was being hailed by some as the only method of instruction and the answer to the failures of our urban schools, despite the substantial evidence supporting systematic phonics instruction, especially for low-income children. But with professional roots in that not forgotten third grade classroom, I regularly applied practical criteria to every new theory or pedagogical implication generated by academic research and found them all wanting.

I first began to sense that writing had a distinctive perhaps crucial role to play in the entire educational process as well as in learning how to read when I read Vygotsky's *Thought and Language* in 1971 (a second minor epiphany for me), particularly his passages on the role of grammar and writing in intellectual development. However, at the time, there was no intellectual context at HGSE for developing this idea. No one had, as yet, tried to make any connections between what was taught in English education departments and reading departments, that is, the connections between the teaching of reading and the teaching of writing. These pedagogical focuses were the responsibilities of two different departments with differently trained scholars and researchers. And since HGSE no longer had an English Education program, cross-disciplinary contacts could not take place within the school.

Two years after reading Vygotsky's work, I stumbled onto the sentence-combining research literature (at that time, people in reading research paid almost no attention to writing or language arts research) and some of the pieces of the puzzle finally began to fit together, so it seemed. I searched for anything that related grammar, writing, and reading to each other, and I was amazed to discover that, at the time, there wasn't even an index card on the psychology of writing in the Union Catalogue at Widener Library. The results of my research and thinking an evaluative review of the research on sentence-combining and its effects on reading comprehension became my qualifying paper for a dissertation and my first publication. However, because, on practical grounds, I was in no position to carry out an experiment on sentence-combining and had to focus on a topic related to the teaching of reading, not writing, I decided to explore some theoretical issues in vocabulary instruction for my dissertation, picking up on an interest that went all the way back to my high school Latin courses. Little did I suspect that the esoteric lexical phenomenon I chose to restrict my research to the prefixed words used in reading instructional materials would lead me right back to the psychology of writing again. Moreover, the very act of writing a dissertation at this point in my thinking occasioned a good deal of introspection about the role of writing in the development of my thinking. It became obvious to me that I wasn't just expressing my thoughts as I wrote my dissertation, but literally working them out.

For part of my dissertation research, I tallied the frequency, in reading instructional texts for grades one to six, of words with "living" prefixes, i.e., words such as transatlantic, pro-labor, and pseudo-intellectual, whose prefixes can be removed (as opposed to etymologically prefixed words such as transpire, propose, and pseudonym whose prefixes cannot be removed because what remains cannot stand alone as independent words in the sense required). The skewed distribution[①] of words with living prefixes in different types of reading material and their increasing number as reading material became progressively more difficult seemed to point to linguistic differences between expository and narrative writing. More words with living prefixes appeared in expository than narrative texts, possibly, I speculated, because of the more learned, Latin- and Greek-based character of the vocabulary of exposition, especially academic exposition, and the constant word-coining that had accompanied the growth of scientific discourse in post-Reformation England (as in ancient Greece itself). These linguistic differences, in turn, pointed to differences in the cognitive demands of each. Yet, the overwhelming emphasis on narrative selections in all instructional readers for the elementary grades meant that, unintentionally, reading skills were being developed for one kind of reading only. As relevant as the differences between narrative and expository writing were for the teaching of reading, I couldn't think of a course, seminar, or

---

① skewed distribution: 偏态分布。

research presentation at HGSE in the six years I had been there that had ever alluded to the stylistic differences between them and to the possible cognitive consequences of these differences. Nor had I ever heard anyone even inquire whether a skewed emphasis on narrative selections might negatively influence reading development. Further, as I thought about why the use of words with living prefixes might well be more characteristic of succinct expository writing than narrative or literary writing, it seemed reasonable to view active prefixation as a more deliberate than spontaneous linguistic choice and hence more likely to take place while writing or revising than while speaking. I concluded that active prefixation was probably a phenomenon that characterized written more than spoken language.

    I couldn't believe that I had come across questions that no one else had ever thought about. So I spent a few days looking through the entire Harvard catalogue, hoping that what I was looking for was not unknown to other scholars, simply unknown to me and the field of reading. I finally found one course description (and that was all) that sounded a little like what I was looking for Morton Bloomfield's course on stylistics. He was the Boylston Professor of Rhetoric, a subject about which I knew very little formally. I took his course as a post-doctoral student and, through it, discovered what those in the field of reading had rarely, if ever, discussed the teaching of rhetoric, questions of style, the theoretical issues engaging those concerned with the teaching of composition, and more broadly the teaching of English. My reading, of necessity, expanded to encompass several disciplines that I had barely known existed in the previous six years.

    At the same time, I obtained a position as the coordinator of the Elementary Education Program at Curry College, a small liberal arts college in Milton, Massachusetts. My professional experiences at Curry College were instrumental in accelerating my transition to becoming a teacher of teachers of writing rather than a teacher of teachers of reading. I was by now convinced that writing was the chief instrument for developing thinking. While reading was still essential for intellectual development, and while I had always seen writing as highly dependent on reading (and still do), writing was (or at least could be, I now believed) the more powerful activity. It required more active, more precise, and more strenuous thinking than reading did. Thus, in the reading and language arts courses I created at Curry College, I incorporated a variety of writing activities designed to enhance my students' reading, thinking, and learning. I also found myself relying on the pedagogical principles I had evolved when teaching third grade years before. Although most of my students were not highly skilled readers or writers, they were willing to work on their reading and writing assignments in the context of a highly individualized, structured, and supportive pedagogical approach.

Unit 9　English Language and Teaching

Exercises

I. Reading Comprehension:

There are four suggested answers marked A, B, C and D. Choose the best answer for each question.

1. All the following statements demonstrate the reasons why the author applied for the graduate school, which one is correct?
   A. Battle between those advocating a sight word approach and those arguing for systematic phonics instruction.
   B. My intellectual curiosity about the nature of reading and about the most successful methods for reading instruction.
   C. The most famous book of all about the controversy over approaches to reading instruction.
   D. The intention of examining the pieces of the reading puzzle from a research perspective.

2. In the sentence "...I stumbled onto the sentence-combining research literature...", the word stumble indicates_____.
   A. the author was uncertain about the literature he had read
   B. the author had accessed to the research literature by coincidence
   C. the author started reading the research literature uneasily
   D. the author had found scarcely mentioned research literature

3. Why did the author decide to explore reading for his dissertation?
   A. Because there had been no relevant literatures on his topic.
   B. Because teaching experiment on writing could not be implemented.
   C. Because it raised an interest of lexis from the author's high school days.
   D. Because the author presumed that reading and writing are correlated.

4. Which one of the following options can not explain the reasons why more words with living prefixes appeared in expository than narrative texts?
   A. Because of the more learned, Latin- and Greek-based character of the vocabulary of exposition.
   B. Because of the constant word-coining that had accompanied the growth of scientific discourse in post-Reformation England.
   C. Because of the different cognitive demands between expository and narrative writings.
   D. Because of the skewed distribution of words with living prefixes in different types of reading material.

5. What research topic did the author argue about?
   A. What reading involves and its implications to English teaching.
   B. What writing involves and its implications to English teaching.

C. How different lexis uses affect the development of English writing.
D. What sentence-combining functions in English reading and writing.

II. Judgments and Implications:

Do the following statements agree with the information given in the passage?
True   if the statement is true according to the passage
False   if the statement contradicts the passage

1. The tenets of transformational grammar dominated reading research, which in turn, had been regarded as the only method of instruction.
2. Writing a dissertation triggered my reflection about the role of writing in the development of my thinking.
3. Words such as transatlantic, propose, and pseudo-intellectual, whose prefixes can be removed are living prefixes.
4. Active prefixation as a more deliberate than spontaneous linguistic choice demonstrates the nature of more cognitive workload in narrative writing.
5. In the reading courses I created at Curry College, I incorporated a variety of writing activities designed to enhance reading, thinking, and learning.

III. Chart Filling:

Read the following chart and fill in each blank with no more than three words.

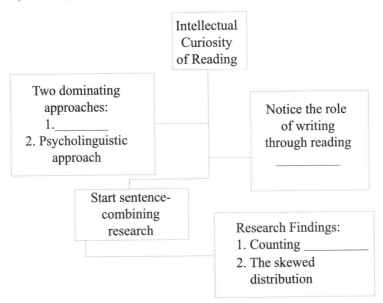

IV. Critical Questions:

Can you summarize how to conduct a classroom-based research in teaching English? Compare your key points with your classmates to find the differences.

Learning Skills

Academic Writing Skills

Thesis

The thesis acts as the main claim of your paper, and typically appears near the end of the introduction. Unless you have a compelling reason to relocate the thesis from the traditional place, put it at the end of your introductory paragraph. Readers anticipate and read closely your thesis, and they want to find a polished statement there. The thesis expresses in one concise sentence the point and purpose of your essay.

Make it arguable

Your thesis must make an arguable assertion. To test whether your assertion is arguable, ask yourself whether it would be possible to argue the opposite. If not, then it's not a thesis — it's more of a fact. For example:

• *Not Arguable:* "Computers are becoming an efficient mechanism for managing and transmitting information in large businesses." (Who's going to dispute this? It's not an arguable assertion — it's a fact.)

• *Arguable:* "Heavy use of computers may disrupt family cohesion and increase divorce in society." (This is arguable because many people may not believe it. It would make a good thesis!)

Be specific

The thesis must also be specific. Avoid broad, vague generalizations. Your thesis should include detail and specificity, offering the reader the why behind your reasoning.

• *Poor Specificity:* "We should not pass the microchip bill." (Hey, not specific enough! It's just a value statement and doesn't provide enough reasoning for the reader.)

• *Good Specificity:* "Because the microchip insert causes serious health hazards such as cancer and brain tumors to those who use it, the microchip should not be passed." (Now the thesis is much more specific, and the reader gets a clear idea of what the essay is going to be about.)

Avoid lists

If your thesis consists of a long list of points, your essay will most likely be superficial. Suppose you had six reasons why WebCT should be adopted in college courses. Instead of trying to cover so much ground in your essay, narrow your focus more to give greater depth to fewer ideas, maybe discussing two or three points instead.

Long lists result in shallow essays because you don't have space to fully explore an idea. If you don't know what else to say about a point, do more brainstorming and research. However, if you're arguing a longer paper, and really need to cover this much ground, still avoid the list in your thesis—just give the reader a general idea of your position, without being so specific.

- *Example of a list*: "The microchip bill biologically damages the health of children, invades the privacy of independent teenagers, increases crime, turns children against their parents, induces a sense of robotry about the individual, and finally, may result in the possible takeover of the government." (Wow, what a list! In a 1,000 words essay, each of these topics will only be explored superficially.)
- *Narrower focus:* "By surgically inserting circuitry similar to cell phone devices that has been known to cause headaches and fatigue, the microchip biologically endangers the health of children." (I've narrowed my focus to just one point—health hazards — instead of the six. Now my job will be to explore this assertion in depth. Academic writing almost always prefers depth over breadth.)

Follow an "although ... actually" format

The "although... actually" format is one of the most effective ways of finding something original and controversial to say. In effect, you are telling someone that what he or she thought to be previously true really isn't. You're saying, *Hey, you thought X? Well, you're wrong. Really, it's Y!* Whenever you look beyond the obvious and give readers something new to consider, you're going to get their attention. Nothing works better than this "although . . . actually" format to set you up in delivering an insight.

- *Example: Although* it appears that computers may help students learn to write, *actually* they can become a detriment to the generation of what creative writers call "flow".
- *Example: Although* many people believe that extraterrestials and crop circles are a figment of the imagination, *actually* there is strong evidence suggested by collective, distinct anecdotes that alien encounters are real.
- *Example: Although* some philosophers profess to lead more pure, thoughtful lives, *actually* philosophers are no different than other publication-hungry academics.

(Note: "actually" isn't always necessary. It is often implied with the clause "although".)

Academic Style

When using ideas or phrases from other writers in your own essay, you must correctly cite in your text exactly where the ideas or phrases come from. Correctly identifying these ideas and phrases is called "in-text citation", and the page at the end of your essay listing the sources you used is called a "Works Cited" page.

Although there are many details and rules about incorporating research into your essay, the following five basic principles will help you correctly integrate sources in your essay.

1. Make sure all authors cited in the body of your essay also appear on the Works Cited page.

If you quote Jones, Smith, and Johnson in your essay, these three authors should appear with full documentation on the Works Cited page. Don't forget them. Likewise, all the authors or sources listed in the Works Cited page should appear in the body of your essay. There should be no sources listed on the Works Cited page that were not cited in your actual essay.

2. Only quote catchy or memorable phrases or sentences.

If the source you're quoting is unremarkable and dry in its expression or opinion, don't bring that unremarkable, dry text into your own writing as well. Paraphrase this material instead, and follow up your paraphrase with the author's name in parentheses (or the article title, if there is no author). Only quote catchy, memorable, quotable phrases, and keep the quotations short—one or two lines usually. In general you want to quote sparingly and preserve your own voice.

3. Don't rely too much on the same source.

If you have four or five quotes from the same author, your reader will eventually just desire to read that author instead. Too much quoting also compromises your own voice and sense of authority about the issue. Rather than limiting your research to one or two authors, draw upon a wide variety of sources, and quote only snippets from each. Having variety will ensure that you are well read in the subject and that you've examined the issue from multiple perspectives.

4. Follow up your quotations with commentary, interpretation, or analysis.

Avoid just dropping in the quotation and then immediately moving on, assuming the reader fully understands the meaning, purpose, and application of the quotation just presented. You almost always should comment on the quotation in some way, even if your commentary is a simple reexplanation of what the quotation means ("In other words..."). Remember that you're taking the quotation from an article you've read, but the reader only gets a glimpse of that whole article and lacks the context that you have, so it might be more difficult for the reader to understand it. Because the essay is supposed to represent your ideas, not just those of another, you must find some way to comment or analyze what you summarize or quote.

5. Use signal phrases to introduce your quotations.

A signal phrase is a clause before the quotation that identifies the author (e.g., "Jones says", or "According to Jones... "). Signal phrases are essential to create a bridge between your own voice and that of another you are incorporating into your essay. If you identify the author in the signal phrase, don't also identify author in parentheses following the quotation. Once is enough.

Also, don't put the article title in the signal phrase unless you want to draw particular attention it. Including the article title in your signal phrase usually results in a long, clunky pre-quote phrase that takes the focus off the quotation.

• *Example of a clunky pre-quote signal phrase:* According to the article "Censorship in American High School Reading Classes", Twain's Huckleberry Finn has been "sacrificed to the gods of political correctness, without any attention to its literary merits". (Avoid putting the article title in the signal phrase.)

• *Better:* According to the *American Quarterly Review*, Twain's Huckleberry Finn has been "sacrificed to the gods of political correctness, without any attention to its literary merits".

• *Even Better:* According to Edmund Wilson, "Twain rewrote the American setting through his character Huck Finn."

• *Example of redundancy:* Mark Twain says the secret to success is "making your vocation your vacation." (Twain) (We don't need Twain identified twice!)

Special note—"*qtd. in*":

Suppose you're using a quotation that appears inside an article written by someone other than the one saying the quotation. In other words, if you're using, say, Judge William's quotation that appears within Mary Jones' article, you cite it by writing "qtd. in" following the quote. If so, write "qtd. in Jones", or whomever.

• *Example:* According to Judge Williams, "just law is the foundation of a just society." (qtd. in Jones)

If Jones is just paraphrasing Williams, then you would omit the "qtd. in" and just write (Jones).

Citation

Source material must be documented in the body of the paper by citing the author(s) and date(s) of the sources. The underlying principle is that ideas and words of others must be formally acknowledged.

- *Wirth and Mitchell (1994) found that although there was a reduction in insulin dosage over a period of two weeks in the treatment condition compared to the control condition, the difference was not statistically significant.*
- *Reviews of research on religion and health have concluded that at least some types of religious behaviors are related to higher levels of physical and mental health (Gartner, Larson, & Allen, 1991; Koenig, 1990; Levin & Vanderpool, 1991; Maton & Pargament, 1987; Paloma & Pendleton, 1991; Payne, Bergin, Bielema, & Jenkins, 1991).*

To cite a personal communication (including letters, emails, and telephone interviews), include initials, surname, and as exact a date as possible. Because a personal communication is not "recoverable" information, it is not included in the References section. For the text citation, use the following format:

- *B. F. Skinner (personal communication, February 12, 1978) claimed ...*
- To cite a Web document, use the author-date format. If no author is identified, use the first few words of the title in place of the author. If no date is provided, use "n.d". in place of the date. Consider the following examples:
- *Degelman (2009) summarizes guidelines for the use of APA writing style.*
- *Changes in Americans' views of gender status differences have been documented (Gender and Society, n.d.).*

Quotations

When a direct quotation is used, always include the author, year, and page number as part of the citation.

1. A quotation of fewer than 40 words should be enclosed in double quotation marks and should be incorporated into the formal structure of the sentence.

- *Example:* Patients receiving prayer had "less congestive heart failure, required less diuretic and antibiotic therapy, had fewer episodes of pneumonia, had fewer cardiac arrests, and were less frequently incubated and ventilated" (Byrd, 1988, p. 829).

2. A lengthier quotation of 40 or more words should appear (without quotation marks) apart from the surrounding text, in block format, with each line indented five spaces from the left margin.

References

All sources included in the References section must be cited in the body of the paper (and all sources cited in the paper must be included in the References section).

Book

Paloutzian, R. F. (1996). Invitation to the psychology of religion (2nd ed.). Boston, MA: Allyn and Bacon.

Informally published Web document

Degelman, D. (2009). APA style essentials. Retrieved from http://www.vanguard. edu/faculty/ddegelman/index.aspx?doc_id=796

Informally published Web document (no date)

Nielsen, M. E. (n.d.). Notable people in psychology of religion. Retrieved from http://www.psywww.com/psyrelig/psyrelpr.htm

Informally published Web document (no author, no date)

Gender and society. (n.d.). Retrieved from http://www.trinity.edu/~mkearl/gender.html

Article or chapter in an edited book

Shea, J. D. (1992). Religion and sexual adjustment. In J. F. Schumaker (Ed.), Religion and mental health (pp. 70–84). New York, NY: Oxford University Press.

Text Citation and References of Henry VIII

"Their conversation is awkward, especially when she mentions Wickham, a subject Darcy clearly wishes to avoid" (SparkNotes Editors, n.d.).

SparkNotes Editors. (n.d.). SparkNote on Henry VIII. Retrieved April 26, 2011, from http://www.sparknotes.com/shakespeare/henryviii/

Plagiarism

Plagiarism—its original meaning, "to kidnap"—is a serious academic offense that can result in your failure of the course and possible suspension from the university. It is important that you know what plagiarism entails so that you can avoid the consequences. Ignorance is no excuse.

In short, plagiarism occurs whenever a student attempts to pass off someone else's ideas or phrasing as his or her own, rather than giving due credit to the author. Even if the student mentions the source, if he or she fails to put quotation marks around phrasing not his or her own, it is considered plagiarism, because the student is attempting to pass off phrasing that does not belong to him or her.

Style

Your style is the fingerprint of your writing and consists of a number of comprising elements. As you edit your essay for style, pay attention to these six areas:

Avoid personal references

Avoid using personal references such as "I" or "In my opinion". It is very easy to say "I feel" or "I think", but this adds little to your essay except a weak argument. If your sentence reads, "I think the Internet is a great source of information", what do the words "I think" add? Rather than supplying a reason for the Internet being a great source of information, the reason given here is "because I think so".

In addition to providing a weak argument, using "I" also takes the focus off the subject and places it on you, the writer, which is sometimes desired in creative writing, but undesirable in an academic essay where the focus is supposed to be on a specific topic. You can usually recast your sentence in a way that omits personal references, but if the sentence just doesn't sound right without "I", then leave it in. It's better to be self-centered than unreadable.

- *Personal References:* In my opinion, gay marriage threatens the institution of marriage and the essential structure of the family, which is the fabric of society.
- *Revised:* Gay marriage threatens the institution of marriage and the essential structure of the family, which is the fabric of society.
- *Personal References:* I think that society is held together by allowing individuals to live as they which, not by constricting laws.
- *Revised:* Society is held together by allowing individuals to live as they which, not by constricting laws.

Diction: Choose the right words

Students learning to use a thesaurus often use it excessively and incorrectly in their selection of words. Knowing that all synonyms do not mean the same thing — that each synonym has a subtle nuance of meaning making it distinct from the other words — will help you avoid random substitutions of words that merely seem to look better. Using good diction in your essay involves choosing exactly the right word for the meaning you want. If you're unsure of a word's meaning, look it up in an online dictionary or download a dictionary to your computer.

- *Poor Diction:* Devlin's essay predicates that a society consists of a group of people brought together by a common set of morals and assurances.
- *Better Diction:* Devlin's essay asserts that a society consists of a group of people brought together by a common set of morals and beliefs.
- *Poor Diction:* Hart responds that Devlin's essay is nothing more than a babble and malentendu of what a society is.
- *Better Diction:* Hart responds that Devlin's essay is nothing more than a confusion and misunderstanding of what a society is.

Vary your sentence length

"Choppiness" is the effect of multiple short sentences in a row giving a sense of breathlessness and childlike simplicity. Contrastingly, the opposite—multiple, successive elongated sentences one after another—gives a sense of never-ending lung power and pompous sophistication. A short sentence can be a good option for the content you're writing, just as a long one can as well. The key is to *mix them up* so that you have some short sentences and some long alternating with each other. This variety will give rhythm to your prose.

- *Choppy sentences:* John turned on the computer. He opened Framemaker. He selected a new document. The document was blank. He opened the graphics panel. He chose the shape tool. It was a polygon. He filled the polygon with red shading. He put a black border on it. It was a nice day. His mother brought him sandwiches. The sandwiches tasted good. (Holy Smokes! I could not take more than about half a page of this before I would go crazy!)

• *Over-elongated sentences*: Turning on the computer, John opened **Framemaker** and, after selecting a blank document and opening the graphics panel, chose a polygonal shape tool which he filled with red shading and a black border while his mother brought him sandwiches, all of which contributed to him having a nice day. Then, deliberating between a black and white or a color layout, John decided that for a publication that would be on the web as well as in print, he would need to create both types of documents, because the print would be too costly for color photos, while the web would be too dull for merely black and white, but this color vs. non-color dilemma was only the tip of the iceberg for John in Framemaker, for he knew neither how to create anchored frames for his graphics, nor how to manipulate the sizes and resolutions of the photos he wanted to import, which was giving him a headache, despite his mother's nice sandwiches. (Combining sentences is fun up to a point, and then it gets ridiculous.)

• *Perfect mix of short and long:* After turning on the computer, John opened Framemaker and selected a blank document. He then opened the graphics panel, chose a polygonal shape tool, and filled it with red shading and a black border. His mother brought him sandwiches, which made his day nice. Then, deliberating between a black and white or a color layout, John decided that for a publication that would be on the web as well as in print, he would need to create both types of documents. The print would be too costly for color photos, while the web would be too dull for merely black and white. But this color... (You get the point by now—variety leads to a pleasing rhythm.)

Avoid sexist pronouns

Although in the past it was acceptable to use "he" when referring to both men and women, it is no longer acceptable to do so now. Why? Because linguists found that language use actually does have an impact on the way people think and act. If pronouns are always "he", and certain professions are always fireman, policeman, chairman, congressmen, etc., then it is more likely that men—by simple virtue of the privileged masculine pronoun and noun use—will fill those positions, and that women will feel that they do not belong in them. Avoiding sexist pronouns will help you find liberation from these restricting gender roles.

Even if you disagree with the above theory, using "he" only pronouns is a practice that is no longer tolerated in academic style. You should instead choose to pluralize your subject and use "they" or "their" when referring back to that subject. Or you can choose "he or she", but if you need to write "he or she" more than twice in the sentence, you might give your reader a headache. Try to avoid "she/he" or "he/she" simply because it is unsightly. Really the best solution is pluralization. (When implementing the plural solution, remember the principle of agreement. "Everyone needs their umbrella" is not grammatical, because "everyone" is a singular subject.)

• *Sexist:* If a medical student wants to succeed, he has to learn to budget **their** time wisely.

- *Liberated:* If medical students want to succeed, they have to learn to budget their time wisely.
- *Sexist:* If one wants to become a DJ, he has to be familiar with the current music styles and have a strong sense of internal rhythm and musical flow.
- *Liberated:* If one wants to become a DJ, he or she has to be familiar with the current music styles and have a strong sense of internal rhythm and musical flow.
- *Sexist:* A good computer programmer has to root his knowledge in practical experience.
- *Liberated:* Good computer programmers have to root their knowledge in practical experience.

Maintain a level of formality

Just as in daily life, in writing you naturally adjust the level of formality of your writing style to the situation and audience. You may use one level of formality with your teacher, and another level with your best friend. In an academic essay, be sure to maintain a formal voice. One way to adjust your level of formality is by avoiding contractions (*i.e.*, using "do not" instead of "don't"). However, it is acceptable to use contractions if you desire to.

- *Hyper-formal*: The degree to which private controversial moralities are decriminalized by the federal government depends on the extent of their injurious repercussions on an otherwise benign society.
- *Too informal*: The feds will start putting pervs and whores in the slammer if they feel their smutty actions are mixin' up good men and women.
- *Just right*: Whether private immoralities are outlawed by the government or not depends on the harm they inflict on public society.

Avoid emotionalism

In addition to a formal voice, you should also maintain a cool-headed, objective tone. Tone usually becomes an issue when you are writing about hot topics you feel strongly about—religion, for example, or cultural values. Even when you strongly disagree with an idea, avoid getting "emotional" in your expression. Avoid seeming angry, or condescending, or rude. Keep your calm and remain scholarly, and try to portray yourself as one who is objectively assessing the situation.

- *Emotional:* We must do everything we can to legalize gay marriage. For the sake of equality, the rights of liberty and freedom that our forefathers fought for—it is essential!!! Don't let conservatives take over your government and impose their puritanical moral values on everyone. This is only going to lead to dozens of more restrictions that those white-haired conservatives will impose in their cozy congress seats!
- *Objective*: Keeping gay marriage illegal poses significant questions about the constitutionality of such laws. The forefathers who wrote the Constitution believed an individual's freedom was vitally important, and that as long as the actions did not cause directly harm to society, the actions should not be decriminalized.

👉 *Group Work Activities*

For each group, you have to complete an academic essay collaboratively.
1. Select one of the units of the textbook as your theme to write an essay with no less than 1,000 words.
2. Hold an online or offline discussion to narrow down your topics.
3. Read all information of the academic writing skills again and pay attention to the key points.
4. The essay has to cover three parts: your writing of the essay, citations and references.
5. All of your essays have been typed in A4 paper with Times New Roman script. (title in 14-pont Front, and text in 12-pint Front)

Sample:

The Advantages and Disadvantages of China's Educational Reforms in Globalization

※※※

※※※

※※※

References:
1. Deutsch, M. (1962). "Cooperation and Trust: Some Theoretical Notes". In M. Jones (Ed.), Nebraska Symposium on Motivation, (pp. 275—319). Lincoln, NE: University of Nebraska Press.
2. Johnson, D. W. (2003). "Social Interdependence: The Interrelationships among Theory, Research, and Practice". American Psychologist, 58(11), 931—945.

Unit 9　English Language and Teaching

☞ *Self-evaluation Form*

What are the main objectives in this unit?

_____
_____
_____

What useful vocabularies or expressions have you learned from this unit?

_____
_____
_____

What key terms and educational knowledge have you learned?

_____
_____
_____

Have you used the learning skills before? Why do you think they are useful or not useful?

_____
_____
_____

If possible, what would you like to add to make learning more interesting and relevant?

_____
_____
_____

Unit 10

Learning Model-inquiry Learning

Introduction

Bibliography of Henry VIII[1]

Henry, the second son of King Henry VII and Elizabeth of York, was born on 28 June 1491 at Greenwich Palace. After the death of his elder brother Arthur in 1502, Henry became heir to the English throne.

King of England

When Henry VII died in 1509, this popular eighteen-year-old prince, known for his love of hunting and dancing, became King Henry VIII. Soon after he obtained the papal dispensation required to allow him to marry his brother's widow, Catherine of Aragon.

In the first years of his reign Henry VIII effectively relied on Thomas Wolsey to rule for him, and by 1515 Henry had elevated him to the highest role in government: Lord Chancellor.

In 1521 Pope Leo X conferred the title of Defender of the Faith on Henry for his book *Assertio Septem Sacramentorum*, which affirmed the supremacy of the Pope in the face of the reforming ideals of the German theologian, Martin Luther.

Military Might

Henry VIII's early military campaigns began when he joined Pope Julius II's Holy League against France in 1511. Wolsey proved himself to be an outstanding minister in his organisation of the first French campaign and while the Scots saw this war as an opportunity to invade England, they were defeated at Flodden in 1513. However war with France ultimately proved expensive and unsuccessful.

Henry VIII is known as the "father of the Royal Navy". When he became king there were five royal warships. By his death he had built up a navy of around 50 ships. He refitted several vessels with the latest guns including the Mary Rose, which sank in 1545.

Henry also built the first naval dock in Britain at Portsmouth and in 1546 he established the Navy Board. This set up the administrative machinery for the control of the fleet.

---

[1] Retrieved from http://www.bbc.co.uk/history/people/henry_viii.

A Male Heir

Henry was acutely aware of the importance of securing a male heir during his reign. He was worried that he had only one surviving child, Mary, to show for his marriage to Catherine, who was now in her 40s. So the king asked Cardinal Wolsey to appeal to Pope Clement VII for an annulment and it soon became clear he wanted to marry Anne Boleyn, who had been a lady-in-waiting to his first wife.

But, unwilling to anger Catherine of Aragon's nephew—the most powerful ruler in Europe, the Holy Roman Emperor Charles V—the Pope refused. Thomas Wolsey's ascendancy was cut short by this failure.

In 1533, Henry VIII broke with the church and married the now pregnant Anne Boleyn in a secret ceremony. Henry was excommunicated by the Pope. The English reformation had begun.

Head of the Church

After Wolsey's downfall, Thomas Cromwell became Henry's chief minister and earned the confidence of the King by helping him to break with Rome and establish Henry VIII as head of the Church of England. This act also brought him much needed wealth through the dissolution of the well-funded monasteries. Over four years Cromwell ordered that 800 monasteries be disbanded and their lands and treasures taken for the crown.

The cultural and social impact was significant, as much of the land was sold to the gentry and churches and monasteries were gutted and destroyed. Henry's personal religious beliefs remained Catholic, despite the growing number of people at court and in the nation who had adopted Protestantism.

Anne Boleyn

In September 1533 Anne gave birth to a daughter, Elizabeth (the future Queen Elizabeth I). Henry had grown tired of her, and after two further pregnancies ended in miscarriages, she was arrested in 1536 on trumped-up charges of adultery and publicly beheaded at the Tower of London.

Henry's third marriage, this time to lady-in-waiting, Jane Seymour, finally produced the son he so desperately desired with the birth of Edward in 1537. Jane Seymour died after childbirth and Henry ordered that she be granted a queen's funeral.

In an attempt to establish ties with the German Protestant alliance, Thomas Cromwell arranged a marriage between the king and German princess Anne of Cleves. The marriage was a disaster and Henry divorced Anne a few months later. Henry blamed Cromwell for this mismatch and soon afterwards had him executed for treason.

Final Years

The final years of his reign witnessed Henry VIII's physical decline and an increasing desire to appear all-powerful. Henry continued with fruitless and expensive campaigns against Scotland and France.

In 1540, the aging King married the teenage Catherine Howard. Their marriage was short lived. It was alleged that she had a previous relationship with Henry's courtier Francis Dereham and an affair with another courtier Thomas Culpeper. Catherine was executed for adultery and treason in 1542.

Henry's final marriage to Catherine Parr, who acted like a nurse, was more harmonious and she would go on to outlive him.

Henry VIII died on 28 January 1547 and was succeeded by his son, Edward VI. He was buried next to Jane Seymour in St. George's Chapel at Windsor Castle.

Questions after reading:

How much do you know about the Tudors? Can you describe the merits and faults of Henry VIII?

Group work:

Topic: Work in groups and listen to the audio materials provided and identify how many wives did Henry marry? Who are they?

Directions: Work as a group and share your ideas with others.

Text A

Brainstorming

The Tudor period is the period between 1485 and 1603 in England and Wales. It coincides with the rule of the Tudor dynasty in England whose first monarch was Henry VII (1457—1509). In terms of the entire century, Guy (1988) argues that "England was economically healthier, more expansive, and more optimistic under the Tudors" than at any time in a thousand years.

Questions before reading:

Why did Henry VIII carry out the religious reformation?

Handling Henry VIII[①]
David Loades & Mei Trow

Because he wasn't the eldest son, Henry VIII should never have become king. Rumours suggested he was destined for a career in the church, but the death of his elder

---

① Excerpt from *The Tudors for Dummies,* John Wiley & Sons, Ltd., 2011.

brother Arthur in 1502 changed all that and meant that he reached pole position by accident. Henry began his reign promisingly enough as a handsome, talented Renaissance prince with a 19-inch waist, but he became a bloated monster who terrified his subjects and whose soul the pope sent to hell.

This chapter gets to the bottom of Henry's transformation, piecing together the man behind the gossipy stories and famous portraits. Unlike Henry VII, who presented a mask to the outside world, his son wore his heart on his sleeve, so we have loads of information about his inner feelings.

Getting to Know Prince Henry

As the only son of Henry VII left standing when Arthur died, it was important that every care was taken with the little boy. This section looks at the kind of upbringing Henry had.

Rocking round the cradle

Only two children in five lived to see their first birthday in the 15th century and mothers and the newly born faced a huge risk. Even among royals death was a constant visitor, so it was just as well that the heir (Arthur) had a spare (Henry).

Henry's theological education almost certainly came from his second tutor, William Hone, and such knowledge was virtually unique in a royal prince. He had a first rate grasp of the most important book of the day, the Bible (still only available then in Latin at all good bookshops). The prince also learned French, Spanish and Italian, vital in the world of power-politics he was to enter later.

As if all that knowledge wasn't enough, Henry was also an excellent horseman, huntsman, jouster, composer, musician, dancer—don't you just hate him already? Henry's dancing first came to the fore when he was 10 at Arthur's wedding in November 1501, when he won the hearts of all spectators. For more on dancing, that vital social accomplishment, see Chapter 1.

Moving up after Arthur's death

Henry's older brother Arthur, the original heir to the throne, had only been married to the Spanish princess Catherine of Aragon for five months when he died of tuberculosis. Arthur's mother Elizabeth comforted her husband by reminding him that "God had left him yet a fair prince, two fair princesses" and that "God is where he was". Henry was now catapulted into the limelight as the duke of Cornwall, and he was made prince of Wales in 1503. He was 11.

For the next six years he cooled his heels with plenty of time for his favourite pastimes—hunting, jousting, eating—but he had no real work to do. Castles in Spain were important to the Tudors. Now that Arthur was dead, Catherine should have gone home to Aragon and Mummy and Daddy (Isabella and Ferdinand), and taken her dowry and the all-important Spanish Alliance with her. But Henry VII's idea was to keep it all in the family by betrothing Prince Henry to his dead brother's wife.

Seeking riches and power

We explain that Henry VII's reputation of being a miserly skinflint isn't quite fair, but the new king on the block, still only 18 when he was crowned after his father's death, spent money like water and had personality and courage as big as the great outdoors. Despite everything that was to happen during his reign, Henry remained amazingly popular with most of his subjects, even though they believed they were going to burn in hell's fire because of him. Like his father, Henry VIII saw that he had two basic ways to make his kingdom rich and powerful:

Go to war and grab somebody's territory (that usually meant the French at the time — everybody hated them).

Arrange a big fat Spanish wedding—which is exactly what Henry VII had done with Arthur and Catherine.

Henry did his duty by carrying out his father's original wish and marrying Catherine of Aragon, keeping her massive dowry and the Spanish Alliance. He could hit France from two directions—by sea across the Channel from the North and by land, taking an army out of Spain over the Pyrenees mountain range.

Taking on the French

One of the key things that Henry did was to renew the conflict with France which had lasted for over a hundred years. In this respect, Henry was quite backward-looking and his role model was Henry V, the all-action hero who'd trounced the French at Agincourt in 1415. Henry was clever enough to join the Holy League, a military alliance Pope Julius II had put together, so he didn't have to risk going it alone.

The only bit of France that England still owned was the town of Calais. To increase his territory, Henry sent the marquis of Dorset to grab Guyenne in south-west France. But there was no support from Henry's fellow League member and father-in-law, Ferdinand of Aragon, so the whole campaign was a disaster.

The First Wife: Catherine of Aragon

You've got to feel sorry for Catherine. The daughter of pushy parents who ruled what would become the superpower of the 16th century, she was a political pawn, bullied by Henry VII, deserted (although that was hardly his fault!) by Arthur and married on the realpolitik rebound to Henry, who eventually divorced her. She was six years older than Henry and produced four children in four years, all of them dying in infancy. The fifth was Mary, who was to remain staunchly loyal to her mother's religion for the rest of her life. Unable to give Henry his much-wanted son, Catherine had to step down in favour of Anne Boleyn, maintaining a dignified silence throughout. She wasn't quite such a goodie two shoes, however, because she had an affair with a disreputable Franciscan monk who may have given her syphilis. She refused the title of princess dowager (which means pretty well *my ex*) and died in retirement in Huntingdonshire in 1536. Next time you're in Peterborough, visit her tomb and pay your respects.

> **The Field of the Cloth of Gold: 1520**
>
> This was a summit conference held near Calais between Henry and Francis. The whole thing was organised by Henry's lord chancellor, Wolsey, and was a chance for both kings to show off their money, weapons and jousting ability. Mock castles were built for war games, fountains ran with wine, tents glittered in gold fabric. Both kings fought five combats on each of ten days, surprise, surprise, beating all combaters. The ostentatious declarations of affection between the two kings was only a veneer, however, and war was soon resumed.

Henry did rather better in 1513, capturing a couple of French towns and winning the Battle of the Spurs (actually, more of a skirmish). This led to a truce and Henry got the city of Tournai to keep him quiet. In exchange, he gave the elderly French king, Louis XII, his 18-year-old sister Mary in marriage. Within months Louis was dead—draw your own conclusions as to why—and Henry was faced with a far more dangerous enemy, Francis I.

Fencing with Francis I

The new French king invaded Italy (then just a collection of states rather than a united country) and the death of Henry's father-in-law, Ferdinand of Aragon, meant that the Spanish Alliance, which Henry might previously have counted on, would be useless against Francis.

So Henry took the advice of Thomas Wolsey, his lord chancellor and righthand man and this led to the Treaty of London of 1518, which:
- Gave Tournai back to France
- Saved everybody's face by agreeing universal peace

The treaty was blown out of the water the following year when the top job of holy Roman emperor was up for grabs after the death of Maximilian of Austria. The three contenders were:
- Charles V of Spain (of the Habsburg family)
- Francis I of France (of the Valois family)
- Henry VIII of England (of the Tudor family)

Charles was elected because of his family connections and the fact that he had more cash than anybody else. The title gave him huge chunks of Europe and, as it turned out, bits of America. Now Charles surrounded France on three sides; Henry controlled the fourth.

> **The Sinking of the Mary Rose**
>
> The Mary Rose was a state-of-the-art warship but it sank in the Solent—the narrow waterway between Portsmouth and the Isle of Wight—in July 1545. We still don't know why. The French claimed (of course!) to have sunk her, but this seems unlikely given the facts. The ship's captain, just before he went down, called to another ship that his crew were "the sort of knaves I cannot rule". Perhaps there was some kind of mutiny on board. We know from DNA evidence from the bodies of the crew who drowned that most of them were Spanish. Henry saw it all happen, riding along the beach and muttering, "Oh, my pretty men. Drowned like rattens!" Check out the hull and artefacts of the Mary Rose in the Historic Docks in Portsmouth. The ship was raised from the sea in 1982.

Putting on a sideshow

Linking with Charles V, Henry sent the duke of Suffolk to attack Paris. Charles was busy in Italy, the weather was awful and Suffolk's army became a rabble. There was better news from Italy, where Francis I was defeated and captured by Charles's army. Even so, broke and unable to capitalise on the opportunity, Henry had to sign a humiliating peace with France in August 1525.

For a while, everything in the Tudor garden was lovely. Henry gave his 11-year-old daughter Mary (by Catherine of Aragon) as a prospective bride to Francis's son, also (confusingly!) Francis, but by 1529 Charles V and the French king were negotiating a new treaty and it looked as if Henry would find himself in a potential war with both France and Spain. It didn't help, of course, that this was the year that Henry began divorce proceedings against Catherine and she was the aunt of Charles V, whose army was surrounding the pope in Rome. The "Ladies' Peace" was signed in the French city of Cambrai to avoid outright war.

Fighting the French (again!)

With Charles and Francis cosying up to each other, Henry put the country on invasion alert. He built forts like Pendennis and Cowes along the south coast, demanded that local troops be mobilised and hiked taxation to pay for all his preparations. European politics change like the wind and Charles and Francis soon fell out, so that there was now *another* two pronged attack by the emperor and Henry on France. This time—the summer of 1544—Henry besieged Boulogne and took it, blowing up part of the town walls. Charles felt betrayed by this posturing—it wasn't part of the joint plan—and promptly defected to Francis.

The French king now launched his own two-pronged attack. One of his armies hit Boulogne and the other arrived off the south coast of England, firing on Henry's fleet off Portsmouth and attacking the Isle of Wight before being driven off.

The war ended tamely with the Treaty of Camp. Henry would keep Boulogne for a fixed period and Francis would then buy it off him.

Making Politics Personal

One of the biggest problems that Henry faced throughout his reign was his "great matter"—his determination to have a son to continue the Tudor line. Inevitably, this involved finding a suitable wife who would provide a male heir for him. We cover Henry's wives in more detail in Chapter 5, but we'll introduce them here, in order of their marriage to the king:

Catherine of Aragon (married Henry June 1509, aged 24, separated 1531, annulled May 1533): See the earlier sidebar "The first wife: Catherine of Aragon" for the lowdown on this sad princess.

Anne Boleyn (married Henry secretly January 1533, aged 26, beheaded May 1536): Henry certainly fell for Anne, the daughter of a Kentish knight, longing, in his own words, to "kiss her pretty dukkys" (breasts), but she was playing hard to get. Not for her was her sister's role of royal mistress; Anne wanted to be Henry's wife—oh, and queen of England too. Various foreign ministers thought her neck was too long, her mouth too wide and her "bosom not much raised", but her long black hair was to die for and Henry was captivated. Think Genevieve Bujold in *Anne of the Thousand Days*. She bore Henry his second daughter, Elizabeth.

Jane Seymour (married Henry 30 May 1536, aged 27, died October 1537): Even before Henry had officially tired of Anne he started flirting with Jane Seymour, who was a lady-in-waiting to both the king's first two wives. The marriage took place only 11 days after Anne's execution and Jane gave birth to Henry's much wanted son, Edward, at Hampton Court on 12 October 1537. Twelve days later she was dead from the all—too common childbed fever and Henry, broken-hearted of course, was on the lookout for a replacement.

Anne of Cleves (married Henry January 1540, aged 25, annulled June 1540). So far, home-grown wives like Anne and Jane hadn't proved a great success, so Henry let Thomas Cromwell suggest Anne of Cleves. This was a purely political marriage because her father John was an opponent of Charles V, the Catholic king of Spain. Cromwell and others hoped that Anne would have some influence on Henry, but they got it hopelessly wrong. She was homely to say the least—Henry called her his "Flanders Mare" only partially because she came from that part of Europe. She had pock-marked skin and spoke virtually no English. In the *Private Lives of Henry VIII* all Charles Laughton's Henry does in bed with Anne is play cards! Henry annulled his marriage to Anne after six months.

Catherine Howard (married Henry secretly November 1540, aged 17, beheaded 13 February 1542). Henry's fifth wife was well connected, the grand-daughter and niece of two powerful dukes of Norfolk, and she herself was a clever woman and a shrewd politician. We don't know if this marriage was ever consummated but Henry became doubtful of Catherine's fidelity and found a way to remove her for good.

Catherine Parr (married Henry 12 July 1543, aged 31; she outlived Henry). Most of the time she acted as Henry's nurse.

Playing Away from Home

The number of his wives and the size of his codpiece have led to the reputation of Henry as a stud. In 30 years he made four women pregnant and three of them were queens of England and his wives at the time. Although Henry certainly had mistresses — it was expected of a king — he wasn't the sex god of legend and certainly nothing like the drooling Sid James in *Carry On Henry!*

During the Middle Ages and into the Renaissance, the nobility were obsessed with the idea of courtly love, in which men wrote poetry, women sighed and accepted presents and everybody flirted for England. In reality, marriages were dynastic, arranged by greedy fathers (like Henry VII himself) to make strong alliances and build huge power bases. What is love got to do with it?

Playing away I — the other Boleyn girl

Mary was the elder daughter of Sir Thomas Boleyn of Hever Castle in Kent. The memorial brass of this social climber is still on show at St Peter's Church there, so check it out. It must be something of a record to have a king bedding both your daughters. The fact that Mary was already married to William Carey didn't bother Henry unduly — after all, the man was only a gentleman of the king's Chamber. Mary may have become pregnant by Henry, but if so it ended in a miscarriage, and the king passed on, with potentially disastrous results, to her feisty little sister Anne.

Playing away II — Bessie Blount

Henry may have turned to Bessie Blount (pronounced Blunt) after disappointment when Catherine gave birth to Mary in 1516. Elizabeth Blount was related to the queen's chamberlain and court gossips noted the pair together at a torchlight masque. By 1518 Bessie was pregnant and Henry Fitzroy was born at Blackmore Abbey in Essex in the spring of 1519. Bastard sons were normally called *fitz* from the old Norman word, and even had their own badge, a bend sinister, on their coats of arms. Being illegitimate carried no shame, but a fitz couldn't legally inherit the throne. Henry Fitzroy was kept away from court, probably because the issue of the king siring a legitimate heir became so acute in the early 1530s (see Chapter 5), and he ended up as duke of Richmond and lieutenant of the north.

Unit 10　Learning Model-inquiry Learning

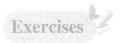

Read the following article and complete the corresponding exercises.

Importance of Inquiry

Memorizing facts and information is not the most important skill in today's world. Facts change, and information is readily available—what is needed is an understanding of how to get and make sense of the mass of data.

Educators must understand that schools need to go beyond data and information accumulation and move toward the generation of useful and applicable knowledge... a process supported by inquiry learning. In the past, our country's success depended on our supply of natural resources. Today, it depends upon a workforce that "works smarter".

Through the process of inquiry, individuals construct much of their understanding of the natural and human-designed worlds. Inquiry implies a "need or want to know" premise. Inquiry is not so much seeking the right answer—because often there is none—but rather seeking appropriate resolutions to questions and issues. For educators, inquiry implies emphasis on the development of inquiry skills and the nurturing of inquiring attitudes or habits of mind that will enable individuals to continue the quest for knowledge throughout life.

Content of disciplines is very important, but as a means to an end, not as an end in itself. The knowledge base for disciplines is constantly expanding and changing. No one can ever learn everything, but everyone can better develop their skills and nurture the inquiring attitudes necessary to continue the generation and examination of knowledge throughout their lives. For modern education, the skills and the ability to continue learning should be the most important outcomes. The rationale for why this is necessary is explained in the following diagrams.

How do I get started using inquiry-based learning?

These following questions should be asked about the planned activity or learning experience:

- ☐ Does it contribute to developing information-processing skills?
- ☐ Does it lead to important content understanding?
- ☐ Does it lead to content understanding in a conceptual context?

Physically, the learning environment should be enriched with learning resources that will both stimulate and help answer the learners' inquiries. The learning environment should contain lots of reading materials — books, pamphlets, journals, and magazines — relating to the topic under study. If a computer with CD-ROM access is available,

CD-ROMs can be important sources of information, and many are interactive and include simulations. If access to the Internet is available, it can be an important source of resource materials and resources for learning. Depending upon the nature of the activity, it might be necessary for the teacher to plan to have supplies and materials available for the students to explore some of their own questions.

In addition, to start using inquiry, you must become familiar with various types of questions and help your students learn to learn from them.

Exercises

You are supposed to design a lesson plan of English to teach Henry VIII, and some important principles have to be observed in your lesson plan:
Teaching objectives (Learning objectives)
Content (skills, language)
Evaluation (questions, essays)

Text B

Brainstorming

Church of England: The Church of England is the officially established Christian church in England and the mother church of the worldwide Anglican Communion. The church considers itself within the tradition of Western Christianity and dates its formal establishment principally to the mission to England by Saint Augustine of Canterbury in AD 597.

As a result of Augustine's mission, the church in England came under the authority of the pope. Initially prompted by a dispute over the annulment of the marriage of King Henry VIII to Catherine of Aragon, the Church of England separated from the Roman Catholic Church in 1534 and became the established church by an Act of Parliament in the Act of Supremacy, beginning a series of events known as the English Reformation. During the reign of Queen Mary I and King Philip, the church was fully restored under Rome in 1555. The pope's authority was again explicitly rejected after the accession of Queen Elizabeth I when the Act of Supremacy of 1558 was passed. Catholic and Reformed factions vied for determining the doctrines and worship of the church. This ended with the 1558 Elizabethan Settlement, which developed the understanding that the church was to be both Catholic and Reformed.

Questions before reading:
Why did the king in Britain have to follow guidance from the Pope? Why did Henry

VIII divorce his first wife?

The Six Wives of Henry VIII

 Catherine of Aragon m. 1509—1533 Divorced	 Anne Boleyn m. 1533—1536 Executed	 Jane Seymour m. 1536—1537 Died
 Anne of Cleves m. 1540 Jan.—July Divorced	 Catherine Howard m. 1540—1542 Executed	 Catherine Parr m. 1543—1547 Widowed
Catherine of Aragon by Michael Sittow 	Born: 16 December 1485 Archbishop of Toledo's Palace, Alcalá de Henares, Spain Married to Prince Arthur: 14 November 1501 St. Paul's Cathedral, London Married to King Henry VIII: 11 June 1509 Franciscan Church at Greenwich Marriage to Henry VIII dissolved: 1533 Died: 7 January 1536 Kimbolton Castle Buried: 29 January 1536 Peterborough Abbey	

---

① Retrieved from http://tudorhistory.org/wives.

Catherine of Aragon: The Most Tragedy

Catherine of Aragon was the youngest surviving child of Ferdinand and Isabella, the joint rulers of Spain, and as was common for princesses of the day, her parents almost immediately began looking for a political match for her. When she was three year old, she was betrothed to Arthur, the son of Henry VII of England. Arthur was not even quite two at the time.

When she was almost 16, in 1501, Catherine made the journey to England. It took her three months, and her ships weathered several storms, but she safely made landfall at Plymouth on October 2, 1501. Catherine and Arthur were married on 14 November 1501 in Old St. Paul's Cathedral, London. Catherine was escorted by the groom's younger brother, Henry.

After the wedding and celebrations, the young couple moved to Ludlow Castle on the Welsh border. Less than six months later, Arthur was dead, possibly of the "sweating sickness". Although this marriage was short, it was very important in the history of England, as will be apparent.

Catherine was now a widow, and still young enough to be married again. Henry VII still had a son, this one much more robust and healthy than his dead older brother. The English king was interested in keeping Catherine's dowry, so 14 months after her husband's death she was betrothed to the future Henry VIII, who was too young to marry at the time.

By 1505, when Henry was old enough to wed, Henry VII wasn't as keen on a Spanish alliance, and young Henry was forced to repudiate the betrothal. Catherine's future was uncertain for the next four years. When Henry VII died in 1509 one of the new young king's first actions was to marry Catherine. She was finally crowned Queen of England in a joint coronation ceremony with her husband Henry VIII on June 24, 1509.

Shortly after their marriage, Catherine found herself pregnant. This first child was a stillborn daughter born prematurely in January 1510, but this disappointment was soon followed by another pregnancy. Prince Henry was born on January 1, 1511 and the was christened on the 5th. There were great celebrations for the birth of the young prince, but they were halted by the baby's death after 52 days of life. Catherine then had a miscarriage, followed by a another short-lived son. On February 1516, she gave birth a daughter named Mary, and this child lived. There were probably two more pregnancies, the last recorded in 1518.

Henry was growing frustrated by his lack of a male heir, but he remained a devoted husband. He had at least two mistresses that we know of: Elizabeth "Bessie" Blount and Mary Boleyn. By 1526 though, he had begun to separate from Catherine because he had fallen in love with one of her ladies (and sister of one of his mistresses): Anne Boleyn.

It is here that the lives of Henry's first and second wives begin to interweave. By the time his interest in Anne became common knowledge, Catherine was 42 years old and was no longer able to conceive. Henry's main goal now was to get a male heir, which his wife was not able to provide. Somewhere along the way Henry began to look at the texts of Leviticus which say that if a man takes his brother's wife, they shall be childless. As evidenced above, Catherine and Henry were far from childless, and still had one living child. But that child was a girl, and didn't count in Henry's mind. The King began to petition the Pope for an annulment.

At first, Catherine was kept in the dark about Henry's plans for their annulment and when the news got to Catherine she was very upset. She was also at a great disadvantage since the court that would decide the case was far from impartial. Catherine then appealed directly to the Pope, which she felt would listen to her case since her nephew was Charles V, the Holy Roman Emperor.

The political and legal debate continued for six years. Catherine was adamant in that she and Arthur, her first husband and Henry's brother, did not consummate their marriage and therefore were not truly husband and wife. Catherine sought not only to retain her position, but also that of her daughter Mary.

Things came to a head in 1533 when Anne Boleyn became pregnant. Henry had to act, and his solution was to reject the power of the Pope in England and to have Thomas Cranmer, the Archbishop of Canterbury grant the annulment. Catherine was to renounce the title of Queen and would be known as the Princess Dowager of Wales, something she refused to acknowledge through to the end of her life.

Catherine and her daughter were separated and she was forced to leave court. She lived for the next three years in several dank and unhealthy castles and manors with just a few servants. However, she seldom complained of her treatment and spent a great deal of time at prayer.

On January 7, 1536, Catherine died at Kimbolton Castle and was buried at Peterborough Abbey (later Peterborough Cathedral, after the dissolution of the monasteries) with the ceremony due for her position as Princess Dowager, not as a Queen of England.

Anne Boleyn: The Most Happy

For a woman who played such an important part in English history, we know remarkably little about her earliest years. Antonia Fraser puts Anne's birth at 1500 or 1501, probably at Blickling (Norfolk) and the date of birth seems to be at the end of May or early June. Other historians put Anne's birth as late as 1507 or 1509.

Anne spent part of her childhood at the court of the Archduchess Margaret. Fraser puts her age at 12—13, as that was the minimum age for a "fille d'honneur". It was from there that she was transferred to the household of Mary, Henry VIII's sister, who was married to Louis XII of France. Anne's sister Mary was already in "the French Queen's" attendance. However, when Louis died, Mary Boleyn returned to England with Mary Tudor, while Anne remained in France to attend Claude, the new French queen. Anne remained in France for the next 6 or 7 years. Because of her position, it is possible that she was at the Field of Cloth of Gold, the famous meeting between Henry VIII and the French king, Francis I.

During her stay in France she learned to speak French fluently and developed a taste for French clothes, poetry and music.

Anne's Appearance

The legend of Anne Boleyn always includes a sixth finger and a large mole or goiter on her neck. However, one would have to wonder if a woman with these oddities (not to mention the numerous other moles and warts she was said to have) would be so captivating to the king. She may have had some small moles, as most people do, but they would be more like the attractive "beauty marks".

A quote from the Venetian Ambassador said she was "not one of the handsomest women in the world...". She was considered moderately pretty. But, one must consider what "pretty" was in the 16th century. Anne was the opposite of the pale, blonde-haired, blue-eyed image of beauty. She had dark, olive-colored skin, thick dark brown hair and dark brown eyes which often appeared black. Those large dark eyes were often singled out in descriptions of Anne. She clearly used them, and the fascination they aroused, to her advantage whenever possible.

She was of average height, had small breasts and a long, elegant neck. The argument continues as to whether or not she really had an extra finger on one of her hands.

Life in England and the Attentions of the King

Anne returned to England around 1521 for details for her marriage were being worked out. Meanwhile she went to court to attend Queen Catherine. Her first recorded appearance at court was March 1, 1522 at a masque.

After her marriage to the heir of Ormonde fell through, she began an affair with Henry Percy, also a rich heir. Cardinal Wolsey put a stop to the romance, which could be why Anne engendered such a hatred of him later in life. It has been suggested that Wolsey stepped in on behalf of the King to remove Percy from the scene because he had already noticed Anne and wanted her for himself. Fraser asserts that this is not the case since the romance between Anne and Percy ended in 1522 and the King didn't notice Anne until 1526. It is possible that Anne had a precontract with Percy.

Somewhere in this time, Anne also had a relationship of some sort with the poet Sir Thomas Wyatt. Wyatt was married in 1520, so the timing of the supposed affair is uncertain. Wyatt was separated from his wife, but there could be little suggestion of his eventual marriage to Anne. Theirs appears to be more of a courtly love.

Exactly when and where Henry VIII first noticed Anne is not known. It is likely that Henry sought to make Anne his mistress, as he had her sister Mary years before. Maybe drawing on the example of Elizabeth Woodville, Queen to Edward IV (and maternal grandmother to Henry VIII) who was said to have told King Edward that she would only be his wife, not his mistress, Anne denied Henry VIII sexual favors. We don't know who first had the idea marriage, but eventually it evolved into "Queen or nothing" for Anne.

At first, the court probably thought that Anne would just end up as another one of Henry's mistresses. But, in 1527 we see that Henry began to seek an annulment of his marriage to Catherine, making him free to marry again.

King Henry's passion for Anne can be attested to in the love letters he wrote to her when she was away from court. Henry hated writing letters, and very few documents in his own hand survive. However, 17 love letters to Anne remain and are preserved in the Vatican library.

The Rise of Anne Boleyn

In 1528, Anne's emergence at court began. Anne also showed real interest in religious reform and may have introduced some of the "new ideas" to Henry, and gaining the hatred of some members of the court. When the court spent Christmas at Greenwich that year, Anne was lodged in nice apartments near those of the King.

The legal debates on the marriage of Henry and Catherine of Aragon continued on. Anne was no doubt frustrated by the lack of progress. Her famous temper and tongue showed themselves at times in famous arguments between her and Henry for all the court to see. Anne feared that Henry might go back to Catherine if the marriage could not be annulled and Anne would have wasted time that she could have used to make an advantageous marriage.

Anne was not popular with the people of England. They were upset to learn that at the Christmas celebrations of 1529, Anne was given precedence over the Duchesses of Norfolk and Suffolk, the latter of which was the King's own sister, Mary.

In this period, records show that Henry began to spend more and more on Anne, buying her clothes, jewelry, and things for her amusement such as playing cards and bows and arrows.

The waiting continued and Anne's position continued to rise. On the first day of September 1532, she was created Marquess of Pembroke, a title she held in her own right. In October, she held a position of honor at meetings between Henry and the French King in Calais.

Queen Anne

Sometime near the end of 1532, Anne finally gave way and by December she was pregnant. To avoid any questions of the legitimacy of the child, Henry was forced into action. Sometime near St. Paul's Day (January 25) 1533, Anne and Henry were secretly married. Although the King's marriage to Catherine was not dissolved, in the King's mind it had never existed in the first place, so he was free to marry whomever he wanted. On May 23, the Archbishop officially proclaimed that the marriage of Henry and Catherine was invalid.

Plans for Anne's coronation began. In preparation, she had been brought by water from Greenwich to the Tower of London dressed in cloth of gold. The barges following her were said to stretch for four miles down the Thames. On the 1st of June, she left the Tower in procession to Westminster Abbey, where she became a crowned and anointed Queen in a ceremony led by Thomas Cranmer, the Archbishop of Canterbury.

By August, preparations were being made for the birth of Anne's child, which was sure to be a boy. Names were being chosen, with Edward and Henry the top choices. The proclamation of the child's birth had already been written with "prince" used to refer to the child.

Anne took to her chamber, according to custom, on August 26, 1533 and on September 7, at about 3:00 in the afternoon, the Princess Elizabeth was born. Her christening service was scaled down, but still a pleasant affair. The princess' white christening robes can currently be seen on display at Sudeley Castle in England.

Anne now knew that it was imperative that she produce a son. By January of 1534, she was pregnant again, but the child was either miscarried or stillborn. In 1535, she became pregnant again but miscarried by the end of January. The child was reported to have been a boy. The Queen was quite upset, and blamed the miscarriage on her state of mind after hearing that Henry had taken a fall in jousting. She had to have known at this point that her failure to produce a living male heir was a threat to her own life, especially since the King's fancy for one of her ladies-in-waiting, Jane Seymour, began to grow.

The Fall of Anne Boleyn

Anne's enemies at court began to plot against her using the King's attentions to Jane Seymour as the catalyst for action. Cromwell began to move in action to bring down the Queen. He persuaded the King to sign a document calling for an investigation that would possibly result in charges of treason.

On April 30, 1536, Anne's musician and friend for several years, Mark Smeaton, was arrested and probably tortured into making "revelations" about the Queen. Next, Sir Henry Norris was arrested and taken to the Tower of London. Then the Queen's own brother, George Boleyn, Lord Rochford was arrested.

On May 2, the Queen herself was arrested at Greenwich and was informed of the charges against her: adultery, incest and plotting to murder the King. She was then taken to the Tower by barge along the same path she had traveled to prepare for her coronation just three years earlier. In fact, she was lodged in the same rooms she had held on that occasion.

There were several more arrests. Sir Francis Weston and William Brereton were charged with adultery with the Queen. Sir Thomas Wyatt was also arrested, but later released. They were put on trial with Smeaton and Norris at Westminster Hall on May 12, 1536. The men were not allowed to defend themselves, as was the case in charges of treason. They were found guilty and received the required punishment: they were to be hanged at Tyburn, cut down while still living and then disemboweled and quartered.

On Monday the 15th, the Queen and her brother were put on trial at the Great Hall of the Tower of London. It is estimated that some 2000 people attended. Anne conducted herself in a calm and dignified manner, denying all the charges against her. Her brother was tried next, with his own wife testifying against him (she got her due later in the scandal of Kathryn Howard). Even though the evidence against them was scant, they were both found guilty, with the sentence being read by their uncle, Thomas Howard, the Duke of Norfolk. They were to be either burnt at the stake (which was the punishment for incest) or beheaded, at the discretion of the King.

The Executions

On May 17, George Boleyn was executed on Tower Hill. The other four men condemned with the Queen had their sentences commuted from the grisly fate at Tyburn to a simple beheading at the Tower with Lord Rochford.

Anne knew that her time would soon come and started to become hysterical, her behavior swinging from great levity to body-wracking sobs. She received news that an expert swordsman from Calais had been summoned, who would no doubt deliver a cleaner blow with a sharp sword than the traditional axe. It was then that she made the famous comment about her "little neck".

Interestingly, shortly before her execution on charges of adultery, the Queen's marriage to the King was dissolved and declared invalid. One would wonder then how she could have committed adultery if she had in fact never been married to the King, but this was overlooked, as were so many other lapses of logic in the charges against Anne.

They came for Anne on the morning of May 19 to take her to the Tower Green, where she was to be afforded the dignity of a private execution. She made a short speech before kneeling on the scaffold. She removed her headdress (which was an English gable hood and not her usual French hood, according to contemporary reports) and her ladies tied a blindfold over her eyes. The sword itself had been hidden under the straw. The swordsman cut off her head with one swift stroke.

Anne's body and head were put into an arrow chest and buried in an unmarked grave in the Chapel of St. Peter ad Vincula which adjoined the Tower Green. Her body was one that was identified in renovations of the chapel under the reign of Queen Victoria, so Anne's final resting place is now marked in the marble floor.

Jane Seymour: Bound to Obey and Serve

Jane Seymour may have first come to court in the service of Queen Catherine, but then was moved to wait on Anne Boleyn as she rose in the King's favor and eventually became his second wife.

In September 1535, the King stayed at the Seymour family home in Wiltshire, England. It may have been there that the king "noticed" Jane. But, it isn't until February of 1536 that there is evidence of Henry's new love for Jane.

By that point, Henry's disinterest in Anne was obvious and Jane was likely pegged to be her replacement as Queen.

Opinion is divided as to how Jane felt about being the new object of Henry's affections. Some see Jane's calm and gentle demeanor as evidence that she didn't really understand the position as political pawn she was playing for her family. Others see it as a mask for her fear. Seeing how Henry's two previous Queens had been treated once they fell from favor, Jane probably had some trepidation, although Anne Boleyn's final fate had not been sealed at that time.

One other view was that Jane fell into her role quite willingly and actively sought to entice the King and flaunt her favor even in front of the current Queen.

However Jane actually felt, we will never know. Henry's feelings were pretty clear though. Within 24 hours of Anne Boleyn's execution, Jane Seymour and Henry VIII were formally betrothed. On the 30th of May, they were married. Unlike Henry's previous two Queens, Jane never had a coronation. Perhaps the King was waiting to Jane to "prove" herself by giving him a son.

Less than two months after Henry and Jane's marriage, the Duke of Richmond, Henry Fitzroy died at the age of 17. Fitzroy was the King's bastard son by his mistress Elizabeth Blount.

It wasn't until early 1537 that Jane became pregnant. During her pregnancy, Jane's every whim was indulged by the King, convinced that Jane, whom he felt to be his first "true wife", carried his long hoped for son. In October, a prince was born at Hampton Court Palace and was christened on 15th of October. The baby was named Edward. Mary, daughter of Catherine of Aragon, was godmother and Elizabeth, daughter of Anne Boleyn, also played a role in the ceremony.

There has been much written over whether or not Jane gave birth to Edward by cesarean section. It seems unlikely that if she had, she would have lived as long as she did after the birth. Jane attended her son's christening, although she was weak. She died on October 24th, just two weeks after her son was born.

Henry had already been preparing his own tomb at St. George's Chapel at Windsor Castle, which was where Jane was buried. In the end, she would be the only of Henry's six wives to be buried with him.

Anne of Cleves: God Send Me Well to Keep

Henry VIII remained single for over two years after Jane Seymour's death, possibly giving some credence to the thought that he genuinely mourned for her. However, it does seem that someone, possibly Thomas Cromwell, began making inquiries shortly after Jane's death about a possible foreign bride for Henry.

Henry's first marriage had been a foreign alliance of sorts, although it is almost certain that the two were truly in love for some time. His next two brides were love matches and Henry could have had little or no monetary or political gain from them.

But the events of the split from Rome left England isolated, and probably vulnerable. It was these circumstances that led Henry and his ministers to look at the possibility of a bride to secure an alliance. Henry did also want to be sure he was getting a desirable bride, so he had agents in foreign courts report to him on the appearance and other qualities of various candidates. He also sent painters to bring him images of these women.

Hans Holbein, probably the most famous of the Tudor court painters, was sent to the court of the Duke of Cleves, who had two sisters: Amelia and Anne. When Holbein went in 1539, Cleves was seen as an important potential ally in the event France and the Holy Roman Empire (who had somewhat made a truce in their long history of conflict) decided to move against the countries who had thrown off the Papal authority. England then sought alliances with countries who had been supporting the reformation of the church. Several of the Duchys and principalities along the Rhine were Lutheran. Holbein painted the sisters of the Duke of Cleves and Henry decided to have a contract drawn up for his marriage to Anne.

Although the King of France and the Emperor had gone back to their usual state of animosity, Henry proceeded with the match. The marriage took place on January 6, 1540. By then, Henry was already looking for ways to get out of the marriage.

Anne was ill-suited for life at the English court. Her upbringing in Cleves had concentrated on domestic skills and not the music and literature so popular at Henry's court. And, most famously, Henry did not find his new bride the least bit attractive and is said to have called her a "Flanders Mare". In addition to his personal feelings for wanting to end the marriage, there were now political ones as well. Tension between the Duke of Cleves and the Empire was increasing towards war and Henry had no desire to become involved. Last but not least, at some point, Henry had become attracted to young Catherine Howard.

Anne was probably smart enough to know that she would only be making trouble for herself if she raised any obstacles to Henry's attempts to annul the marriage. She testified that the match had not been consummated and that her previous engagement to the son of the Duke of Lorraine had not been properly broken.

After the marriage had been dissolved, Anne accepted the honorary title as the "King's Sister". She was given property, including Hever Castle, formerly the home of Anne Boleyn.

Anne lived away from court quietly in the countryside until 1557 and attended the coronation of her former step-daughter, Mary I.

She is buried in a somewhat hard to find tomb in Westminster Abbey.

Catherine Howard: No Other Will than His

Catherine Howard was the daughter of Lord Edmund Howard, a younger brother of Thomas Howard, Duke of Norfolk. She was also first cousin to Anne Boleyn, Henry's ill-fated second Queen. She was brought up in the household of the Dowager Duchess of Norfolk. As part of the Duchess' household, she would have spent most of her time at Lambeth and Horsham.

Catherine came to court at about the age of 19 as a lady in waiting to Anne of Cleves and there is no doubt that the spirited young girl caught Henry's attentions. Catherine uncle probably encouraged the girl to respond to the King's attentions and saw it as a way to increase his own influence over the monarch. The Duke of Norfolk also took advantage of the debacle of the Anne of Cleves marriage as a chance to discredit his enemy, Thomas Cromwell. In fact, Cromwell was executed shortly after the marriage was nullified.

Sixteen days after he was free of Anne, Henry took his fifth wife, Catherine Howard, on July 28, 1540. Henry was 49 and his bride was no older than 19.

For all that can be said against this match, Catherine did manage to lift the King's spirits. Henry had gained a lot of weight and was dealing with the ulcerated leg that was to pain him until his death. The vivacious young girl brought back some of Henry's zest for life. The King lavished gifts on his young wife and called her his "rose without a thorn" and the "very jewel of womanhood".

Less than a year into Catherine's marriage, the rumors of her infidelity began. In a way, one couldn't blame her for seeking the company of handsome young men closer to her own age. But to do so, even if only in courtly flirtations, was dangerous for a Queen, especially one who came from a powerful family with many enemies. Catherine didn't help matters much by appointing one of her admirers as her personal secretary.

By November 1541, there was enough evidence against the Queen that Archbishop Cranmer informed the King of Catherine's misconduct. At first Henry did not believe the accusations, but he agreed to allow further investigations into the matter. Enough evidence was gathered that the Queen had been promiscuous before her marriage and may have had liaisons after becoming Henry's wife. She was executed on the Tower Green on February 13, 1542 and laid to rest near her cousin Anne Boleyn in the Chapel of St. Peter ad Vincula at the Tower of London.

Catherine Parr: To Be Useful in All That I Do

Catherine Parr was the eldest daughter of Sir Thomas Parr and his wife Maud Green, both of whom were at the court of Henry VIII in his early reign. Maud was a lady-in-waiting to Queen Catherine of Aragon and named her daughter, born in 1512, after her. So, Henry VIII's last wife was named after his first. Thomas Parr died in November 1517, leaving his three children, William, Catherine and Anne in the care of their mother. Maud managed the children's education and the family estates and must have left an impression on her daughter of the greater role an independent woman could have in society. The education that Maud arranged for the children was similar to that of other noble figures of the time and at least in the case of Catherine, it ignited a life-long passion for learning. She was fluent in French, Latin and Italian and began learning Spanish when she was Queen.

Catherine Parr's first marriage was to Edward Borough, the son of Thomas, third Baron Borough of Gainsborough in 1529 when she was 17 years old. Edward died only a few years later, probably in early 1533. It was during this marriage that Catherine's mother Maud died, in December 1531. Catherine's second marriage was to John Neville, third Baron Latimer of Snape Castle in Yorkshire, whom she married in the summer of 1534 when he was 41 and she was 22. Latimer had two children from his previous marriages so Catherine also became a stepmother for the first time. During the Pilgrimage of Grace a rebel mob forced Latimer to join them and later took Catherine and her stepchildren hostage at the castle. Latimer was able to eventually secure their freedom and managed to escape arrest for his associations with the rebellion after it was finally put down.

Catherine's ailing husband died in March 1543, leaving her a widow for the second time, now at the age of 31. It was around this time that Catherine was noticed by not only the King, but also Thomas Seymour, brother of the late Queen Jane Seymour. Catherine expressed her desire to marry Thomas Seymour after Latimer's death, but the King's request for her hand was one that Catherine felt it was her duty to accept. Catherine and Henry VIII were married on July 12th in the Queen's closet at Hampton Court Palace in a small ceremony attended by about 20 people.

Catherine was interested in the reformed faith, making her enemies with the conservatives of Henry's court. It was Catherine's influence with the King and the Henry's failing health that led to a plot against her in 1546 by the conservative faction. Catherine and her ladies were known to have had banned books which was grounds for arrest and execution on charges of heresy. To gain evidence against the Queen, Anne Askew, a well-known and active Protestant, was questioned and tortured, but refused to recant her faith or give evidence against Catherine and her ladies. However, there was enough other evidence against the Queen to issue a warrant for her arrest. The warrant was accidentally dropped and someone loyal to the Queen saw it and then quickly told her about it. This is a well-documented incident that has made its way into many historical fiction accounts. Sometimes the history itself is the best drama! After learning of the arrest warrant, Catherine was said to be very ill, either as a ruse to stall or from a genuine panic attack. Henry went to see her and chastised her for her outspokenness about the reformed religion and his feeling that she was forgetting her place by instructing him on such matters. Catherine's response in her defense was that she was only arguing with him on these issues so she could be instructed by him, and to take his mind off other troubles. Playing to Henry's ego no doubt helped and Catherine was forgiven.

Catherine was close with all three of her stepchildren as Henry's wife and was personally involved in the educational program of the younger two, Elizabeth and Edward. She was also a patron of the arts and music. Catherine's own learning and academic achievements, as alluded to previously, were impressive, and in 1545, her book *Prayers or Meditations* became the first work published by an English Queen under her own name. Another book, *The Lamentation of a Sinner*, was published after Henry VIII's death.

Henry VIII died in January 1547 and Catherine had probably expected to play some role in the regency for the new nine-year-old king, Edward VI, but this was not to be.

Only a few months after Henry's death, Catherine secretly married Thomas Seymour, but the quickness and secret nature of the union caused a scandal. Catherine was still able to take guardianship of Princess Elizabeth and Seymour purchased the wardship of the king's cousin, Lady Jane Grey. It was during this time that the rumors of a relationship between Elizabeth and Seymour arose and Elizabeth was sent to another household in the spring of 1548.

After three previous marriages and at the age of 37, Catherine was pregnant for the first time and in June 1548, she moved to Sudeley Castle in Gloucestershire to await the birth of her child. On August 30th she gave birth to a daughter named Mary. Catherine soon fell ill with puerperal fever, which was to claim her life in the morning hours of September 5th. Catherine was buried, with Lady Jane Grey as the chief mourner, in the chapel at Sudeley Castle, where the tomb can still be visited today.

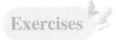

Exercises

Read the following article and complete the corresponding exercises.

What Does It Have to Do with My Classroom?

Inquiry learning can turn information into useful knowledge. It stresses skill development and nurtures the development of good habits of mind. Information, lacking a useful context, often has limited applications beyond passing a test. Learning plans and teaching materials need to include a relevant context for new information to lead to broader understandings. It is often hard for students to understand the connections between activities within a particular subject. This confusion is heightened when students struggle to understand the connections between different subjects within traditional schools.

Questions, whether self-initiated or "owned", are at the heart of inquiry learning. While questions are also a part of the traditional classroom, the sources, purposes, and levels of questioning are quite different. In the traditional classroom, the teacher is frequently the questioner. Questions are usually intended to provoke feedback about a reading or activity assignment. In an inquiry classroom, the teacher asks questions that are more open and reflective in nature. Appropriate questioning techniques are important in an inquiry-based classroom, especially in the lower grades where they become a foundation for self-initiated questioning.

Inference questions

These questions ask students to go beyond immediately available information. For example, a high-school photography teacher held up a black-and-white portrait of a machinist taken by Paul Strand and asked, "What do you know by looking at this photograph?" Through careful questioning and discussion, his students realized the image contained hints that implied a whole network of information: clues to content (where and when the photograph was taken), technique (where the photographer stood, where the light sources were located), and meaning or attitude (what Strand felt about industry and workers). To push beyond the factual in this way is to ask students to find clues, examine them, and discuss what inferences are justified.

Interpretation questions

If inference questions demand that students fill in missing information, then interpretive questions propose that they understand the consequences of information or ideas. One day, when her English class was struggling to make sense of Frost's poem "The Silken Tent", a teacher asked, "Imagine if Frost compared the woman to an ordinary canvas tent instead of a silk one. What would change?" Faced with the stolid image of a stiff canvas tent, students suddenly realized the fabric of connotations set in motion by the idea of silk—its sibilant, rustling sounds; its associations with elegance, wealth, and femininity; its fluid motions. In a similar spirit, during a life-drawing class, a teacher showed his students a reproduction of Manet's "Olympia" and asked them, "How would the picture be different if the model weren't wearing that black tie around her neck?" A student laid her hand over the tie, studied the image and commented, "Without the ribbon, she doesn't look so naked. She looks like a classical model. With the ribbon, she looks undressed, bolder."

Transfer questions

If inference and interpretation questions ask a student to go deeper, transfer questions provoke a kind of breadth of thinking, asking students to take their knowledge to new places. For example, the final exam for a high-school film course contained this question: "This semester we studied three directors: Fellini, Hitchcock, and Kurosawa. Imagine that you are a film critic and write a review of 'Little Red Riding Hood' as directed by one of these individuals."

Questions about hypotheses

Typically, questions based on what can be predicted and tested are thought of as belonging to sciences and other "hard" pursuits. But, in fact, predictive thinking matters in all domains. When we read a novel, we gather evidence about the world of the story, the trustworthiness of the narrator, the style of the author, all of which we use to predict what we can expect in the next chapter. Far from letting their students simply soak in the content of dances, plays, or fiction, skilled teachers probe for predictions as a way of making students actively aware of their expectations.

Exercises:

After reading some information on Henry VIII, would you raise some questions and exchange your ideas with your classmate. While questioning, some important rules have to be followed, for example:

Why are you interested in the question?

What is the correlation between this question and other questions?

What kinds of questions are you asking for?
Where can you find further information?

Text C

Brainstorming

The Catholic Church, also known as the Roman Catholic Church, is the largest Christian church, with more than 1.2 billion members worldwide. It is among the oldest religious institutions in the world and has played a prominent role in the history of Western civilisation. The Catholic hierarchy is headed by the Bishop of Rome, known as the Pope. The Catholic Church teaches that it is the one true Church founded by Jesus Christ, that its bishops are the successors of Christ's apostles and that the Pope is the sole successor to Saint Peter who has apostolic primacy. The Church maintains that the doctrine on faith and morals that it presents as definitive is infallible.

Question before reading:
What do you know about Thomas More?

Who Were the Early Reformers in England?[1]
Alison Weir

As yet in England there were few who looked beyond the correction of abuses and wanted a complete overhaul of the doctrine of the Church. Typical of the kind of reforming spirit in the early sixteenth century were men like Thomas More, the lawyer and future chancellor, and John Colet, dean of St Paul's. Heavily influenced by the humanism of Desiderius Erasmus, men such as there were not afraid to criticize the Church but were intent on remaining within it. The humanism or "New Learning" that Erasmus championed built upon a revival of the study of pagan, classical writers and a deep textual criticism. Erasmus, while publishing a number of satirical works which were sharply critical of the clergy and the Church, made his most significant contribution in a new translation of the New Testament. Returning to the original Greek texts, his version was more accurate than that commonly used, the Vulgate, and his corrections served "to undermine the scriptural authority of the priesthood and the papacy". Armed with new critical tools, humanists in England attempted to revitalize the Church.

More's great work *Utopia* satirized contemporary Christian values by imagining a

---

[1] Excerpt from *The Six Wives Of Henry VIII*. Vintage, 2007.

society which was essentially humane yet not Christian. His ironic point was that this imaginary, pagan society was superior to, and had much to teach, sixteenth-century Christian European society. While More's subtlety was not lost on his readers, John Colet took a more direct approach. Invited to preach before the Convocation of Canterbury in 1511, Colet was scathing in his criticism of the clergy and of the bishops. The clergy were guilty of worldliness, lush, greed and ambition, and the bishops, who ought to have been attempting to rectify these problems, were setting poor examples themselves. These attacks were not welcomed by the Ecclesiastical establishment, but it was always clear that neither Colet nor More desired to do any more than reform the existing structure from within it. Colet was never a "Protestant", and More became the scourge of those who challenged the doctrine of the Church. However uncomfortable the humanist critique may have been for the leaders of the Church, the followers of this "New Learning" were not heretics.

As noted earlier, England had its own tradition of heretical teachings. John Wyclif had first advanced his ideas at Oxford towards the end of the fourteenth century. That was a time when confidence in the Church was a very low ebb: the papacy had earlier moved from Rome to Avignon (prompting English suspicions that the Pope was no more than a French Chaplain), and there were at one time three separate and competing popes. Wyclif's teachings had called for a Bible in English and the dissolution of monasteries, had attacked Church property and had argued for a rolling-back of priestly and papal power. He also had a vision of "a new order of society...in which citizens obeyed the lay prince as priest and king". In fact, Wyclif's programme for reform anticipated many of the criticisms that reformers in the sixteenth century were to level at the Church.

However, Wyclif's reforms, although interesting to the powerful John of Gaunt, who became his protector, were never instituted, not least because the English government in the late fourteenth century was unstable enough as it was without embarking on so ambitious a project as Wyclif proposed. The support that he had among the nobility and middle classes gave his ideas a certain respectability until they became associated with the rebellion of Sir John Oldcastle in 1414. Wyclif's followers now began to be persecuted and were forced underground. There they remained, known as Lollards, only surfacing periodically to be tried for heresy.

How extensive a community the Lollards were in the sixteenth century is a matter open to question. By the eve of the Reformation they appear to have existed in some regions of the country primarily among the merchant and artisan classes. The complicated and elegant ideas of John Wyclif had degenerated somewhat over the course of a century into a very simplistic attack on ceremony, the veneration of images, belief in purgatory, and priest, and the identifying badge of Lollardy was the translation of the Bible into English known as the "Lollard Bible". Lollardy seems to have been largely a phenomenon of southern England. London, Essex and Kent in particular appear to have had strong Lollard communities. Bristol in the southwest and Coventry in the Midlands were also centres of Lollard support. However, the Lollards were hardly representative of common public opinion, and whether Lollardy provided any real leadership in the Protestants did not always consider themselves fellow travelers. However, there were those in England who took matters a step further than either the Lollards or the humanists.

In the early part of the sixteenth century a new breed of reformed thinker was emerging. It must be stressed that they were few, and it is as a result of the ultimate victory of Protestantism over Catholicism in England that these early reformers have been given the prominence by historians that they have received. At the time, they were on the margin, even if their attacks did sometimes provoke responses from the highest levels of government.

The centre for this group of reformers was Cambridge, its leader the Augustinian prior Robert Barnes. Barnes was an intelligent and vocal critic of the clergy and the bishops and, although forced to recant his views in the 1520s, continued as an important voice for reform under the protection of Thomas Cromwell until 1540. Barnes and his followers initially gathered at the White Horse Tavern, where they discussed, and were influenced by, the writings of Martin Luther and other continental reformers. From this group would emerge two of the future leaders of the church in England: Thomas Cranmer and Hugh Latimer.

Perhaps the best known of these new Protestants was William Tyndale, because he published his criticisms and his English translation of the New Testament. Horrified by what he saw as the ignorance of the clergy, particularly in his West Country home, and influenced by the writings of Luther on salvation, Tyndale began a campaign of criticism which attracted followers in the 1520s. He was persuaded by the Lutheran concept of salvation by faith alone and, as a consequence, attacked the doctrine of purgatory and the practice of indulgences. More than that, he developed a political theology challenged the power of the priesthood and vested the power to reform the Church in the king, who, after all, was chosen by God to govern. Although these opinions, and especially Tyndale's antagonism towards the papal authority, were attractive to a king who wished to challenge that authority, there was no question but that Tyndale's opinions were considered heretical, especially after the publication of his translation of the New Testament in 1525. It was Tyndale's most important contribution to the reformation. This Bible in English, based on Erasmus' translation from the Greek, added much that was antipapal and anticlerical in the margins, although the translation itself was faithful. In 1524, he was forced to flee to the continent, where he carried on a violent pamphlet battle with Thomas More until he was captured and executed for heresy by the forces of the Holy Roman Emperor Charles V in 1536. In Tyndale's thinking, the ideas of the Lollards and humanism amalgamated and grew. His reliance on Scripture as the final and most important authority made him uncompromising in his positions. Therefore, although his opinions on the authority of the Pole were much to the liking of Henry VIII, he was unable to support the king's wishes for a divorce because he could find no Scriptural justification for it.

The issues were not raised by Tyndale alone. Others, such as Thomas Bilney, Thomas Arthur and John Frith, found themselves in trouble with authorities for their outspoken opinions. Frith, a devoted disciple of Tyndale, was expelled from Oxford for his views and fled to the continent in 1528 to join his mentor. Returning to England to organize support for the Protestant cause, he was captured and burned at the stake in 1533. Bilney and Arthur were both tried for heresy at Cambridge in 1527. While Arthur, who had criticized ecclesiastical jurisdiction, admitted his error, Bilney proved a much more difficult case. On most matters very orthodox, indeed hardly a Protestant at all, he was outspoken in his opposition to the veneration of images, which he deemed idolatry, and to papal pardons on the grounds that these seemed to denigrate the sufficiency of Christ in the matter of salvation. Was Christ's on the cross not enough to ensure forgiveness of sins? Recognising his peril, Bilney managed to answer carefully the questions put to him, but in the end was forced into a humiliating recantation. The recantation was half-hearted, however. Soon thereafter Bilney was distributing Protestant books and preaching without a licence in Norfolk. For this he was burned at the stake in 1531 and was immortalized by Protestant historians (most notably John Foxe) as a martyr to a cause to which he was only ever marginally committed.

The importance of these early reformers was inflated later by Protestant historians. The reformers reached only a small percentage of the population and, as often as not, preached to the already converted or the disaffected. They were primarily influenced among the young scholars at Cambridge during the halcyon days of the White Horse Tavern. Important though their influence was among the future leaders of the Church of England, they were not particularly influential with the general population.

What Were the Issues?

Just as the newly formed Parliament of 1529 was about to meet, a Protestant firebrand, Simon Fish, published his tact *A Supplication of Beggars*. He painted a dismal picture of the clergy and the state of the Church, as did his fellow common lawyer, Christopher St German, who built a case against the clergy by listing known examples of clerical abuse. We have already noted John Colet's criticism of the clergy abuse. We have already noted John Colet's criticism of the clergy in 1511. All these have been seen as evidence of the reality of violent anticlerical sentiment in England and the abuses that were laid at the door of the clergy.

But what were those abuses, and what were the issues that the reformers focused on in their attack on the Church? There were two levels of criticism directed at the Church. First, there was criticism of abuse of practice—aspects of Church discipline which were violated and either ignored or not dealt with effectively by the existing structures within the institution. Second, there was criticism of practices which the reformers felt to be intrinsically wrong—ceremonies, traditions, and "superstitions" based on an incorrect analysis of Scripture or a faulty theological interpretation. While Thomas More or John

Colet might agree that there were problems of discipline that cried out for reform, they would not agree that the theology of the Church was in error.

The problems that existed in ecclesiastical discipline in the early sixteenth century were nothing new. The Church had been wrestling with these persistent breaches of discipline for centuries: sometimes effectively, sometime not. The abuses most commonly cited were simony, pluralism, non-residence, nepotism, sexual misconduct, ignorance and benefit of clergy.

All of these been recognized as abuses from very early on and for good reason. Often used as a means of unfair advancement in the Church, simony had been outlawed by early councils of the Church, but it proved very difficult to control. Pluralism was frowned upon because it meant that some parishes might be neglected by clergy who were busy elsewhere. However, one benefice might not produce sufficient income for the clergyman's support, and so dispensations were granted by Rome if this was the case. Assurances were required that all parishes would be looked after adequately by curates, but there were abuses of this system: some clergy held more than two benefices, some bishops held more than one diocese. The curates hired by pluralists were not usually of the best quality, as they were paid only a small percentage of the income of the parish, such a position was not attractive to the best candidates. In some cases, no curate was provided at all. The main complaint was that the people of the parish were not being served adequately.

Non-residence might be the result of pluralism, but a more common cause was that the priest might be employed elsewhere. It was not uncommon for the clergy to serve as stewards, managing the estates or affairs of the wealthy. In addition, the clergy often served the government in a variety of positions which drew them away from their parishes or divorces on a regular or even permanent basis. Even a casual glance at the men who served Henry VIII as diplomats reveals that many were either bishops or priests. If they were conscientious, they left men adequate to look after their cures but sometimes this did not happen. Again, those who suffered were the people whose spiritual needs the Church existed to serve.

The more powerful among the clergy were often guilty of nepotism as they often had a number of benefices at their disposal to dispense as they saw fit. (Thomas Cardinal Wolsey, chancellor of England and archbishop of York, for instance, secured benefices for his son Thomas Winter even though Winter was studying in Paris.) As a consequence, nepotism was followed by non-residency and, because one benefice was often not enough to provide a comfortable living, by pluralism.

Sexual misconduct was simply that: the clergy had all taken a vow of celibacy and were not supposed to have sexual relations of any kind. By the sixteenth century clerical celibacy had been in force for some five hundred years, although it had not always been part of the tradition of the Church. Sometimes local custom accepted clergy who had female companions and even families, despite the overall ban on such behavior. The bulk of sexual charges (and there were few of these) brought against the clergy had to do with behavior far more scandalous than simple cohabitation.

Ignorance was a charge which was made especially against the poorer clergy who served as curates in parishes held in plurality. While some of the clergy had university education, a great number had only rudimentary training. The issue was not whether, in some cases, they were able to read the services and understand them. After the break with Rome, it was discovered in Gloucester that ten of the clergy could not recite the Lord's Prayer. This was taken as an indication of how badly standards had slipped in the pre-Reformation Church. Charges of ignorance raised real questions about the ability of the clergy to perform their parochial function.

Originally designed to protect the clergy and extended even to the minor orders, benefit of clergy was a privilege where the opportunities for abuse were plentiful. The Church had recognized this and took steps to curtail abuses—even going so far as to brand the hands of those who had claimed benefit of clergy and were not entitled to do so again. But the apparent injustice of this privilege could still provoke anger among the laity. In 1514, when the coroner's jury returned a verdict of murder and charged several of the bishop of London's officers after Richard Hunne was found hanged in a cell in the bishop of London's palace, the accused escaped trial by claiming benefit of clergy. London was outraged at the time, and the case had not been forgotten by those who assembled in Parliament in 1529.

In addition to these abuses, there were long-standing grievances to do with the way the Church raised money to maintain its ministry, and the way it administered justice in its courts. The Church raised its money through a tax known as the tithe, and through fees that it charged for a variety of spiritual services. Refusal to pay could result in arrest and prosecution before the Church courts. Richard Hunne, for instance, found himself in the bishop of London's gaol because he had refused to pay one such fee—the mortuary fee. Some questioned whether it was possible for the church to dispense justice fairly where its own financial interests were involved or where its own officials were in jeopardy.

While these issues of practice tended to be eye-catching—everyone understood what the sexual misconduct of the clergy meant—the more specifically theological issues were equally, if not more, important in the debate. Here we find a number of issues which causes serious disagreement. Most of these were based on an understanding of Christian theology which relied on the ultimate authority of Scripture and on the insights of Martin Luther. The central problem was how one could come to eternal life, and the question that the reformers asked was simply: what is necessary for salvation?

Like Luther, they found the answer in *Bible*. They argued that only those requirements for eternal life found specifically in Scripture were necessary. Anything else was superfluous, of human invention, or even antithetical to the pursuit of salvation. For some reformers this appeal to Scriptural authority meant that any observance, custom or belief that could not be supported by Scripture was not to be accepted; indeed, acceptance might be harmful to one's spiritual health. Others, like the writer Thomas Starkey, would argue that some of the traditions of the Church, while not being necessary, might be useful to one's spiritual life. This moderate position was not generally shared by radical reformers although the Church of England would ultimately follow the middle way that Starkey first enunciated.

The key to understanding all the issues raised by the early reformers, however, is the doctrine of salvation by faith alone. Once a theologian accepted the notion that there was nothing one could actively do to achieve eternal life except have faith, then the structure that the Church had built around the doctrine of salvation began to crumble. The doctrine of purgatory, the half-way house between heaven and hell, was objected to as a human invention without Scriptural authority or proof. Indulgences were objected to because they implied that the love of God as demonstrated in the sacrifice of His son was not enough and that somehow the human agency of the Pope or the Church might have some control over the benefits of God's love. The veneration of the saints, nowhere commanded in the *Bible*, was seen as denying that Christ himself was sufficient to intercede for our salvation. The veneration of images was seen as idolatrous and completely contrary to Scripture. Pilgrimages were seen as superstitious and not required of Christians. Finally, transubstantiation, the doctrine that the consecrated bread and wine of the Eucharist actually became the body and blood of Christ (despite their appearance), was attacked as absurd and lacking Scriptural authority.

As the central text on which the reformers based these criticisms was the Bible, the refusal of the English Church to allow the Bible to be published in the vernacular was seen as an attempt by the Church to keep the Christian religion in the hands of the Church and away from the people. Access to this essential Christian text was believed by reformers from Wyclif to Luther to be vitally important to the development of faith. Up to a point, the people were encouraged by the reformer to make up their own minds. While the Bible was available in the vernacular in several countries, the Council of Oxford in 1407, moved by hostility to the Lollard Bible, had outlawed English translations. In fact, parts of the Bible in translation did exist and many reformers included in their tracts large sections of Scripture in translation, but no complete and official version existed. The established Church feared unorthodox interpretations which could lead to heresy, such as Lollardy, and wanted to maintain control of the central text.

The debate over the vernacular Bible, especially when seen from a distance, would seem to be evidence of great dissatisfaction with the Church, but was it? We have already suggested that the traditional view of a decrepit Church riddled with corruption will no longer stand the test of the evidence and we have argued that those who were so vocal in their criticisms were an unrepresentative minority. What was the state of the Church in England in the early sixteenth century? What did the people think?

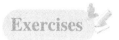

Read the following samples and complete the corresponding tasks.

Students Doing Inquiry Learning

What does inquiry-based learning look like? Much of what is said about science and inquiry learning can be applied to all subjects. The following list describes some of what inquiry learning looks like in practice.

Students raise questions, propose explanations, and use observations.
- They ask questions (verbally and through actions).
- They use questions that lead them to activities generating further questions or ideas.
- They observe critically, as opposed to casually looking or listening.
- They value and apply questions as an important part of learning.
- They make connections to previous ideas.

Students plan and carry out learning activities.
- They design ways to try out their ideas, not always expecting to be told what to do.
- They plan ways to verify, extend, confirm, or discard ideas.
- They carry out activities by: using materials, observing, evaluating, and recording information.
- They sort out information and decide what is important.
- They see detail, detect sequences and events, notice change, and detect differences and similarities.

Students communicate using a variety of methods.
- They express ideas in a variety of ways, including journals, drawing, reports, graphing, and so forth.
- They listen, speak, and write about learning activities with parents, teacher, and peers.
- They use the language of learning, apply the skills of processing information, and develop their own "ground rules" appropriate for the discipline.

Students critique their learning practices.
- They use indicators to assess their own work.
- They recognize and report their strengths and weaknesses.
- They reflect on their learning with their teacher and their peers.

Learning Skills

Inquiry Learning Skills

What Is Inquiry-based Learning?

An old adage states, "Tell me and I forget, show me and I remember, involve me and I understand." The last part of this statement is the essence of inquiry-based learning, says our workshop author Joe Exline. Inquiry implies involvement that leads to understanding. Furthermore, involvement in learning implies possessing skills and attitudes that permit you to seek resolutions to questions and issues while you construct new knowledge.

What Are the Key Principles of Inquiry Learning?

To recap, the key principles of inquiry learning are listed below. You can use them to guide the creation of your inquiry facilitation plans.

Principle 1:

All learning activities should focus on using information-processing skills (from observations to synthesis) and applying the discipline "ground rules" as a means to learn content set in a broad conceptual context.

Principle 2:

Inquiry learning puts the learner at the center of an active learning process, and the systemic elements (the teacher, instructional resources, technology, and so forth) are prepared or aligned to support the learner.

Principle 3:

The role of the teacher becomes one of facilitating the learning process. The teacher also becomes a learner by finding out more about the learner and the process of inquiry learning.

Principle 4:

What is assessed is what is valued. Therefore, more emphasis needs to be placed on assessing the development of information-processing skills, nurtured habits of mind, or "ground rules" of the discipline, and conceptual understandings—rather than just the content of the field.

Step-by-step Facilitation-plan Creation

The following is an outline for developing each step of an inquiry facilitation plan of your own. You can use the blank boxes to fill in your own ideas for your facilitation plan. The outline below starts with a focus on short-range activities, but most of what is outlined is appropriate for all ranges of activities.

Unit 10 Learning Model-inquiry Learning

1. Learning Objectives and Expected Outcome

In this space, you should provide the focus of skills development for the lesson. These can include observation skills, research skills, synthesis skills, etc.

2. Habits of Mind/Ground Rules Being Emphasized

List the rules of the discipline being studied that you wish to reinforce here. For example: in science, these would include particular aspects of the scientific method; for English, these would include literary ideas and ideals.

3. Conceptual Theme Most Important to This Lesson

In this space, include the themes that connect the lesson to previous lessons and the important ideas in the framework of the discipline that you wish to stress. Examples could include the way the discipline explores change, the way it makes connections between one idea and another, or the way theories or ideas can be applied to different levels of analysis.

4. Specific Content

List here the content that your students need to know by the end of the lesson. You may want to include the academic standards you are seeking to meet here as well.

5. Sources and Resources Needed/Available

Note sources here like libraries, professional journals, local colleges/universities, the Internet, other professionals, etc. Also list any materials you may need.

6. Potential Roadblocks to Learning

List any problems you see with helping students learn this material. Also list possible solutions. Include several alternatives. This section will grow as you progress.

7. Inquiry Attributes Already Possessed by Learners

Answer the questions here as a guide for pre-assessment and taking the learners to the next level:

- What are the skill levels of the learners?
- What nurtured habits of mind do the learners possess?
- What are the levels of conceptual understanding of the learners?
- What are the levels of content understanding of the learners?

8. Questions and Types of Questions to Be Raised and Explored

Fill in here the main questions that you hope learners will explore, bearing in mind the various types of questions (inference, questions about hypotheses, etc.).

9. Ongoing Assessment

Once students have begun to explore the questions and content of the lesson, observe them during the activity, examine aspects of their work, and find out where they are having difficulty. Make efforts to judge each learner's progress from where he/she started to where he/she has progressed. Keep records of this progress for later comparisons.

10. Appropriate Sources and Resources to Effectively Monitor Progress

List here the ways you will assess your students at the end of the activity (i.e., reports, exams, etc.).

11. Professional Preparation

List here things that you, as a teacher, need to find out before starting this lesson.

What Are the Benefits of Inquiry-based Learning?

One of the important missing pieces in many modern schools is a coherent and simplified process for increasing knowledge of a subject from lower grades to upper grades. Students often have difficulty understanding how various activities within a particular subject relate to each other. Much more confusion results when the learner tries to interrelate the various subjects taught at school.

Too little effort is devoted to defining important outcomes at the end of high school and planning backwards and across subjects. Inquiry-based learning can help make these connections.

Specific content such as photosynthesis has much more relevance for the learner if set in a larger context of understanding the interrelationship of the sun, green plants, and the role of carbon dioxide and water. Social studies content, such as industrial development, set in the context of interrelating changes in the human-designed world can add new perspectives to this important natural process. Students can still learn content of both science and social studies, but through a series of well-planned experiences, they will grasp the larger conceptual context and gain greater understanding.

Within a conceptual framework, inquiry learning and active learner involvement can lead to important outcomes in the classroom. Students who actively make observations, collect, analyze, and synthesize information, and draw conclusions are developing useful problem-solving skills. These skills can be applied to future "need to know" situations that students will encounter both at school and at work.

Another benefit that inquiry-based learning offers is the development of habits of mind that can last a lifetime and guide learning and creative thinking.

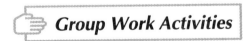

Group Work Activities

Work in groups and complete the following tasks.
Task 1: What I'm looking for
- Use your knowledge and understanding to develop lines of enquiry.
- Evaluate historical sources[①] and fill in the forms.
- Identify those sources that are useful.
- Use sources to reach and support conclusions.
- Evaluate and reflect on the work carried out and the method you used in the enquiry.

---

① Historical source can be found at the end of the activity.

Task 2: Areas to cover
You will need to discuss about one of the followings:
- **The young Henry**—What was his education, skills, personality and image? Did these make him sound like a great king or not?
- **Henry VIII's government**—Did he rule or just reign? Who did most of the work, Henry or ministers such as Thomas Wolsey? Did this mean he was great?
- **Henry, the people and his rule**—How popular was Henry with the people? Was he a cruel king or just a king trying to ensure peace?
- **Henry and religion**—Why did Henry make himself the Head of the Church? How did he show he was the rightful Head of the Church? Did Henry make changes to the church for the benefit of the country or himself?
- **Henry and Wales**—What did he do for Wales? Were the Acts of Union an attempt to destroy the Welsh language?
- **Anything else you would want to find out.**

Finally:
At the end of this investigation you will need to write an essay of Henry VIII with no less than 1,000 words. In this essay you will assess whether Henry VIII deserves to be called "Great" or not. You will need to make use of some of the sources you have been provided with and collect your own information.

Essay Outline:
You are now ready to write an academic essay. Remember that an academic essay tells the question of a topic and analyses it. It looks at what other researchers achieved in the field, how this information influenced your inquiries, and if your inquiries have been made sound illustrations.

Historical Enquiry: Henry the Great: Image or reality?

Introduction:
Background knowledge or information

For example:
Explain briefly why Henry VIII was called "Great" and why he is remembered and what image people have of him.
Explain why you decide the question of the topic to write or why the question of the topic has its special significance or features.

Main Part:
Write paragraphs on one of the followings. Possible mention some of the sources

that you have studied:
- **The young Henry**—What were his education, skills, personality and image? Did these make him sound like a great king or not?
- **Henry VIII's government**—Did he rule or just reign? Who did most of the work, Henry or ministers such as Thomas Wolsey? Did this mean he was great?
- **Henry, the people and his rule**—How popular was Henry with the people? Was he a cruel king or just a king trying to ensure peace?
- **Henry's foreign and defensive policy**—How did he try to make England stronger? Did he only do this because he was successful in his foreign policy?
- **Henry and Wales**—What did he do for Wales? Were the Acts of Union an attempt to destroy the Welsh language?
- **Include anything else you have find out or line of investigation you have followed.**

You now need to refer to at least **two** sources that you found to be **useful** to your enquiry and **two** that were **not so useful**. **Citations** have to be used to illustrate your point of views.

Conclusion:
Write a conclusion in which you decide whether Henry VIII deserves to be called great or not.

Enquiry Worksheet

Name	Form

Historical Enquiry: Henry the Great: Image or Reality?

Henry VIII who ruled England and Wales between 1509 and 1547 is perhaps the most well known king in British history. He was known for "display". When he met one of his rivals, King Francis I of France, just outside Calais in 1520, a complete town of tents and timber was built for the meeting. Yards of velvet, satin and cloth of gold were sent to decorate the temporary palaces. It was called "The Field of the Cloth of Gold". Henry loved all this display: by the end of his reign he had fifty-five palaces, two thousand tapestries, one hundred and fifty paintings and nearly one thousand eight hundred books. He also spent vast sums fighting wars and made every effort to be known as a warrior king. Nearly 72,000 people were

Unit 10　Learning Model-inquiry Learning

executed during his reign. So is there any wonder he is remembered.

During the reign of Elizabeth I, Henry VIII was called "Henry the Great" of "Great Harry". The question is does he deserve to be remembered as "Great", or was this more a matter of image than reality? You are going to carry out an enquiry to decide how he should be remembered.

What do I KNOW about Henry VIII?

What would I WANT to know about Henry VIII?

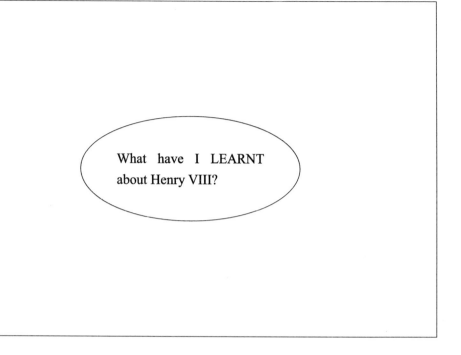

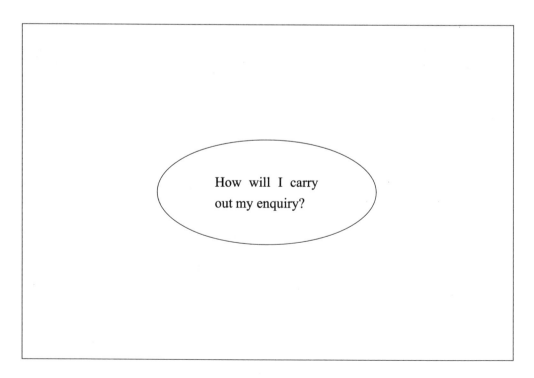

Unit 10　Learning Model-inquiry Learning

What do I learn about the image of Henry from the source?

What else would you want to know about the source?

How will the source help your enquiry?

Source 1—A copy of a portrait of Henry painted by the artist Hans Holbein the Younger in 1536.

What are the strengths and weaknesses of the source?

What do I learn about the young Henry from the source?

What else would you want to know about the source and its content?

His Majesty is the handsomest ruler I ever set eyes on; above the usual height, with an extremely fine calf to his leg, his complexion very fair and bright, auburn hair combed straight and short, in the French fashion.... He speaks French, English and Latin, and a little Italian, plays well on the lute and harpsichord, sings from book at sight, draws the bow with greater strength than any man in England and jousts marvellously.... a most accomplished Prince.

Source 2—The Venetian Ambassador describing the young Henry VIII in 1509

How will the source help your enquiry?

What are the strengths and weaknesses of the source?

Unit 10 Learning Model-inquiry Learning

What do I learn about the young Henry from the source?

What else would you want to know about the source?

How will the source help your enquiry?

Source 3—A portrait of Henry from about 1520 when he was 29 years old and young and healthy.

What are the strengths and weaknesses of the source?

What do I learn about Henry's interests from the source?

What else would you want to know about the source?

Source 4—Henry, jousting during a tournament held in 1511 to celebrate the birth of Prince Henry (who soon died). The image comes from a roll on jousting. Henry was more interested in jousting rather than running the country.

How will the source help your enquiry?

What are the strengths and weaknesses of the source?

Unit 10 Learning Model-inquiry Learning

What do I learn about Henry's government from the source?

What else would you want to know about the source and its content?

Cardinal Thomas Wolsey (c1472—1509) was Henry's most trusted minister until his fall in 1529—30. He was the son of an Ipswich butcher and grazier, and his governmental and political skills led to swift advancement in the Church and State, including the acquisition of rich offices and the office of Lord Chancellor (the King's head of government).

Source 5—(Adapted) The historian Susan Doran writing in *The Tudor Chronicles, 1485—1603 (2007)*

How will the source help your enquiry?

What do I learn about the rule of Henry from the source?

What are the strengths and weaknesses of the source?

Henry VIII... was very fond of having his own way... those who suffered most... were his ministers and the great nobles... But to tell the truth, the common people in England were often not sorry to see the great nobles who lived among them lose their heads or their properties, as long as King Henry... did not tax them too heavily. Whatever may have been his faults, and he had many, there can be no doubt that by far the greatest number of the people in England loved him.

Source 6—Historian H. O. Arnold-Forster, writing in *A History of England* (1897)

What else would you want to know about the source and its content?

How will the source help your enquiry?

What are the strengths and weaknesses of the source?

Unit 10 Learning Model-inquiry Learning

What do I learn about Henry's personality and popularity?

What else would you want to know about the source and its content?

Henry is so greedy that all the riches in the world would not satisfy him... to make himself rich he has impoverished his people. This King... does not trust a single man... and will not cease to dip his hand in blood as long as he doubts the people.

Source 7—The French ambassador to England writing to the King of France in 1540. The King of France was a rival of Henry VIII.

How will the source help your enquiry?

What do I learn about Henry's rule from the source?

What are the strengths and weaknesses of the source?

What else would you want to know about the source and its content?

According to Holinshed, who wrote 25 years after Henry's death, 72, 000 thieves and vagabonds were hanged during his reign. It is over 2 per cent of the 2,800,000 inhabitants of England, which equals the proportion of the 6, 000,000 Jews exterminated by Hitler.

Source 8—Historian Jasper Ridley in his book *Henry VIII* (1984)

How will the source help your enquiry?

What do I learn about Henry's rule and how he responded to protests?

Unit 10 Learning Model-inquiry Learning

What are the strengths and weaknesses of the source?

What else would you want to know about the source and its content?

Cause such dreadful executions upon a good number of the inhabitants hanging them on trees, quartering them, and setting the quarters in every town, as shall be a fearful warning.

Source 9—Orders given by Henry VIII in 1537, about what should happen to those who took part in a protest against him known as the Pilgrimage of Grace.

How will the source help your enquiry?

What do I learn about Henry's rule? How does the source differ with other sources?

What are the strengths and weaknesses of the source?

What else would you want to know about the source and its content?

His rule was humane, his executions sporadic... he never killed anyone with his own hand... The number of victims... was not large.

Source 10—Historian John Bowle in his book *Henry VIII* (1964)

How will the source help your enquiry?

What do I learn about Henry's religious changes from the source?

Unit 10 Learning Model-inquiry Learning

What are the strengths and weaknesses of the source?

What else would you need to know so as to understand the source?

Changes to the church in England began with Henry VIII. His reformation of the church was caused by his desire for power and money but above all the need for a male heir.

When the Pope refused to end Henry's marriage with Catherine of Aragon, Henry reacted by passing laws to limit the Pope's power and to take any church money for himself. In 1534 Parliament recognized Henry as their "only and supreme lord and even supreme head." in the Act of Supremacy.

Source 11—A description of some of the changes made to the Church by Henry VIII. This account was written by a secondary school history teacher.

How will the source help your enquiry?

What does the source tell us about Henry's religious policies?

What are the strengths and weaknesses of the source?

What else would you need to know so as to understand the source?

How will the source help your enquiry?

Source 12—A gold medal from 1545. Henry is shown wearing a jewelled cap, ermine robe and jewelled collar, with a inscription Latin around the edge reading "Henry VIII, King of England, France and Ireland, defender of the faith, and under Christ, the supreme head on earth of the Church of England and Ireland".

What are the strengths and weaknesses of the source?

Unit 10 Learning Model-inquiry Learning

What do I learn about what Henry did for Wales?

What else would you want to know about the source and its content?

Henry's religious changes and his treatment of Queen Catherine had upset many of the Welsh who remained loyal to the Pope. Henry believing that the Welsh posed a threat to his crown ordered his Chief Minister Thomas Cromwell to pass laws to bring Wales under English control. The result was the Acts of Union of 1536 and 1543 which divided Wales into thirteen shires, destroyed the unruly Marcher lordships and brought the whole of Wales under English law.

Source 13—A description of the Acts of Union written by a history teacher.

How is the source different to other portraits of Henry?

What are the strengths and weaknesses of the source?

What do you learn about what Henry did for Wales?

What else would you want to know about the source and its content?

The people of Wales... do daily use a speech nothing like the natural mother tongue used in England... From henceforth no persons that use the Welsh speech or language shall enjoy any... office or fees within this realm of England and Wales.

Source 14—An extract from the Act of Union of 1536.

How is the source different to other portraits of Henry?

What are the strengths and weaknesses of the source?

Unit 10　Learning Model-inquiry Learning

✋ *Self-evaluation Form*

What are the main objectives in this unit?
_____
_____
_____

What useful vocabularies and expressions have you learned from this unit?
_____
_____
_____

What key terms and educational knowledge have you learned?
_____
_____
_____

Have you used the learning skills before? Why do you think they are useful or not useful?
_____
_____
_____

If possible, what would you like to add to make learning more interesting and relevant?
_____
_____
_____

References

Almond, G. A., and S. Verba. (1965) *The Civic Culture.* Boston: Little, Brown.

Amabile, T. M. (1996) *Creativity in Context.* Boulder, CO: Westview.

Amsterdam, A. and Bruner, J.S. (2000) *Minding the Law.* Cambridge, MA: Harvard University Press.

Apter, D. E. (1968) *Some Conceptual Approaches to the Study of Modernization.* Englewood Cliffs, N.J.: Prentice Hall.

Barbour, R. (2007) *Doing Focus Groups.* London: Sage. *Behaviour* 6: 114—43.

Berliner, D. (2008) "Research, Policy, and Practice: The Great Disconnect" in S.D. Lapan and M.T. Quartaroli (eds.), *Research Essentials: An Introduction to Designs and Practices.* N.J.: Jossey-Bass, Hoboken, pp. 295—325.

Berstecher, D. (1970) *Zur Theorie und Technik des internationalen Vergleichs: Das Beispiel der Bildungsforschung.* Stuttgart: Klett.

Bruner, J.S. (1996) "Meyerson aujourd'hui: quelques reflexions sur la psychologie culturelle", in F. Parot (ed.), *Pour une psychologie historique: Ecrits en hommage à Ignace Meyerson.* Paris: Presses Universitaires de France.

Bruner, J.S. (1997) "Celebrating divergence: Piaget and Vygotsky", *Human evelopment,* 40: 63—73.

Bruner, J.S. and Lucariello, J. (1989) "Monologue as Narrative Recreation of the World", in K. Nelson (ed.), *Narratives from the Crib.* Cambridge, MA: Harvard University Press.

Claypole, M. (2010) *Controversies in ELT. What You Always Wanted to Know about Teaching English but Were Afraid to Ask.* Norderstedt: LinguaBooks/BoD.

Craft, A. (2005) *Creativity in Schools — Tensions and Dilemmas.* London: Routledge.

Craft, A. (2008) "Tensions in Creativity and Education". In *Creativity, Wisdom and Trusteeship—Exploring the Role of Education,* ed. A. Craft, H. Gardner, and G. Claxton. Thousand Oaks: Corwin Press, pp. 16—34.

Craft, A., H. Gardner, and G. Claxton. (2008) "Nurturing Creativity, Wisdom, and Trusteeship in education." In *Creativity, Wisdom and Trusteeship—Exploring the Role of*

Education, ed. A. Craft, H. Gardner, and G. Claxton. Thousand Oaks: Corwin Press, pp. 1—13.

Cropley, A.J. (2008) *Creativity in Education and Learning—A Guide for Teachers and Educators*. London: Routledge.

Csikszentmihalyi, M. (1996) *Creativity—Flow and the Psychology of Discovery and Invention*. New York: Harper Perennial.

Debeauvais, M. (1970) *Comparative Study of Educational Expenditure and Its Trends in OECD Countries since 1950*. Paris: OECD.

Dieckmann, B. (1970) *Zur Strategie des systematischen internationalen Vergleichs: Probleme des Datenbasis und der Entwicklungsbegriffe*. Stuttgart: Klett.

Driscoll, M. (2002). *Blended Learning: Let's Get Beyond the Hype*. Available at http://www-07.ibm.com/ services/pdf/blended_learning.pdf (accessed on 5 July 2010).

Fasko, D. (2000—2001) "Education and Creativity". *Creativity Research Journal* 13, No. 3/4: 317—27.

Flyvbjerg, B. (2006) "Five Misunderstandings about Case Study Research". *Qualitative Inquiry* 12, No. 2: 219—45.

Fraser, S. (1964) *Jullien's Plan for Comparative Education, 1826—1827*. New York: Teachers College, Columbia University.

Geertz, C. (1999) "A Life of Learning". *The Charles Homer Haskins Lecture for 1999*. American Council of Learned Societies, Occasional Paper.

Glâveanu, V. (2010) "Principles for a Cultural Psychology of Creativity". *Culture and Psychology* 16, No. 2: 147—63.

Kvale, S., and S. Brinkmann. (2008) *Interviews: Learning the Craft of Qualitative Research Interviewing*. Thousand Oaks, CA: Sage.

Levy, M. and G. Stockwell. (2006) *CALL Dimensions: Options and Issues in Computer-Assisted Language Learning*. Mahwah, N.J.: Lawrence Erlbaum.

Lillejord, S., and O. Dysthe. (2008) "Productive Learning Practice—A Theoretical Discussion Based on Two Cases". *Journal of Education and Work* 21, No. 1: 75—89.

Lindström, L. (2009) "Produkt-og procesvurdering i kreativ virksomhed". In *Kreativitetsfremmende læringsmiljøer i skolen,* ed. L. Tanggard, and S. Brinkmann. Frederikshavn: Dafolo Forlag, pp. 151—70.

Looney, J. (2009) *Assessment and Innovation In Education,* OEC D Education Working Paper No. 24, July, p. 61.

Macridis, R.C. (1968) *The Comparative Study of Politics*. New York: Random House.

Mason, J.H. (2003) *The Value of Creativity: The Origins and Emergence of a Modern Belief.* Aldershot: Ashgate.

Mayer, R.E. (2004) "Should There Be a Three-Strikes Rule Against Pure Discovery Learning?", *American Psychologist,* Vol. 59, No. 1, pp. 14—19.

Merritt, R., and S. Rokkan (eds.). (1966) *Comparing Nations: The Uses of Quantitative Data in Cross-National Research.* New Haven: Yale University Press.

Moultrie, J., and A. Young. (2009) "Exploratory Study of Organizational Creativity in Creative Organizations". *Creativity and Innovation Management* 18, No. 4: 299—314.

OEC D (2000) *Knowledge Management in the Learning Society.* Paris: OEC D Publishing.

OEC D (2003) *Networks of Innovation: Towards New Models for Managing Schools and Systems.* Paris: OEC D Publishing.

OEC D (2004) *Innovation in the Knowledge Economy: Implications for Education and Learning.* Paris: OEC D Publishing.

OEC D (2006) *Personalising Education.* Paris: OEC D Publishing.

OEC D (2007) *Evidence in Education: Linking Research and Policy.* Paris: OEC D Publishing.

OEC D (2008a) *Improving School Leadership—Volume 2: Case Studies in System Leadership* (edited by Beatriz Pont, Deborah Nusche, and David Hopkins), Paris: OEC D Publishing.

OEC D (2008b) *Innovating to Learn, Learning to Innovate.* Paris: OEC D Publishing.

OEC D (2009a) *Beyond Textbooks: Digital Learning Resources as Systemic Innovation in the Nordic Countries.* Paris: OEC D Publishing.

OEC D (2009b) *Working out Change: Systemic Innovation in Vocational Education and Training.* Paris: OEC D Publishing.

OEC D (2010a) *Are the New Millennium Learners Making the Grade?: Technology Use and Educational Performance in PISA 2006.* Paris: OEC D Publishing.

OEC D (2010b) *The OECD Innovation Strategy: Getting a Head Start on Tomorrow.* Paris: OEC D Publishing.

Oliver, M. and K. Trigwell. (2005) "Can 'Blended Learning' Be Redeemed?". E-learning 2/1: 17—26.

Pope, R. (2005) *Creativity—Theory, History, Practice.* Oxon: Routledge.

Przeworski, A., and H. Teune. (1970) *The Logic of Comparative Social Inquiry.* New York: Wiley.

Rokkan, S. (ed.). (1968) *Comparative Research Across Cultures and Nations.* Paris/The Hague: Mouton. (Especially papers by H.R. Alker, Jr., L. Benson, A.J.F. Köbben, D. Lerner, G. Ohlin, E.K. Scheuch.)

Russett, B.M. et al. (1964) *World Handbook of Political and Social Indicators.* New Haven: Yale University Press.

Saywer, R.K. (2004) "Creative Teaching: Collaborative Discussion as Disciplined Improvisation". *Educational Researcher* 33, No. 2: 12—20. Downloaded By Schön, D.A. 1987. *Educating the Reflective Practitioner.* San Francisco: Jossey-Bass.

Scarrow, H.A. (1969) *Comparative Political Analysis.* New York: Harper & Row.

Sharma, P. and B. Barrett. (2007) *Blended Learning: Using Technology in and Beyond the Language Classroom.* Oxford: Macmillan.

Sharpe, R., G. Benfield, G. Roberts, and R. Francis. (2006) *The Undergraduate Experience of Blended E-learning: A Review of UK Literature and Practice.* Retrieved from http://www. heacademy.

Shoup, P. (1968) "Comparing Communist Nations: Prospects for an Empirical Approach". *American Political Science Review* 62.

Smyth, J., and R. Hattam. (2002) "Early School Leaving and the Cultural Geography of High Schools". *British Educational Research Journal* 28, No. 3: 375—97.

Sternberg, R.J. (2006) "Introduction". In *The International Handbook of Creativity,* ed. J. C. Kaufman, and R. J. Sternberg. Cambridge: Cambridge University Press, pp. 1—9.

Tanggaard, L. (2009) "The Research Interview as a Dialogical Context for the Production of Personal Narratives and Social Life". *Qualitative Inquiry* 15, No. 9: 1498—515.

Tanggaard, L. (2010) *Fornyelsens kunst.* København: Akademisk forlag.

Torrance, E.P. (1972) "Can We Teach Children to Think Creatively?" *Journal of Creative.*

Tyack, D. and W. Tobin (1994) "The 'Grammar' of Schooling: Why Has It Been So Hard to Change?", *American Educational Research Journal*, Vol. 31, No. 3, 453—479.

Westbrook, K. (2008) "The Beginning of the End for Blended Learning?". IATEFL CALL Review Summer 2008: 12—15.

Willis, P. (1977) *How Working Class Lads Get Working Class Jobs.* Farnborough: Saxon House.